Robert Russa Moton

OF HAMPTON AND TUSKEGEE

Dr. Robert Russa Moton

Robert Russa Moton

OF HAMPTON
AND TUSKEGEE

Edited by

WILLIAM HARDIN HUGHES
FREDERICK D. PATTERSON

Chapel Hill

THE UNIVERSITY OF NORTH CAROLINA PRESS

❧ *Preface* ❧

THE EDITORS are pleased to present this volume of tributes to the
life of Dr. Robert Russa Moton, the long time associate and
successor to Booker T. Washington. The idea that such a book as
this should be written occurred to the administrative officers of
Tuskegee Institute several years ago after it was decided that a
regular feature of Tuskegee Institute's program should include a
memorial service to Dr. Moton to be held during the fall of each
year.

The first of these tributes are offered by those who knew Dr.
Moton personally. They are interesting glimpses of Dr. Moton as
a person as well as of his life and labors. It was decided that, without
waiting for the passage of years to accumulate the number of such
tributes required to make a volume of reasonable size, an attempt
should be made forthwith to have the many distinguished persons
who knew Dr. Moton and worked with him under a variety of
circumstances contribute to a volume which would be entitled
MOTON OF HAMPTON AND TUSKEGEE. Therefore, in
developing this type of volume consisting of a number of essays or
personal tributes, it was recognized that a more distant period
would doubtless require a scholarly evaluation of Dr. Moton's life
by a distinguished man of letters. However, it was agreed a volume

of general interest might be created from statements by those who held Dr. Moton in highest esteem and who, because of the distinguished services they rendered in coordination with his, would offer estimates of his life which would be of compelling worth.

The wisdom of getting started on this effort as soon as possible is more than evident for, in the comparatively short period since 1950 when the first invitation to contribute to such a volume was written, several of those who furnished statements are now deceased. It would have been most unfortunate to have been denied the splendid contributions of A. L. Holsey and Alvin J. Nealy.

The selected statements from Dr. Moton's own writings, along with the tributes from contributors to the volume, offer direct and indirect commentaries on the period in which Dr. Moton served. They reveal clearly the optimism and hope which were part of his reaction to problems in race relations. They also reveal the generousness of heart which he felt for all mankind.

Dr. Moton's life of public service in education and national affairs began in 1890, continued through World War I, and lasted until 1935, just before active preparation began for World War II. During these years his concerns were wide and varied. They touched the educational, social, economic and spiritual aspects of Negro life and, without exception, this had a salutary and often decisive effect. An instance, perhaps not sufficiently detailed in this volume, is the fact that Dr. Moton was one of those chiefly responsible for bringing the Interracial Commission into existence shortly after World War I to combat serious tensions, wide-spread at the time. Also, his direct appeal to Mr. George Eastman of Rochester, New York, resulted in the gift of $50,000 which provided substantial underwriting for the program of the Commission. Dr. Will W. Alexander, who gave brilliant leadership to the Commission as its Director, repeatedly attributed his success to Dr. Moton's personal friendship, guidance and inspiration.

Because so much has happened to alter racial and human relationships over the past few years, the editors feel that this volume serves as a running commentary on the period 1890 to 1935. It was in the latter year that Dr. Moton retired from the Presidency of Tuskegee Institute. At the close of his career he stated that the changes which had occurred during his lifetime were far in excess of those envisioned in his fondest dreams. Persons who read of his labors can judge the extent to which he helped bring about changes for the better in human understanding and good will, and will note the extent to which he stood firm against the protests of white and Negro alike in support of positions he believed represented the larger good. It is only as what he had to say and do are examined in terms of the circumstances under which progress had to be made at the moment, that proper appreciation of his contribution is possible and his stature as a sane, generous-hearted and courageous leader is revealed.

Some effort has been made to reduce repetition in the contributions from the several writers. The extent of this effort had to be balanced against the value of having each contributor pay his special tribute and in terms of the importance of having more than one expression concerning the importance of a given event.

Warm thanks are due to each contributor. Their prompt and effective response to the invitation to write chapters on Dr. Moton's life without monetary compensation were in themselves tributes of a high order. More than this, in every statement it is possible to detect a depth of feeling and a sense of personal indebtedness to Dr. Moton which adds strength to each contribution. Appreciation is expressed to President Luther H. Foster of Tuskegee and President Alonzo G. Moron of Hampton Institute for their interest and their willingness to recommend the appropriations required for the preparation and publication of the volume. In like manner the Trustees of Hampton and Tuskegee are deeply thanked. Special thanks are due to Canon Anson Phelps Stokes who kindly read the manuscript and made many valuable and detailed suggestions.

We are pleased to close this introductory statement with a comment contained in a paragraph from a letter written by Dr. Stokes. After examining the entire manuscript Dr. Stokes commented: "Dr. Moton ... was really one of the strongest characters I have ever known and it is perfectly clear that it would have been impossible to secure a better successor to Dr. Washington of Tuskegee."

W. H. Hughes
F. D. Patterson

ᵛᵉ Contents ᵉᵛ

[ix]

CONTENTS

✬ *Illustrations* ✬

[xi]

ILLUSTRATIONS

Robert Russa Moton

OF HAMPTON AND TUSKEGEE

CHAPTER 1

❧ *Ancestry and Early Life** ❧

About the year 1735 a fierce battle was waged between two strong tribes on the west coast of Africa. The chief of one of these tribes was counted among the most powerful of his time. This chief overpowered his rival and slaughtered and captured a great number of his band. Some of the captives escaped, others died, others still committed suicide, till but a few were left. The victorious chief delivered to his son about a dozen of this forlorn remnant, and he, with an escort, took them away to be sold into slavery. The young African pushed his way through the jungle with his bodyguard until he reached the coast. Arrived there, he sold his captives to the captain of an American slave ship and received his pay in trinkets of various kinds, common to the custom of the trade. Then he was asked to row out in a boat and inspect the wonderful ship. He went, and with the captain and the crew saw every part of the vessel. When it was all over they offered him food and he ate it heartily. After that he remembered no more till he woke to find himself in the hold of the ship chained to one of the miserable creatures whom he himself had so recently sold as a slave, and the vessel itself was far beyond the sight of land.

After many days the ship arrived at the shores of America; the

* From Robert Russa Moton, *Finding a Way Out* (New York: Doubleday, Page & Company, 1920).

[3]

human cargo was brought to Richmond and this African slave
merchant was sold along with his captives at public auction in the
slave markets of the city. He was bought by a tobacco planter and
carried to Amelia County, Virginia, where he lived to be a very old
man. This man was my grandmother's great-grandfather.

According to the story as he told it to my grandmother, he
brought more at auction than any other member of the party. He
was a very fine specimen of physical manhood, weighing somewhere around two hundred pounds, and standing about six feet
two inches in height. My grandmother said of him that he learned
very little of the English language and used that little always with
a pronounced foreign accent. He never grew to like America or
Americans, white or black; and certain days, after the passing of
so many moons, he observed religiously throughout his life. These
were feast days with certain ceremonies of their own, in which,
when possible, two other members of that same party though not
of his tribe would join him. Each understood the tribal language of
the others. These days, so my grandmother said, which occurred
about three times a year, his owner permitted him to take off, leaving him undisturbed, for at other times he was entirely faithful and
conscientious in his work. His great-granddaughter—my mother's
mother—was not, I should judge, very unlike this great-great-great-
grandfather of mine, for in her youth she was a magnificent type of
womanhood, both physically and mentally; and even to her death,
at ninety-six years of age, she was possessed of remarkable physical
and mental vigour. She "carried the keys" on her owner's, Doctor
Craddock's, plantation, and stood next on the female side of the
household to his wife, superintending the making of the clothes,
caring for the children on the plantation, and in later years conducting what would in the present day be called a Day Nursery;
that is, caring for the children of the mothers who were in the field,
seeing to their food and dress, and to their conduct, of course.
Frequently these old mothers were very clever in story telling, so
that "Uncle Remus," "Brer Fox," and "Brer Rabbit" were familiar
to the children of the South, both white and black, many years
before they got into print.

My father's mother, who lived to be 108 years old, was also
brought directly from Africa, and was finally sold to a planter who

lived in Charlotte County, Virginia. It was there my father was born. He was owned by Doctor Alexander of the county, and when he died, about 1850, and the estate was divided, my father was sold to John Crowder of Prince Edward County, and, I think, presented to his wife as a Christmas present. I have many times heard my father tell of his experiences as a slave; of the many hardships through which he passed, and of the many good times he had even as a slave, for one of the fortunate traits of the Negro is his jovial nature, his ability to see humour even in adversity, and to laugh and sing under almost any circumstances. I have often thought that most other races, had they gone through the difficulties which the Negro faced, would have produced much more insanity than has been found in the past among Negroes; unfortunately, however, insanity is increasing very much indeed among my people, an indication in all probability that they are taking life much more seriously than they have done in the past.

There were many kind masters during slavery days; and there must have been such a thing as kindness even between master and slave. The overseers who were generally of the poorer class of white people were, as a rule, the cause of much of the contention and usually made most of the trouble; at least the Negroes thought so. They were night patrollers, or, as the Negroes called them, "patter-rollers," and were paid by the hour in many places to catch and whip any slave found off his master's plantation after nightfall without a pass. Not infrequently these people received from the master less consideration even than the slave, and in most cases the bitterest animosity and hatred existed between the overseers and the slaves. It was not unusual that Negroes considered themselves superior in every respect to the overseer class, whose members were generally referred to among them as "po'h white trash." This expression was "the last word" in degradation, infamy, and general contempt that Negroes could command. Even today, when Negroes refer to people as "poor white trash," it has a meaning all its own, and I am of the opinion that much of the ill feeling between the races in our country today had its origin in these unpleasant relations between overseer and slaves before Emancipation.

On the Crowder plantation there was an overseer who had a particular dislike for my father, probably because he thought that my father received entirely too much consideration from his master and mistress; in short, there was a kind of jealous rivalry between them. It is unnecessary to say that the dislike on the part of the overseer was generously reciprocated by my father. If there was any difference, it was that the hatred on my father's part was the stronger—if that were possible; and without doubt, being in the confidence of his master, he used his opportunity to the disadvantage of the overseer. It was the rule of the plantation that no slaves except such as the master designated should be whipped by the overseer. My father, of course, was thus exempted. On one occasion the overseer, unfortunately, and against the order of his employer, insisted upon whipping my father. The scene took place in a tobacco barn where my father was engaged with perhaps fifty other slaves in sorting and stripping tobacco. In the scuffle, in which several other slaves helped the overseer in response to his call, my father easily got the upper hand, for he was a man of unusual strength. He not only overpowered the overseer but the men who undertook to assist him, maiming the overseer and one of the men seriously. This was in the midst of a severe snow storm. My father took the only course, as it seemed, that was open to "obstreperous" slaves—he took to the woods. This was in early December. Here he remained, picking up what food he could at night in cabins and elsewhere, until March, when, for want of food and sufficient clothing, his feet having been frost bitten, he was obliged to give in. He returned one snowy afternoon, slipped into the stable, and hid himself in the loft under the hay. His hat was discovered by his master's two sons whose conversation, which he overheard, showed that they were afraid of him. They ran to the house and told their father of his return, and he came out to the barn and urged him to come to the house and be looked after, for the entire family was really very fond of him. He was taken back to the house where his mistress, the mother of the two boys, treated him most kindly. Indeed, he said, they all wept over his pitiable condition. His feet, after careful nursing for several months, were finally in shape to permit him to resume his duties. He promised that he would not commit the same offence again, provided, however, no "po'h white trash" attempted again to whip him. He apologized to the overseer, and the two agreed that there would be no further trouble. But a few weeks afterward he went to his master and told him he was very sorry it was not possible for him to get along with that overseer and asked that his master sell him to a nearby planter, who had agreed to give him better treatment. This time it would appear that he and the master came very near the "parting of the ways." This seems strange, I know, but it was not infrequent that slaves of the more intelligent type would make definite arrangements with some near or distant planter to buy them; thus slaves very often picked their own masters. But in this case Mr. Crowder made it plain to him that they could get along; that he was unwilling to sell him; that he belonged especially to his mistress and that she depended on him. My father insisted, however, that the overseer be discharged. Whether his attitude in this case produced the desired result my father did not know, but in any case within a few weeks the objectionable overseer left and a new overseer took his place, who established better relations, not only as between himself and my father, but with the other slaves as well, in consequence of which the master got better and more efficient service with very much less friction.

From that time forward my father lived pleasantly on the Crowder plantation, neither he nor the master nor the overseer breaking their mutual promise—my father's being that he would not fight again unless someone attempted to whip him; and the overseer's, that he would not attempt to whip him. My father used to say that one man could not chastise another, although two men might fight and one might get the better of the other. That idea was very strong in his mind.

When the Civil War broke out my father went with Mrs. Crowder's brother—Captain Womack of Cumberland County, Virginia, who was afterward Colonel Womack—into the fray as his "body servant." I think they would say "valet" today. He was with him during the first three years of that bitter struggle, suffering all the privations and hardships so familiar to those who know what the Southern Army endured.

One experience he used often to relate was that near Petersburg he accidentally got within the Union lines and was told that he might remain with the Yankees if he so desired; but he told them that he could not do so at the time because he had given his definite promise that he would stand by Colonel Womack until the war was over. He could not break his promise. He had also sworn to see to it, so far as he could, that no harm came to his master and he felt that he would remain true to that pledge so long as Colonel Womack was equally true to his promises to him. I am told that the friendship between the two men, one black, one white, was very strong; that nothing ever separated them save Colonel Womack's death which, as I recall my father's account of it, occurred in one of the famous charges near Petersburg.

When the war was over my father "hired himself" to the Crowders, where he remained until Christmas of 1866 when he married mother, Emily Brown. They were married in the old plantation house of the Hillmans of Amelia County. The Hillmans, as I recall, were Scottish Presbyterians and like many other Southerners, had lost everything during the war except their name and honour and the pride of aristocratic ancestry.

My mother, like her own mother, was a woman of very strong character in many ways, very much like my father. Among my early recollections is the fact that my mother frequently, after working in the field all day, would hurry us through the evening meal in order to get the cabin ready for the night school which met regularly in our simple home. I recall now the eagerness with which some twenty-five or thirty men and women struggled with their lessons, trying to learn to read and write while I was supposed to be asleep in my trundle bed, to which I had been hurried to make room for this little band of anxious, aspiring ex-slaves, some of whom came as far as six miles in order to take advantage of this rare opportunity which but a few years before had been denied them. The teacher of this night school was my mother's brother, who, in spite of the penalties attached, had learned to read and write from his young master, picking up here and there snatches of information while they played and worked together, ofttimes without the young master's realizing the gravity of his actions. All this took place but a few years after the close of the war and before any schools had been established for coloured or white children in that section. My mother was one of the most enthusiastic of the students, while my father, who was much older than my mother, although giving his unqualified approval and encouragement to the school, sat by and listened and once in a while in a mischievous mood threw in an ejaculation which upset the order and dignity of the school, much to the embarrassment and annoyance of the teacher and, I fear, sometimes to the indignation of the more serious-minded students, especially my mother.

Thinking of the experiences through which my ancestors passed, along with thousands of other slaves, in their contact with the white people of America, I have often felt that somehow—in spite of the hardships and oppression which they suffered—that in the providence of God, the Negro, when all is summed up dispassionately, has come through the ordeal with much to his credit, and with a great many advantages over his condition when he entered the relationship. The white man, on the other hand, has reaped certain disadvantages from which the whole country still suffers and from which it will probably take several generations to recover completely.

In January, 1867, my father hired himself to Mr. Samuel Vaughan of Prince Edward County, and was made foreman or "head man" on the Vaughan Plantation while his family continued to live in Amelia County. It was in Amelia County that I was born on the 26th day of August of the same year. Among my earliest recollections is one of my father appearing on a Saturday morning with a team of four mules hitched to a large farm wagon in charge of a coloured man, Beverley Jones, who rode one of the mules. My father and my mother, assisted by friends, packed our few belongings into this wagon and took me with my mother to the Vaughan plantation in Prince Edward County where my father had been working. I remember perfectly the long drive and how they wrapped me in an old gray blanket and a blue military overcoat—which were very common in those days—in order to protect me from the bitter cold. Here in an old house, in the rear of a Virginia mansion known as "Pleasant Shade," I spent most of the years of my early youth. My mother for many years was cook, and my father "led the hands" on the plantation. It was here that I caught my first glimpses of real culture and got my first inspiration as to what I would like to be and something of what I would like to do.

On account of my parents' relation to the household, and because I was the only child near the "big house," I naturally received much attention from the Vaughan family. I can never forget Mrs.

Vaughan—"Miss Lucy" we called her, as was the custom not only among the coloured people but among the white folks also—and her three daughters, Misses Patty, Jennie and Mollie. I was soon big enough to carry Miss Lucy's key basket. This was considered a great honour for a small Negro boy before the war and immediately afterward. I felt the "dignity and responsibility" of my office. As I grew older my duties increased until I assisted her and her daughters in the care of the fowls, of which she had a great number— turkeys, geese, ducks, and a great many chickens. But proud as I was of these duties, I have never since so sincerely envied any one his position as I did Sam Reed, the general house boy and waiter in the family. Miss Lucy had promised me that when Sam was big enough he would be transferred to the farm, as was the custom, and I could have his place. Sam helped the cook, made all the fires, was in the "big house" much of the time, and generally wore "good clothes." He was a favourite on the plantation. Besides all this, Sam was a remarkable acrobat. He could turn somersaults, stand on his head, turn a cart wheel, go wheelbarrow fashion, and could per- form what were to me many very wonderful acrobatic feats, in addition to being a wonderfully good reel and jig dancer and a re- markably fine singer. He must have inherited his ability to sing from his father, "Uncle Jim," who was a noted "shout singer" in the neighborhood. Sam was not a "Christian" and so sang anything; and he did it very effectively. Under Sam's direction I practised many of his accomplishments, and with his careful tutelage became a close second. As a result, he and I were frequently called into the "big house" to perform. But there was one thing I had against Sam. He grew so slowly it seemed that I would soon be bigger than he, and would lose my chance to get his place when he should be sent on to another. Fortunately for me, but perhaps unfortunately for Sam, his father now insisted that it was time for him to leave the house, as he considered him too old to devote himself to "doing chores"; and being only a house boy, his pay was too small. He would earn more by working on the farm. So Sam had to go.

I shall never forget the joy I felt when told that I was to wait on the table at breakfast the following morning, and how Sam and my mother instructed me until late in the night how to perform my new duties; how I should stand; and how to all appearances I was to pay no attention to the conversation. I remember how they sat at the table and had me pass things—empty plates and dishes—I do not recall whether from the right or left side, but judge now it must have been from the left. In any case, I got through my first day with some show of success and proved myself fairly equal to my new responsibilities. As a compliment to the honours of the post, the young ladies at the house made me a couple of suits which I should wear only on special occasions. I think I have never had a position since then in which I took any more pride than in this youthful promotion to the place to which I had aspired for several years. Yet there was more in my position than was at first apparent. "Mr. Willie" Vaughan, the only son, I took in many things as a model. I copied his laugh, his walk, his dress, the way he handled his knife and fork, and other characteristic manners of his in a fashion that must have sometimes amused those who observed me. But aside from its humorous aspects, this contact with the Vaughan family meant for me a certain kind of most valuable training and education.

About this time a rather interesting incident happened. While my work was new, my mother made me devote an hour at night to my blue-backed Holmes's Primer. She was my teacher, being one of the very few coloured women in our neighborhood who could read at all. There was a popular belief that the Vaughans, notwithstanding their kindness and aristocratic ideas, objected to and opposed Negroes' reading and writing. My mother was very careful, therefore, that they should not know that she was teaching me to read, or even that she herself could read. For several years she had kept from them the fact that she even knew one letter of the alphabet from another; but one night after the day's work was done there was a gentle rap at the door of our two-roomed house. I remember that we were sitting before a big, open fire—my father, my mother, and I—my mother teaching me by the light from the fire. As the custom was in those days my mother called out to learn who was there. Imagine our consternation when the answer came back: "Miss Lucy." My mother was tempted to hide the book when she discovered who was at the door, but my father objected, saying we were free and that he would leave the Vaughans if they made any objections; that he could find plenty of work at good pay at any one of a dozen plantations in the district. So the door was opened and in walked "Miss Lucy," to find us in the very act. She expressed the greatest surprise when she discovered what was taking place, but she astonished us equally when she indicated that she was very much pleased, and commended my mother on the fact that she could read and told her she was very wise to teach her son to read. The next day we were even more astonished and of course pleased when Miss Mollie, her youngest daughter, said to my mother that Mrs. Vaughan had asked her to give me a lesson for one hour every afternoon and to do the same for my mother if my mother would care to have her do so. So the next time my father went to Farmville, eight miles away, he bought the necessary books both for my mother and me, and my lessons began in a more systematic way with Miss Mollie as teacher and my mother as my "classmate" for one hour each afternoon. My mother finally dropped out but I continued for some time, though intermittently.

One of the saddest recollections of my childhood was the death of Mrs. Vaughan. I can never forget the impression it made upon me, the wailing of the coloured women on the plantation and the sadness of the coloured men. There must have been between three and four hundred people on the Vaughan estate, including men, women, and children. Mrs. Vaughan, like her husband, possessed a very beautiful character and was beloved of everybody on the plantation. While I did not then appreciate the full gravity of the situation, I wept along with the others; for in spite of my youth I realized somewhat the loss that this death was to me as well as to others. For there was not a family on the plantation and scarcely a person who had not at some time been helped by her kindly personal attention to their needs and difficulties. Several years later Mr. Vaughan was married again—to Miss Pattie Perkinson, a daughter of Captain Perkinson, the head of another of Virginia's fine families, who owned a large estate a few miles away. I confess that I did not entirely approve of the marriage. The truth of the matter was I shared the feelings—perhaps in less degree—of most of the people on the plantation, especially the women; though my own feelings were more personal than general. I was not so worried about the marriage itself as I was anxious that whoever took "Miss Lucy's" place should not interfere with the position I was occupying in the Vaughan household. I was certain that no one could be so kind as "Miss Lucy" had been to me, and I felt sure that "Miss Pattie" would not be; and what I had heard of the dealings of certain members of her family with coloured people rather tended further to disquiet than to allay my youthful anxiety about my own future. My position at this time in the Vaughan household was, in my mind, of a very important sort. I was doing, so I supposed, just about as I wished, and running things much to my own liking. I carried the keys all day and hung them at the head of Mr. Vaughan's bed the last thing at night. I issued the corn for the stock and frequently helped in weighing the rations to the scores of men who came up Saturday afternoon for their allowances. I went hunting with Mr. Vaughan, visited the rabbit traps in the morning, and also went fishing with him on the Appomattox River. He rode a magnificent bay mare we called Fannie, while I rode a mule, blind in both eyes, named Kit. It is not surprising, therefore, that I should have been more or less jealous of my position and anxious that the new mistress of the house should be of a kind to meet my approval, for by this time the three daughters had all married and only Mr. Vaughan's son, Mr. William S. Vaughan, was left.

My mother was still the cook, and my father was running things as headman on the farm, but neither my father nor my mother counted very much in my mind so far as this situation was concerned; indeed Mr. Vaughan and his son did not count very much looking at it from the mental angles of my youth. I was, however, very pleasantly surprised when "Miss Pattie" came to "Pleasant Shade." The things that had been prophesied regarding her were not fulfilled. She did not take the keys from me and I had just about as much leeway as before, in some respects more. She was more careful than the men folks had been about setting the table and cleaning the house, pulling up weeds, the clearing of the garden, and such things. She made me sweep off the porches once and sometimes twice or three times a day—I had gotten to the place where I swept them perhaps twice and sometimes only once a week. And besides all this, the new Mrs. Vaughan insisted that my mother should continue my lessons, and encouraged me in various other ways.

In the fall following this important event a school was opened for coloured children a few miles from the Vaughan plantation. This was the first school for Negroes in that neighbourhood; indeed the first school of any kind, for there had been no public schools of consequence for either white or coloured children before that time. In the fall of the previous year the coloured people had been urged to vote with the promise that if they did so a public school for their children would be established in our district. They voted according to instructions and the promise was kept.

In early October a free school was opened for coloured people, and with Mr. John Morrisette, a white man, as teacher. My father and my mother decided that I should go. They consulted the Vaughans, particularly Mrs. Vaughan. She readily approved. Forthwith she and my mother fitted me out and I appeared in school the opening day. I recall how I felt when I observed that there were so many children bigger than myself who could not read. Because of my instruction at home I was in the highest class in the school. And I had special pride in the fact. I think I was reading in the third reader. But reading at all by a coloured boy in those days was rather unusual; and a coloured free school, with fifty or sixty children on the opening day, and meeting in the daytime as well, was a real marvel. Mr. Morrisette, who, by the way, had been an officer in the Southern Army, was most kind and thoughtful and very patient, and took a great deal of care and pains, even on the opening day, to classify us. He brought many books of various kinds, and his wife, who was a very unusual woman, came in later to help him in the difficult task of organizing this large number of Negro children into a real school. His task no doubt was a hard one, not only because of the children directly, but because of the parents as well, many of whom, as time went on, troubled him very much. All of us naturally thought the more books the student carried the more he knew, and many parents were therefore willing to get the fourth, fifth, and even the sixth reader for their children without any protest at the expense so long as they were carrying "bigger" and "higher" books. My father shared this feeling along with the rest. He was not altogether happy at my having only a third reader; but Mrs. Vaughan, who knew what I was doing, came to the rescue and assured him that I would have "bigger" books in ample time, and that I would probably learn more than many others who had many more books.

I continued my work in the Vaughan family, before and after school, at intervals for many years, and without doubt what I learned from my contact with them was worth quite as much to me as what I learned at school. Indeed, my own idea has always been that the one supplemented the other. My work before and after school was being correlated unconsciously with what I was learning in books; which was true also of my contact with the nearly four score children whom I met daily at school.

The Vaughans were of the finest type of Southern families—kind, thoughtful, and generous. They were people of considerable wealth and at the top of the social scale in that community; but at the same time they were of all the white people the most popular among the Negroes of the neighbourhood. They visited Negro churches and prayer-meetings, and Negroes frequently visited the old Jamestown Presbyterian Church to which the Vaughans belonged and of which Mr. Vaughan, I think, was an elder, as was also his son in later years. For many years they conducted Sunday School in the afternoon at Jamestown Church for coloured people. This school was taught by the leading ladies of the community with the help of some of the leading white men. In this connection it is significant that the Vaughans never suffered for want of adequate and faithful help on the farm or in the household, and it is certain that their influence on the coloured people on their place and in that section was of the best. This was true of them in that day. It is equally true today of their three daughters and was true of their son and his wife, both of whom have died within the last few years. The Vaughans never lost prestige or social standing in the community by being kind and helpful to coloured people.

The pastor of the Jamestown Presbyterian Church, to which I have referred, was the Rev. George H. Denney, a minister who lived in Amelia County, some twenty miles away, and usually came to the community on Saturday afternoons in a sulky. He generally made his home with the Vaughans, remaining over from Saturday until Monday. Occasionally he came earlier or remained later for certain special services. I was always glad to have him come, even though it added to my duties somewhat, because of the extra shoes to polish and the extra pail of water that I had to bring from the spring some distance away. At the same time he was very kind to me; it was he who gave me the first Bible that I ever had and took pains to interpret certain passages with which I had become somewhat familiar but whose meaning was as yet rather vague to me. But my joy at his coming lay in the fact that frequently, especially in the summer season, he brought with him his son George. He was about my own age which accounted for our having many good times together. Sometimes we were joined by Ernest Morton, another white boy, and Lee Brown, a coloured boy, but George and I were especially friendly. Many a day he would sit at the table with the family and I would be keeping the flies off and waiting on the table, when we would wink at each other and make plans as to what we would do when dinner was over and my other work done. Often he would pitch in and help me through and then off we went fishing on Sailor Creek, famous for one of the skirmishes between Lee and Grant, on the way to Appomattox after the evacuation of Richmond.

We not only enjoyed our boyish play, but we worked many examples in arithmetic together and discussed history as well. I remember that we differed frequently. One of the discussions we used to have most often was about which was the greater general, Grant or Lee. He was for Lee; I for Grant. We often discussed the merits of the conflict between the states, which culminated in the war. I could never swerve him from his position on this question and he never swerved me from mine. We never found it profitable to discuss this issue. He would sometimes lose his temper, and I frequently lost mine. There came a time when we ceased to discuss it at all and I think our relations were consequently very much pleasanter. He had a most excellent father and the son was of the same type—very bright, always frank, always generous—and he never swerved in his friendship for me.

I sometimes feared that the Vaughans and the Reverend Mr. Denney, George's father, were a little annoyed that he preferred apparently to be out in the fields where I was with the cows and sheep, or even to help me with my chores, to being in the house among the guests—for the Vaughan household was a very popular meeting place for young people and old. It was a great social centre and the scene of many parties.

Mr. Vaughan's death, which occurred about this time, made everything different at "Pleasant Shade" thereafter. The farm was divided among the children. Most of the coloured people moved away. My father went to live with a family of Mortons who were by marriage connected with the Vaughan family. Mr. J. X. Morton, who afterward became a professor at the Virginia Polytechnic Institute, had a son Ernest, to whom I have referred. Our friendship grew stronger; indeed he left parents and everything else to be with my coloured chum Lee and with me, and we, in the same spirit, neglected everything that we could with impunity, in order that the three of us could be together. We fished and hunted together and engaged in many boyish sports and pranks. Nothing in his possession was too good for us, and nothing in ours was too good for him. As we grew older my father did not wholly approve of this intimacy, and used often to say that we were "too thick to thrive." In the course of time there did come a parting. Ernest went off to school and my chum Lee and I were left on his father's farm. The weeks immediately following his leaving for the Virginia Polytechnic Institute were dull and dreary for us at home. This I think was in October. I continued to work on the farm, for I was now too big for chores, and went to school when the weather did not permit working on the farm. I was anxiously awaiting the Christmas holidays when our friend Ernest would return and we would again have some good times together. He would tell us no doubt of his college experiences and we had some experiences that we could relate to him. At last the day came. Lee and I were at the house when they brought him in the carriage from Rice's depot. He had with him also his room-mate, I think, who had come to spend the holidays with him. They both wore gray uniforms with brass buttons. Lee and I, as soon as Ernest alighted from the carriage, rushed up to shake hands. He not only did not shake hands with us but his manner was as cold and frigid as the north wind that we were breathing. He did bow, but it was quickly done. Lee went home. I went into the kitchen with Aunt Viny, the cook. I was feeling bad; so was Lee. I was thinking. Sometimes I wonder if I ever thought quite as seriously on life as I did that night. A few moments later he came out into the kitchen in his splendid spick-and-span uniform with brass buttons and polished shoes. Aunt Viny, the old cook of sixty or seventy years, rushed up to him and threw her arms around him, exclaiming, "My chil'! My chil'!" and he in turn threw his arms around her. He was not more demonstrative toward his mother; in fact, not even so much so, because his mother was not so demonstrative as the cook. I sat unhappy, puzzled, thinking. Finally, through the darkness of the night, I stole down through the ravine, across the brook, and up to our cabin on the hill. I went to bed early that night. My father, who always saw and realized much more than he ever expressed, asked me the one question that I did not care to have him ask, and he made just the one ejaculation which cut keen and deep. He said, "Did you see Ernest?" "Yes, Sir," I said. "What did he say to you?" "Nothing," said I. "I told you to stay away from there," he said. I made no answer. He said no more. He knew how I felt, for he probably imagined what had happened. I went immediately to bed, as I have said, earlier than was my custom, and I think remained in bed later next morning, but I slept less than usual. I was thinking that night. I arose next morning more weary than when I went to bed; but I was wiser and more resolute than ever before in my life. I went through my usual day's work on the farm and looked after the hogs for the Mortons, and did what I had to do with reference to the feeding, but did not go to the house except as I was obliged to do. I met Ernest and his chum face to face. I looked the other way. I do not think they noticed where I was looking. I am sure they did not care. I was trying to snub them both. It had no effect, so far as I could judge, on either. But before going to bed the following night I had firmly resolved that getting an education was the best thing toward which I could bend my efforts in the future.

The next morning I asked my father about the school for coloured people, which was being projected under the influence of General Mahone at Petersburg, now a State Normal School. He told me much about it. It was to open the following fall. The Hon. John M. Langston, he said, a coloured man who was as well educated as any white person that he knew of, was to be the president. He said I might go if I wished and that he would do what he could to help me. It being a state school, and he having certain strong friends in the Republican Party (General Mahone among them), Hon. B. S. Hooper, a member of Congress from the Fourth Congressional District of Virginia, would probably arrange for me to have a scholarship. He also told me much about Hampton Institute but he was not enthusiastic about my going to Hampton. He said

Hampton was a "work school" and that he could teach me as much about work as Hampton could; but as he thought I could go to Hampton without any money, he would permit me to go if I insisted, though it was against his inclinations. During the winter I did much thinking, and much talking, too, with those people whose judgment I thought I could trust, about going to school, either at Hampton or at Petersburg. Mention was also made of some other schools. Captain Frank Southall, whose brother, Dr. J. W. Southall, was later Superintendent of Public Instruction of Virginia, learned through some source that I contemplated going to school. He had somehow been impressed with my knowledge of the Bible and my interest in the Sunday School at the Jamestown Presbyterian Church, to which I have referred, and of which he was superintendent. He wanted me to go to a school at Tuscaloosa, Alabama, to fit myself for the ministry in the Presbyterian Church. He said he would gladly arrange this and that the entire expense would be provided. This did not appeal to me very much, because I was unwilling to sign an agreement that I would enter the ministry or join the Presbyterian Church. All of my people were Baptists and we were living in a strongly Baptist community, that is, so far as Negroes were concerned. The Negroes, at least in my community at that time, looked with more or less suspicion upon the religion of white people anyway, and the feeling between denominations was strong; so, while I was determined to get an education, I replied that I preferred to be an ignorant Baptist rather than an educated Presbyterian. In my youthful zeal I told others of the offer I had had from Captain Southall and of my determination to keep the faith, repeating the expression that I preferred being an ignorant Baptist rather than an educated Presbyterian, and this expression never failed to bring forth much approval and applause from the coloured people of the community.

The following spring I joined a party of young men and secured work in Surry County in a lumber camp near the James River. My hope was to save sufficient money to pay my way through school. I had talked very frankly with my friends regarding schools, and had about decided that I would enter the school at Petersburg. I worked in this camp about two years, and succeeded in making my way up successively from piling lumber, through the grade of an experienced tree chopper—which meant that I had a pretty thorough knowledge of the quality of lumber in a tree before it was cut down, knowing by certain definite signs evident to a lumberman whether a tree was sound or decayed—to the post of foreman of a squad, having in charge the sorting and grading of lumber.

One is apt to think of seventy-five or more lumbermen as a rough, lawless, and undesirable group, fitted only for the heavy work connected with lumbering. As a matter of fact, there were a few rough men, who, in every sense, lived up to that reputation, but in the Ferguson camp there was a large number of honest, hard-working, thrifty men who came mostly from Prince Edward, Amelia, and Dinwiddie counties in Virginia. Many of them were ambitious for schooling. Some few had had some experience in politics and therefore kept posted on what was going on in Virginia.

The "Readjuster Movement" had just been introduced. This had caused the fusion of many Republicans and Democrats into what was known as the Readjuster Party. We had little or nothing to do with the people native to Surry County; the truth of the matter was, they didn't permit us to, because of our reputation. A few of us went to Sunday School and attended church services at Cypress Baptist Church, five miles away, and got somewhat into the social life of the coloured community. Beyond this a number of the men, in order to spend their leisure time profitably, organized a debating club, holding at intervals a mock court or a mock assembly, copying as nearly as we could the Virginia Legislature. Almost every night in the week there was something going on in connection with some one of these organizations.

I remember one man from Dinwiddie County, George Edwards, who had for many years served as magistrate in his precinct. He was reasonably well educated and had been a school teacher. He was well versed in politics and everything else that had to do with public affairs in Virginia. He it was who guided us for the most part in these activities. There were others almost as well trained. I think I have never had any experience I enjoyed any more than the winter nights in that camp; and I got from this experience a certain sort of training that I have since in many ways found very useful. I got also a taste for politics and other civic affairs that might have changed my career but for certain conscientious scruples of my mother's.

I recall also how shocked we were at the tidings that President Garfield had been shot. When we later learned of his death, we thought it proper to suspend all public activities in the camp for a week as a mark of respect to the President.

Evening meetings, especially on Saturdays, brought out sometimes large numbers of local people, white and coloured; and the manager of the camp became so well pleased with the effect that he gave us Saturday afternoon once a month, and invited many people from surrounding communities as well as from other saw-mills—and there were many saw-mills in the neighbourhood—to witness these monthly public exercises.

During the two years that I spent in that camp in Surry County, I saved comparatively little money; but I got something from the work itself, and the intimate contact with this group of men—the debating societies, the glee club, the prayer meetings, and other activities—which has had a very strong influence upon my later life.

An attack of malaria fever made it necessary for me to leave this marshy section on the James River. At the doctor's suggestion I returned to my home in Prince Edward County. My return home was in the late summer of 1882 and I found the political atmosphere very "thick and heavy." I was asked frequently to speak at political mass meetings, and I pitched in with vigour, taking up the cudgels for the "Readjuster Movement," about which, however, I knew little. This was a movement on the part of the Fusion Party for the readjustment of the state debt. All Negroes had a vote in those days. Negro Democrats were very few, only about a half dozen or so being found in a county. I remember the impression created on the mass of coloured people—and white people, too, for that matter— when I appeared at a picnic in the Vaughan woods and made a surprisingly effective political speech. I knew little about the subject, and was as much surprised as any one at the impression made and the enthusiasm over my speech displayed by the large number of people present. But the impression was so strong that when the meeting was over I was taken aside by three or four white men and as many coloured, who decided then and there that I should have the nomination for the Lower House of the State Legislature from my district. They decided what the ticket should be; that there should be certain white men and myself as the one coloured man. I was especially urged to this step by Walker Blanton, a shrewd, keen, coloured man, who did not know one letter of the alphabet from the other, but who was nevertheless the political leader of the district among the coloured people and withal a very useful citizen. I was inclined to accept the proposition, but there were one or two strong obstacles in the way. One was that I had planned to go to school, but the really serious one was that I was not yet twenty-one years of age. The white people in the group said that they could arrange the age situation, that nobody could prove exactly when I was born, and that I was large and mature in appearance, so that question would hardly arise in any case; and one gentleman in the group said that he knew my mother and father and the whole family connection and, moreover, had the family Bible record of all of them, so that he could easily adjust them in a way that would stand any test. The coloured men were equally zealous, making their plea on the ground that I had more education than any coloured man in the precinct, which was enough; that I could at least read and write and figure, and that was not true in Virginia of all the legislators even. The temptation was very great. I had just about decided to accept. Everything was to be arranged by the leaders of the Read-juster Party in the county. The only thing then left would be the formal notification a few weeks afterward. But my mother when approached said that she could not raise my age, and would be un-willing to swear to anything but the truth; that she knew exactly the day and year and hour of my birth. My father was non-com-mittal. He felt that my mother was too conscientious and that there were lots of probabilities of her being mistaken, and, too, that she would be perfectly safe in saying she was not absolutely sure and leaving it to the white people to settle the rest. But my mother stood firm, so the committee, finding that they could not get her to agree to sign the affidavit, concluded that the matter was at an end. Another coloured man was nominated and later elected. I confess I was somewhat relieved and not very sorry that my mother had taken such a firm stand. To be sure there was some disappointment, but I am confident that I slept better as a result of my mother's decision.

About this time a young man by the name of Edward D. Stewart, a graduate of Hampton Institute, came to teach in the school in our district which I had attended at intervals for some years. I was able to get from him first-hand information about Hampton. He gave me facts regarding the inner working of the school: how a student could enter, the kind of work he would do, the studies he would have, and something of what the men accomplished after graduating. He felt sure that I would have no difficulty in entering and in completing the course of studies. He thought my greatest difficulty would be in overcoming the popularity which I had achieved in my home community. He suggested that I would have to put all that behind me and assume that I did not know so much as I thought I did or as others in my community thought I did. He feared it would be difficult for me to adapt myself to the discipline of the school at Hampton. I was at this time leader of the church choir, superintendent of the Sunday School, and might have been deacon, but was considered too young for that particular place. In some ways I was considered a very important man in what was then a rather backward community.

I wrote to General Armstrong, the principal of Hampton, my letter being endorsed by Mr. Stewart. General Armstrong gave me an immediate reply in his own handwriting, saying that I might come to Hampton and work in the knitting room. Mr. Stewart advised that I had better wait until I could get work on the farm at Shellbanks or at the saw-mill. He knew something of my knowledge of lumber and experience in farming, stock-raising, and similar lines. He advised against my learning to knit mittens or working in the house under any circumstances. He had the feeling that knitting-room boys at Hampton did not succeed very well, for some fell into bad ways, a good many were disciplined severely, and a few suspended. So, at his suggestion, I wrote asking that I might have a place either on the farm or at the saw-mill, which work, I considered, was better adapted to my size and strength. Not long afterward I received a letter to the effect that I might come and that they would find satisfactory work for a boy who showed such good sense in his choice of occupation.

I took my departure on Sunday morning from the cabin where we were then living. The night before I was given a "party." It would be called "reception" now. To be sure, it was in a log cabin and there were a great many people present. The young folk indulged in games of various kinds but the older ones, the church members especially, took the whole matter more seriously. I recall that just before we parted there were many speeches. They were all crude, as I think of it now, yet I have seldom witnessed a more sincere and touching farewell reception. One old pastor, Armstead Berkely, who was perhaps seventy-six years of age, officiated as master of ceremonies. He had a wonderfully fine voice, strong and melodious. He was a great singer and had all the qualities necessary to make him a fervid, emotional speaker. I have known him at revival meetings to offer prayer, and again and again I have seen educated white people present who could scarcely control their features for the tears which ran down their cheeks. He made the final speech and closed the affair with a very earnest and touching prayer; and while there had been much levity among the young folk the early part of the night, he left them all in a very serious mood. I could not respond when called upon, but the impression of the sincere affection and good will of those simple, earnest people with whom I had lived from childhood has always remained with me.

My old chum, Lee Brown, and a few friends took my little trunk on a mule cart next morning, and we drove about five miles to Rice's Depot where I took the train for Norfolk, Virginia. Here I transferred to the Baltimore steamer which ordinarily touched at Old Point about seven o'clock at night. It so happened that because of a very severe storm the captain of the steamer decided that he would not touch at Old Point, so I was carried on with many other passengers to Baltimore. This was entirely against my wishes and naturally I was much annoyed. The ship's crew were very kind to all of us and gave us our meals and made no additional charge for the extra trip. This being my first experience on a steamboat, I suffered the discomforts that are common to the average passenger sailing on a stormy night. I spent a most interesting day in Baltimore strolling around, but did not get very far from the wharf.

CHAPTER 2

❧ *Doing and Learning*❧

That night I took the same steamer on which I had arrived and landed at Old Point the following morning, the 13th of October, 1885. I took a hack, which carried me and my little trunk past Fortress Monroe and up through the little town of Phoebus, then Mill Creek, and on to the grounds of the Hampton Institute. It was to me the most beautiful place I had ever seen. We drove up through the school farm past the old Butler School. This was a school that had been built under the direction of General Butler during the Civil War for the children of the freedmen, out of the lumber that had been used, much of it, in hospital barracks. We passed on through many acres of vegetables which Hampton had cultivated, and past the National Soldiers' Home cemetery, where stood some four thousand or more marble headstones, marking the final resting place of men who gave their all to preserve the Union. It is interesting that in that same cemetery, cared for by the Federal Government, there are many hundreds of Confederate soldiers also. Looking upon the well-kept grounds of the Institute, the water front, the neat and imposing buildings and farm lands, I felt almost as if I were in another world. A few mischievous boys took occasion to have some fun at my expense. They were already calling out

* From Robert Russa Moton, *Finding a Way Out* (New York: Doubleday, Page & Company, 1920).

"fresh fish," and two or three of them yanked my small trunk out of the carriage and balanced it on their fingers as waiters balance their trays in hotels. Some suggested that it weighed ten pounds; others, five. One little fellow, by the name of Bates, as I remember, whom I afterward found to be a fine baseball player, wanted to bet it would weigh not over two and three fourths pounds. I must confess that the small trunk was entirely out of proportion to the size of its 175 pound, eighteen-year-old, and somewhat awkward, owner. But I went through the ordeal good naturedly, and finally one of the older boys was kind enough to show me to the office where I presented myself to the commandant. He sent me for examination to Miss Anna G. Baldwin, the head teacher in the night school. She seemed to me very cold and unsympathetic, but I found afterward that I had misjudged her. She was, in fact, kind and very sympathetic; though her manner, like that of many New Englanders, was cold, austere, and very businesslike. The white women with whom I had dealt before had in their manner and speech a certain sympathetic quality that put one rather at ease than otherwise. Anyhow, I failed utterly to pass the entrance examination, though it seemed even at that time to be easy. I think I was bewildered. Everything was new and confusing. Baltimore experiences, my sea sickness, so many students, the battalion and band—all were so strange that I found it difficult even to see the print which was given me to read or the figures with which I was working. I was very much upset over my failure. I returned to the office and handed Mr. Curtis the note which announced it. He, too, seemed very much disappointed. He was at the same time sympathetic and told me frankly that he was very sorry that I had not passed. From what I had told him of the work I had done in school he had thought I would have no difficulty in passing, but would make a rather high class. He passed the note to Mr. F. C. Briggs, then the business agent of Hampton Institute, who sat at a desk near him. The two whispered some words, to which, at the time, I did not think it improper for me to listen. Mr. Briggs remarked and, by the way, I thought all the time Mr. Briggs was General Armstrong—in an undertone to Mr. Curtis, "it is too bad. I like his face. He has a very honest look," adding, "I think you had better keep him if you can." Mr. Curtis then turned to me with the words, "Well, young man, what are you going to do? You have failed to pass your examination to enter even the lowest class." I told him that I had come to stay at any cost, and that I thought my failure was due to my new surroundings; that I had not been in school for about two years, but had read an occasional newspaper and an occasional book when I could get hold of one, but had done no work in arithmetic except of the simplest kind and had written only an occasional letter, so that I thought I was "rusty." He wanted to know if I had any objection to hard work. I assured him I was not afraid of hard work, that I had worked hard all my life; so he said he would give me a choice of work, asking whether I would like to go to the kitchen or to the farm or whether I would prefer the saw-mill. As I had worked at a saw-mill and had some knowledge of lumber, I preferred the saw-mill, and was so assigned. I found this mill much larger and much more complicated than any I had seen before. I was put under the charge of a student, Edward R. Jackson, whom the boys called "Big Jack." He was to instruct me in Hampton's methods of grading and piling lumber. I was also admitted on trial to the lowest class in the night school.

I remember very well my first Sunday night at Hampton. Six hundred or more students—Negroes and Indians—with a hundred or more white people, assembled for evening prayers. A modest, unassuming gentleman, with a soothing voice, conducted the services. I do not remember the passage he read, but there were two or three petitions in his prayer that stirred my youthful emotions and brought over me a feeling hard then and hard now to describe. ... The students sang plantation songs, the religious folk songs of the Negro. I had been brought up on this kind of music and was very familiar with many of the songs that were sung, but somehow there was something about this singing—led by a tall, very handsome black man with a deep and melodious baritone voice—with the four parts blending almost as if there were just one great voice singing, that almost carried me into a new world. I had never heard such singing, but somehow, notwithstanding my thorough enjoyment of the music, the dress, and manner of the pupils, and my real appreciation of being in such a wonderful institution, I was disappointed to hear these songs sung by educated people and in an educational institution. I had expected to hear regular church music such as would be sung by white people mostly, and such as was written as I supposed by white people also. I had come to school to learn to do things differently; to sing, to speak, and to use the language, and of course, the music, not of coloured people but of white people.

One of my newly made friends, Thomas B. Patterson, who sat next to me in chapel, and with whom I worked at the saw-mill, and who to this day is noted for his frankness of expression, whispered to me saying, "What do you think of that music?" My reply was, "The singing is all right but this is no place for it." As the group of us walked on toward our quarters I did not hesitate to express my opinion regarding this music and most of the new boys agreed emphatically with my attitude. One or two of the older students argued that the songs were beautiful and people enjoyed them so why should we not sing them. The only reply I could give was that they were Negro songs and that we had come to Hampton to learn something better; and then, too, I objected to exhibiting the religious and emotional side of our people to white folks; for I supposed the latter listened to these songs simply for entertainment and perhaps amusement. I had frequently seen white people at Negro gatherings in my own community, and had the feeling that many of them came merely to be entertained. I remember how strongly I felt many years before when I attended Robinson's circus in our little village of Farmville. I remember the animals, of which I had only seen pictures before, and also the ring performances—fancy riding, antics of the clowns, and so forth. At the close of the main performance a concert was announced and my last ten cents was paid for it. Some twenty or thirty men with faces blackened appeared in a semicircles with banjoes, tambourines, and the like. The stories they told and the performances they gave were indeed most interesting to me, but I remember how shocked I was when they sang, "Wear dem Golden Slippers to Walk dem Golden Streets," two men dancing to the tune exactly as it was sung by the people in the Negro churches of my community. This song was as sacred to me as "Nearer, My God, to Thee" or "Old Hundred." I felt that these white men were making fun not only of our colour and of our songs, but also of our religion. It took three years of training at Hampton Institute to bring me to the point of being willing to sing

Negro songs in the presence of white people. White minstrels with black faces have done more than any other single agency to lower the tone of Negro music and cause the Negro to despise his own songs. Indeed, the feeling of the average Negro to-day is that the average white man expects him to "jump jim-crow" or do the buffoon act, whether in music or in other things. It is a source of gratification, therefore, to Negroes generally that Fisk University, Hampton Institute, Tuskegee Institute, and many other Negro educational institutions, have persistently preserved and used the folk music of their people, in keeping with the spirit of its origin, thus not only elevating it in the estimation of coloured people, but causing others also to appreciate its value and beauty.

A few Sunday evenings later, when General Armstrong had returned to the Institute, he spoke in his own forceful manner to the students about respecting themselves, their race, their history, their traditions, their songs, and folk lore in general. He referred them to the Negro songs as "a priceless legacy," which he hoped every Negro student would always cherish. I was impressed with him and with his address, but I was not entirely convinced. However, I was led to think along a little different line regarding my race. The truth is it was the first time I had ever given any serious thought to anything distinctively Negro. This also was the first time in my life that I had begun to think that there was anything that the Negro had that was deserving of particular consideration. This meant a readjustment of values that was not particularly easy for a raw country lad.

I think it was in December 1885 or late in November that a group of boys, of which I was one, was returning from the Soldiers' Home, which is separated from Hampton Institute only by a creek. We had noticed, before going over, a coloured man going through the engine room and boiler room and over the lumber yard looking at the machinery, lumber, saw-mill, planing-mill, etc., and we met this same man on our return going through the orchard, the farm, and the truck garden. We wondered who this man could be who seemed rather familiar with things at Hampton, and at the same time appeared to be very much interested in all the work of the place. When we went to chapel that night this gentleman sat next to General Armstrong on the platform in the old Whitin Chapel.

There were many visitors from the hotels and the town as well as the regular audience, and there were more teachers in chapel than usual. It was the first time I had seen a coloured man on the speaker's platform. We were glad, and took much pride, as the Negro students generally did, in any honour that came to a coloured man at Hampton; that is, any special recognition that came from General Armstrong.

After the usual devotional exercises General Armstrong, in his characteristic way, introduced this gentleman to the audience. He presented him as Booker T. Washington of Tuskegee. I remember now what a beautiful introduction General Armstrong gave him. He spoke of the possibilities of the work at Tuskegee and felt very sure that Tuskegee would some day be as large as Hampton, if not larger, and he predicted that Booker T. Washington would eventually be recognized as one of America's most distinguished citizens. He made this statement, he said, because he was thoroughly acquainted with the man of whom he was speaking. Booker T. Washington, he said, had been one of his boys; that he had served as his private secretary, and that he had recommended him for the work in Alabama. That during the past five years he had had wonderful success in gaining the good will of the white people and the coloured people surrounding the Institute and that the North had responded to his appeals for aid. Indeed General Armstrong had given no one so strong and, it seemed to us, so flattering an introduction, though many distinguished visitors had already appeared on that platform since I had entered school. There was not much known then of Booker T. Washington, though General Armstrong and others had frequently referred to him and the work which he had started at Tuskegee in Alabama. Even at this time General Armstrong had pointed him out as a sample of what he hoped the Hampton students would look forward to becoming after completing their education. He hoped they would start schools on the Hampton plan in rural communities.

While we were pleased at the introduction, we were anxious that this coloured man should measure up with his address to what General Armstrong said in the presence of so many white people, to say nothing of the coloured people. It made us all the more anxious that the coloured man should appear to good advantage, and I confess, as I think of it now, the appearance of the speaker did not impress us strongly. I remember some boys whispered "We're gone to-night."

There is something pathetic sometimes, I think, about the anxiety on the part of coloured people that one of their number shall show up to good advantage. The conditions under which we live, the early predictions that the Negro would not succeed, and the persistent comment that he is an inferior individual, have created in the race an anxiety and an earnest desire that every effort the Negro puts forth shall be of the best. We were especially anxious therefore, that on that occasion he should "hit the Bull's eye," as we used to say. He had not spoken many minutes before all of our anxiety had disappeared. He started off by telling a story which I do not recall at this time, but I know it was something about eating partridges. He spoke of what he was trying to do at Tuskegee Institute and said, modestly, that he was trying to carry out, as any graduate should do, the ideas of General Armstrong and Hampton. He spoke clearly of the importance and value of trade education and pointed out the fact that the men who had learned their trades in slavery were passing and that white men were taking their places.

As I think of it now, and as I thought of it then, we considered it perhaps the most remarkable address we had ever heard, and coming from a coloured man, about whom we had felt so much anxiety, it was all the more impressive. We were not expected to applaud in chapel at Sunday evening services, but there was a spontaneous outburst of applause from the audience when he sat down, and it was prolonged. General Armstrong arose, remarking, "I am glad you had the good sense to break the rule on such an occasion." He added, "This is for me as well as for you a very happy hour." It is unnecessary to remark that that address was the talk of the year among the students and teachers. We had some Indian friends who used to come to our rooms after meetings of this sort. I recall now that until "taps," some eight or ten of us, with our Indian friends, discussed that speech. One of the latter, John Archambeau, remarked to the group that the only fault he found with Booker Washington was the fact that he was not an Indian.

My twelve months' work at the saw-mill was hard and difficult, but I got out of it a great deal of pleasure and satisfaction. I, with my associates, learned a great many things, especially about lumber and machinery. I learned among other things to fire a huge boiler, something of the quality of coal, and how to get the most out of it. I learned to run the big Corliss engine, much about steam fitting, and a good deal about carpentry work, though I had worked for a while as a carpenter before.

I closed my year at the saw-mill in October, 1886, when I entered the regular day school. During the previous year I had worked in the day and attended school at night. This was customary among students who did not have the means to enter the day school directly.

Soon after this I was made an officer in the battalion and was given charge of one of the boys' buildings, being responsible to the commandant for the physical care of the building as well as for the conduct of its occupants. I recalled that my father yielded under protest to my coming to Hampton as a work student, urging me to wait another year while he and I saved sufficient money so that I could go to Petersburg and not be obliged to do work in the school. He felt, and I shared his feeling to some extent, that I knew all there was to know about work, but somehow I discovered during my year as a work student that I was constantly running against new things and new ways of doing old things: in the care of my own room, in the drill, at the saw-mill, in the night school; and even in the dining room and on the playground my vision grew continually wider and larger and I became more skilled in many ways with many and various things. That work year was a sort of initiation into an entirely new life, new surroundings, new people, different races, new standards, new ideas and ideals; and I have always been glad that, in spite of my father's protest, I had come—not because I wished to work, but rather because I did not wish to delay another year in getting an education—and had taken this year of work at Hampton Institute. But the first year in day school was different. I assimilated, perhaps unconsciously, many of these new ideals. While I learned many valuable lessons from books during this first year, they were insignificant as compared with the indescribable something which I gathered outside of books, very real at Hampton, and very real to me, too, which I cannot accurately describe in writing, but which was nevertheless very pronounced and very definite.

In my next year I came in daily contact with a half dozen or more lady teachers of the sturdy, austere, exacting, yet very kindly New England type; and while many of the subjects which they taught were not entirely new, the presentation was so different and they brought in so many practical, daily-life problems, not put down in books, that I found myself for the first few months in a realm almost as strange and different as my first year. One of the most striking subjects, as I think of it, was natural history or zoology, which was taught by Miss Ford, who afterward became the wife of General Armstrong. Our collection of numerous specimens, the investigation and dissecting of various insects and animals, the use of the microscope, were all a constant revelation to me of my dense ignorance concerning the common, every-day things with which I had been dealing and about which I had thought I knew so much. Mrs. Armstrong was a wonderfully strong teacher, able to arouse tremendous enthusiasm among her pupils, not only to master what was in the text book, but also to augment this by their own investigation and research in order to test the accuracy of the text book. I think also that my work in mathematics under Miss J. E. Davis, a graduate of Vassar College; in geography, under Miss Mary E. Coates; in grammar, under Miss M. J. Sherman, a graduate of Wellesley College, together with my work under others made for me a most interesting, inspiring, and helpful year.

At the close of the middle year, with seventy-eight other students, I was passed on to the Senior Class and was provided with a certificate to teach in the schools of Virginia, provided, of course, that I could pass the county examination satisfactorily. It occurred to me that, before teaching, inasmuch as I had never been outside of Virginia, except on my enforced visit to Baltimore, it would strengthen my position in my school community, wherever it might be, if I could at least say that I had lived outside of Virginia; so I secured a position as head waiter in a hotel in Pennsylvania. I had what the boys would call in those days "a very successful season." While my work was not very hard from some points of view and my pay was very generous, at least in gratuities—"tips"—there was something about the life that did not appeal to me, because the conduct of some of the guests differed greatly from what I had expected. So far as the treatment received from the guests was concerned, I had no cause for complaint, but many things about them and their manner of living were disappointing, not to say shocking, to one who had set up a very high standard and rather high ideals for people of means and education who lived amidst such pleasant and apparently wholesome surroundings.

At the close of the summer season I returned to Virginia and was appointed to teach in the school at Cottontown in Cumberland County. In this community, as in most other country communities, everybody knew everybody's else business, or thought he did. It was therefore soon known throughout the community that I had returned from school and secured a first-grade certificate, and that the county superintendent, Mr. Irving, a lawyer, had also spoken several times to groups of people on the streets of the town of Farmville and other places of the excellent record I had made in my examination; indeed that he had felt obliged to grant me a first-grade certificate even though I had had no practical experience as a teacher. I think I must have shocked the whole district by working as a day labourer on a farm after having been appointed to teach. It thoroughly upset the residents, white and coloured. No coloured teacher in that locality had up to that time ever been known to do such a thing. Many white friends, also neighbours, who had heard of it mostly through coloured people, rode over to Mr. Walthall's place to see if the rumour were really true. I was a sort of curiosity, but deep down in the heart of the people I am sure that there was a feeling of genuine satisfaction that I was doing this. Mr. Walthall, who was one of the leading farmers in that section, did not hesitate to express his approval in no uncertain terms. After the first few days, he increased my pay to nearly twice what he was paying the others, saying that he felt that I was worth more than they. Furthermore, he did not hesitate to tell all of his men about it, and after two weeks gave me entire charge of the squad of some twenty people. The truth of the matter is I was earning more on the farm than I did later when I began teaching.

It was a very busy year but I managed to find time for reading and study. I had had up to that time a more or less vague desire to study law. I had an idea that perhaps some day I might follow that profession, so the superintendent of schools for Prince Edward County, whose office was in Farmville nine miles away, was kind enough to give me lessons in law and lend me such of his books as I needed. He declined to accept any pay but allowed me to work in his office on Saturdays, copying deeds, contracts, and similar work, which saved time for him and was, of course, excellent training for me. This enabled me to occupy my evenings in a more or less definite systematic way. On Saturdays when I came to town he frequently catechized me very minutely on various phases of the week's work which he had given me to do.

The following spring, Mr. Irwin, the superintendent, told me I had sufficient knowledge to pass the bar examination. It was the law in Virginia then that a candidate for the bar could receive a certificate to practice after examination by two circuit judges. I never shall forget the time I appeared before Judge Frank Irving, the father of Mr. Irving under whom I had been reading law during the winter. I had come to the court-room late one afternoon. There must have been thirty people there, many attorneys among them. The cases had all been disposed of for the term. The judge was swapping stories with some of the attorneys. He finally turned to me and said "By the way, Moton, I understand that you want to take an examination to practice law." I told him that I did, and he said "I might as well examine you now." I told him I was not prepared to be examined then, that I would prefer to be given another appointment. He said "No, I can refuse you a certificate now as well as any time. I have had only one Negro in my court and he did not belong there. He was permitted to practice by courtesy, so I will examine you now. Come up here." I was certainly unprepared, but I thought I might as well face the ordeal. His son who sat over within the enclosure gave me some encouragement by saying, "You had better come over and try it anyhow. Many men have failed and you will have company."

I remember that the judge asked me to tell him first what a "demurrer" was, I undertook to tell him. He differed with me. I argued with him. In ten minutes I had forgotten that I was arguing with "His Honour," so we argued the "demurrer" in all its phases until dark. All the attorneys remained and were intensely amused, apparently. After we had spent perhaps two hours and a half in arguing this, the only question that the judge asked me, he said, "I will give you a certificate. Call up at the office tomorrow morning." And turning to the clerk of the court he said "Write him a certificate, Claxton, and I will sign it tomorrow."

But I had to pass another examination, before a judge who was reported to be more gruff than this one. A few days later I drove fifteen miles to the home of this other circuit judge, who lived in another county. I reached the house at breakfast time, somewhere around seven o'clock, just as the bell rang for him to come in to breakfast with the family. He saw me drive up, asked what my business was, whether I had had breakfast, and other questions. I assured him that I had had a very early breakfast and told him what my errand was. He gave me a seat on the front porch and went in to breakfast. Presently the cook came out with a tray on which was a very good breakfast, with steaming hot biscuits and other appetizing dishes. I did not send it back.

Later the judge came out and apparently in a very indifferent manner talked of many things and asked many questions, not at all along the line of the law, as I had expected. The fact is, I was all prepared for this examination. I was prepared to give the definition of law, something of the history of law, the various divisions of the law, and to answer the questions likely to be asked. I was prepared to make up briefs, indictments, and everything else that I had been able to find after much study in law books; but the judge asked about President Cleveland, who was then president; what I thought of him, of Congress, the tariff, the Republican Party, Mr. Lincoln, the Secession Movement. He asked my opinion of General Lee, General Jackson, and General Grant. He asked questions about Hampton Institute, General Armstrong, the relation of the races, as well as many other subjects. A famous case was then pending in an adjoining county: he asked me about the merits and demerits of both sides. It so happened that I was familiar with the case. He had seen me in the courtroom a few weeks before when he was the presiding judge. He asked me what I thought of the arguments of the opposing attorneys, and I did not hesitate to pick flaws in them and commend what I thought to be their good points. I also told him I thought one of the attorneys had been unwise in one of the questions he had asked his client, almost losing his case himself, in my judgment. The judge expressed no opinion whatsoever. Finally he excused himself a moment, went into the house and came back and handed me a certificate. I came away with a sense of disappointment that here I had been handed a license to practise law and had never been properly examined. I decided, therefore, to continue my studies, but as I think of it now I can understand that the examination, while technically deficient from my viewpoint, was in every sense adequate from the standpoint of this experienced jurist.

The apparent success which came to me that year brought many thoughts to my mind with reference to what I should do when I had finished my course at Hampton. Cumberland County and Cottontown—the name by this time had been changed to Adriance—seemed to me an ideal place for a small industrial school on the Hampton plan. Within a radius of perhaps ten or fifteen miles there were concentrated something like three or four thousand coloured people who could buy land, and many of whom had already secured substantial holdings. The white people were very kindly disposed toward them and anxious to sell land to coloured people. Also there were four churches. In every way it was an ideal community for a little school; so I got some of the more thoughtful coloured men together and we went over a scheme for such a school. I called on some of the leading white people and they also approved the plan, offering their support, and one gentleman offered to give ten acres of land. The county superintendent, Mr. Corson, assured us that the county would do at least as much as it had been doing, and he felt sure that they would provide the salary for the teacher. I wrote General Armstrong at Hampton and Miss Mary F. Mackie and some others of my Hampton teachers, setting forth my plans. They strongly advised against it, and urged me to return to the Institute and to complete my course. Some of them wrote me frankly that I did not have sufficient education to undertake such a work. One lady teacher, Mrs. I. N. Tillinghast, who is at present a warden at Vassar College, wrote me very frankly that my education was exceedingly deficient; that I did not know enough about any thing to succeed; that I had the ability to get up before a crowd and to make a certain kind of show, but that there was not nearly so much to what I was doing as I thought. I shall always remember that letter, for her argument, though hard to accept, was convincing. I therefore decided for the present, at least, to abandon the scheme.

The following summer I went to Philadelphia and succeeded in securing work in John Wanamaker's store, through the kindness of a friend who gave me a letter of introduction to Mrs. Robert C. Ogden. This, too, was a very interesting experience. I worked in what was called the housekeeping department for the first two months with a gang of about fifty men. There were but two coloured men, of whom I was one. The others were mostly Irishmen and Italians, but there were also two Dutchmen and two or three American white men. We had all of the noon hour and other off-hours when we had a chance to discuss many very interesting questions from different points of view. I never knew before that white men had so much fault to find with other white men. These men complained of the trusts, were down on both the Democratic Party and the Republican Party, as well as on Mr. Wanamaker, who was then the Postmaster General under President Harrison. It was hard for me to understand how these men could be working for a firm that gave what seemed to me so much consideration to its employees, and yet be so bitter against every person in authority. Mr. Wanamaker had just called together all of his employees who had been in the service more than ten years and presented each of them with a purse; and several of the men in our group were among this number; yet these very men were more bitter in their criticism afterward than before. We saw Mr. Wanamaker occasionally on Saturday and sometimes on Monday mornings. Mr. Robert C. Ogden, the manager, we saw daily. It was rather interesting to me to observe that the Irish and the native Americans of the group were generally the most outspoken in their denunciation of the rich and of all office holders. The Italians said very little, and the Dutchmen said nothing unless their opinion was asked. Later in the summer I was transferred to the Bureau of Information, where I remained until the middle of September, when I left Philadelphia for Hampton.

Having had my year at teaching, as required by the course at Hampton, I was now eligible for membership in the Senior Class. I began my work in October, 1889. Of the seventy-eight students who had been promoted to the Senior Class with me, only forty-eight returned to complete the course. I had reached the rank of Captain in the Middle Year; but things had somewhat changed during my fifteen months away from the school. Mr. George L. Curtis, who as Commandant had been most kind and friendly to me, had resigned his position and Mr. Charles W. Freeland had succeeded him. I was not sure that I would receive as much consideration from Mr. Freeland as I had from Mr. Curtis. In fact, I was reasonably sure that I would not, because the boys had already prejudiced my mind against him. He was an Episcopal minister and they said he came from Georgia, and was much worse, as we understood it, than a real Georgian, because, as they said, he was a "re-constructed Northerner." The idea was prevalent then as now among coloured people that when Northern people came South, and change from the Northern to the Southern attitude on the race question they are much more intolerant, from the Negro's point of view, than native Southerners. My prejudice against him therefore was very strong, and I had about reached the conclusion that he and I could never get along together. All of us had some resentment against General Armstrong for having brought such a person into the work. The young men did not hesitate to express the opinion that if General Armstrong meant to have a Southerner he should have gotten a real Southerner, and if he were going to have a Northerner he ought to have a real Northerner. It so happened that several boys from Savannah, Georgia, where Mr. Freeland had had a parish, entered school that fall, and those young men, I noticed, spoke very well of him and of his mother. They said he had been very popular with the coloured people in Savannah and with white people also. This report had to some extent the effect of allaying what was growing to be considerable bitterness on the part of the students generally. I soon found, however, that, while Mr. Freeland was very strict and very exacting, he was most kind and generous and that students who lived up to his rules had no difficulty in getting on with him.

When I entered Hampton in 1885, except for a slight inclination toward the legal profession, I did not have any very definite plan or notion as to what I wanted to do, but I was clear in the desire to return home and continue in the same activities in the school, church, and other local movements in which I had engaged before going off to school. My thought was to get sufficient education to do these things better and to save myself the embarrassment which I frequently underwent because I did not know as much as many people in the community thought I did. But when I entered the Senior Class my mind was pretty definitely set on the legal profession, and though I had passed the examination and been licensed to practice in Virginia, and while the teachers at Hampton did not oppose my plan exactly, they did raise the question freely and frankly, and I might add frequently also, as to whether I could thus render my people the greatest service, and whether legal advice at that time was the greatest need of an uneducated, struggling people in the rural districts of the South.

There was never any question, even from my earliest youth, I think, as to my desire to be helpful to my people, but exactly how it should be done was not wholly clear. My heart was pretty definitely set on going back to Prince Edward County, and the little town of Farmville was to me an ideal place. Something about the atmosphere of the locality appealed very strongly to me. I had been in Philadelphia, Washington, and Baltimore, and had seen a little of Norfolk, Richmond, and Petersburg, but somehow they did not compare in importance to my mind with Farmville, nor seem nearly so attractive as a place to live in as this little town on the Appomattox River.

Being the ranking captain, besides filling other places of responsibility in the school, somehow or other I was able to gain the confidence of most of the student body. I was made president of the Young People's Christian Association, an organization nominally under the chaplain, Mr. Frissell, but it took in all of the religious organizations of the school, the officers being elected by the student body. I was also made president of the Old Dominion Debating Society, the Boy's Glee Club, and the Senior Class, as well as president of the Temperance Society. These honours carried with them of course, certain responsibilities which I rather shrank from because I did not wish to have anything hamper my studies. In former years my class work had been somewhat along the lines of previous reading, but the Senior work was almost entirely new, except perhaps general history in which I had had no systematic instruction. Owing to this fact it was necessary for me to give closer attention to my studies than ever before.

I recall that after my election as president of the Temperance Society one of my very kind teachers, Miss Davis, to whom I have previously referred, met me as we came down from the assembly room, and calling me into her classroom said, "Moton, I hope you won't accept any other office. It would be very bad for you; a number of your friends among the teachers are afraid that your head is going to be turned; because you are receiving too much attention." While this was somewhat of a shock to me I received it with good grace, because, as my Sunday-School teacher, I had learned to value her opinions, though they were often expressed with embarrassing frankness. I carried my new honours as best I knew how, and had to face no serious difficulties, for as a matter of fact most of the details were looked after by the teachers, who were on the administrative committees of many of these organizations.

CHAPTER 3

❧ *Black, White, and Red*[*] ❧

O n a Saturday night just before the close of school, General
Armstrong invited the Senior boys to spend an evening at his
home. He told some fascinating stories of his war experiences with
Negro soldiers, the Ninth U.S. Coloured Troops which he recruited
and commanded at the Battle of Gettysburg. He showed us his uniform with a colonel's shoulder straps, which his mother had just
sent on to him from California, together with his sword. He told
with frankness of the weaknesses which he had observed in Negro
soldiers and of their strong points as well, but he showed clearly,
though apparently unconsciously, what wonderful growth these
men made under kind yet positive discipline. We had a most interesting and instructive evening. As the party was leaving, he asked
me to remain for a few moments, saying that he wished to speak
with me. I supposed, of course, that he wished me to do some errand
for him, but to my great surprise he began by asking what my plans
were for the future. I told him something of what had been on my
mind with regard to the school plan for Cumberland County and
my desire to help those people who had been so responsive to and
appreciative of my year's work, and who were very desirous of
having me return, for throughout the year I had been receiving

* From Robert Russa Moton, *Finding a Way Out* (New York: Doubleday,
Page & Company, 1920).

letters from committees as well as individuals urging me to come back. He commended the scheme and pointed out very clearly how it could be done, what a good thing it would be, how we could work in cooperation with Hampton and bring students to a certain degree of academic as well as industrial development, fitting them for entrance into the Junior Class, at Hampton, he thought, without examination. He also pointed out many essential details which I had overlooked. While in a general way he heartily approved of the plan, he nevertheless strongly advised against my undertaking it for at least a year. He did not hesitate to tell me that I needed more experience, and suggested that I could be very much more useful to my race and would conduct my school in a very much more satisfactory way if I would remain at Hampton for the present and help in the training of teachers for the large number of public schools that were being opened up throughout Virginia and the South. He would accept no decision at that time; in fact, he did not give me much chance to say anything. He simply took for granted what I would do and how I should do it. "You can think this over," he said, "and let me know if there is any reason why you should not take up your duties at the close of school as assistant to Mr. Freeland, the Commandant of the school cadets."

I took General Armstrong's suggestion and accepted work at Hampton as assistant to the Commandant, but decided not to enter upon my duties until the opening of school. I therefore again secured work through Mr. Robert C. Ogden, then in the John Wanamaker store at Philadelphia. In the meantime, it seemed advisable that Mr. Freeland, the Commandant, should go out through the Indian country and select Indian students for Hampton, this custom having obtained ever since Captain (now General) Robert H. Pratt brought on the first party of Indians in 1878. It was Captain Pratt who, after serving for a short time at Hampton with the Indians, founded the famous Carlisle School over which he successfully presided for many years.

Mr. Freeland's absence made it desirable for me to begin work at Hampton in the summer as Acting Commandant in charge of the three hundred or more Negro and Indian boys. Mr. Ogden readily released me from my engagement, saying he always doubted the wisdom of the Hampton graduates coming North so soon after graduation, for fear the fascination of Northern city life would incline them to remain, and congratulated me that I had escaped this temptation. I took up quarters in the "Wigwam," the building in which the Indian boys were housed. General Armstrong used to call the person who lived in the building the "House Father." It so happened also that one of the teachers who had been engaged to teach in the Indian school for the summer was obliged to resign her position because of illness, so I was to fill her place.

While I had, during my four years, been in more or less intimate contact with Indian students on the parade ground, in classroom, dining room, and elsewhere, and had some very intimate friends among the young men, I had never before taught Indian pupils, neither had I gotten a very clear insight into the Indian's attitude and viewpoint on matters in general. I learned for the first time how different it was from my own. I was surprised to find how hard it was for many Indians to adapt themselves to the customs of the white man, for they thought the old way, their way, better and in many cases gave very good reasons to support their view. Their opinion, for example, about the white man's religion was that he preached one thing and frequently practised another; that he preached human brotherhood, for instance, while very few whites, so far as the Indians could observe, actually practised human brotherhood. This thought was firmly fixed in the minds of many of them. This was a new experience for a Negro, for while many of us shared this view about the inconsistencies of the white man and how far he was from actually practising his religion, we had nevertheless adapted ourselves to the white man's ways, and had, consciously or unconsciously, and sometimes anxiously, absorbed the white man's civilization. The nearer we came to it, it seemed, the happier we were. I learned for the first time that peoples other than the Negro had problems and race feelings and prejudices, and learned to sympathize with another race, one, too, that was more nearly on a plane with my own and whose difficulties and handicaps seemed much greater than those of my own race. Living in the building with the Indian boys and being in their prayer meetings, and often acting as pitcher on their baseball team, along with contact in the Sunday School and in the day school classes of boys and girls, all gave me occasion to study more or less minutely the Indian character, especially by way of contrast with the Negro. I had taught Sunday School at intervals during my entire school career in one of the neighbouring coloured schools, and I remember with what enthusiasm my immature Biblical interpretations were received by the pupils and how comparatively easy it was to drive home a Bible lesson from every-day life. Not so with the Indians, however. They agreed that the point was well taken, but frequently I would find some pupil raising his hand—sometimes a girl who, I thought, was paying no attention to what was going on— and she would ask why Christian white people had cheated the Indians. Such interpretations, of course, frequently took all of the "wind out of my untrimmed sails."

In this connection, I remember that General Nelson A. Miles, then major-general of the United States Army on an official inspection of Fortress Monroe, sent up to say that he would inspect the cadets at Hampton on Sunday morning. During this inspection, as the adjutant read the orders for the day, General Miles heard the name of "Paul Natchee" and asked if Natchee came from Fort Sill and if he had been at Mount Vernon barracks. He was told that he had. The General then said, "This is the son of the old Chief Natchee whom, I am sorry to relate, I was obliged to kill because of persistent treachery." He asked how the boy was getting along and expressed a desire to see him before he left the grounds.

We then marched into the chapel and instead of the usual Sunday morning sermon, General Miles delivered a most helpful address. I had given orders to have Natchee remain after church and speak to me, which he did. I brought him up to General Miles with all of the deference due to the General's position, accompanied as he was by a large retinue of army officers and many prominent civilians as well as several naval officers, there being at that time some war vessels anchored in Hampton Roads. I presented Paul to General Miles. Extending his hand he greeted this boy of about seventeen years of age very cordially, unusually so for the ranking general of the United States Army, and in the presence, too, of a number of his subordinate officers. Paul looked him straight in the eye, did not salute, and refused to shake hands. I thought he had not observed the General's extended hand, and in a whisper I said, "The General wants to shake hands with you," but in typical Indian fashion he said, "Know it." General Miles, who had won his fame as an Indian fighter and who always observed every movement about him, turned to me and said, "Never mind, Major. He is an Indian. He will not shake hands." The General lectured him in a very kindly way on his stubbornness, telling him that his father might have been of great service to his race but for his indomitable and unconquerable stubbornness, which undoubtedly Paul had inherited. I was very much humiliated. So was Doctor Frissell. I think General Miles was the only person present who was not. I made up my mind to punish this young man very severely, and evidently General Miles knew it, though I said nothing. After I had dismissed Paul the General turned to me and said, "Do not punish him. He inherits that spirit. It can never be gotten out of him." As soon as I had an opportunity I called Paul in. When he walked into the office he said: "I ready go guard house. I stay there thousand years, never shake hands wid him. He killed my father." He broke down and wept, and through tears he murmured, "He killed my father. I never shake hands wid him. I never speak to him."

During that same year, when I was travelling with the Hampton Quartette as a singer and speaker, while en route between Albany and Boston, General Armstrong took the opportunity to ask me many rather interesting and searching questions. I had been acting as assistant disciplinarian under Mr. Freeland. I did not know whether my work had been satisfactory or not. The General among other things asked whether I thought, with the year's experience, if left entirely alone with the discipline, I could handle the situation at the school. He wanted to know if I had the organization of the battalion clearly in my mind and if I could handle it successfully. He asked me many questions about the school in general: what my attitude was; if I had noticed any differences between the races, the white, the coloured, and the Indian; if I had noticed any difference between the Northern white man and the Southern white man. He finally ended more or less abruptly by saying, "I want you to familiarize yourself very thoroughly with all phases of the work of the school, not only with reference to the discipline of the young men, but everything else that has to do with the work." I was very much disturbed because from the tone of his remarks I was rather inclined to feel that I had failed in my work.

We went on to Boston, where we spent many days holding meetings in the interest of Hampton's work. On my return to the school a few weeks later I went directly to Mr. Frissell, the chaplain, and did what everyone in the school usually did—teachers and students alike when in trouble—I asked him what General Armstrong had in his mind. I told him that I had been much disturbed by the questions which the General had asked me. He assured me that I had no need to be disturbed, that my year had been satisfactory, and that the General, as well as others, was very much pleased, so much so that he had had in mind asking me to assume charge of the Department of Discipline and Military Instruction of the Institute. Mr. Freeland had resigned and General Armstrong had made up his mind to place a coloured man for the first time in this very responsible position. He said that it was believed by many that Negro students would not respond to authority from one of their own number; but that Booker Washington's success at Tuskegee Institute, and the very satisfactory way in which I had handled some delicate situations during the year between the teachers and the students, as well as between Negroes and Indians, had convinced the General, as well as himself, that there would be much less trouble and friction in the school if I were placed in charge of the discipline. I confess this was a very great surprise to me. Instead of appealing to my pride it almost frightened me that I should for a minute have been considered for such a position. On the other hand, it was not my intention to remain at Hampton for more than two years. My idea was to get the larger experience which General Armstrong had suggested in the conversation at his house the year before and then go into some pioneer work among my people. The truth is I had never given up the idea of starting the school in Cumberland County, and was also interested still in the study of law.

In the following November General Armstrong, while in the midst of an address near Boston, was stricken with paralysis, from which he never wholly recovered, remaining an invalid for about two years thereafter, but entering more or less actively into the school's affairs, though it was necessary for him to be moved about in a wheel-chair. During this period Mr. Frissell performed the more active duties of Principal. I learned during these years to know General Armstrong very much better than ever before. I had previously been with him much in the North, and had observed many things about him that had struck me as unusual. It was difficult to understand how a man who was always as busy as he and who lived under such continuous pressure could be always solicitous for the comfort of the young men who were with him, Negroes and Indians, for there was usually at least one Indian in the party. He looked personally into our quarters to see whether they were comfortable or not. He did the same with respect to our meals, as well as other matters affecting our welfare. Frequently it happened at railroad stations, when it was necessary to hire a hack for ourselves or wagon to carry luggage, that he picked out the man who had the poorest horse and the most dilapidated vehicle. One day when Mr. Wm. H. Daggs, who generally managed our party, questioned the wisdom of our piling into a hack which looked as if it would break down at any minute, the General remarked that he always selected the poorest horse and hack because it was evident that this man needed the money more than the others. He added, jokingly, that this might not always hold for the reason that sometimes the evidences of poverty on the part of the hackman might be due to his own prodigality.

One day in May, 1893, when he was very ill, he sent for me to come over to the Mansion House, but this was against the doctor's orders; so Mrs. Armstrong and I agreed that it was wiser for me not to see him, but he insisted. He wanted to see me because he had noticed latterly that students, in passing his home to and from their meals, had been much quieter than previously. During his confinement to the house he had enjoyed the hearty laughter of the young men as they passed and their singing of plantation melodies and other songs. He asked me the very direct question if I had given orders that they should be more quiet because of his illness. There was no way to evade the question so I had to admit that such an order had been given. With some emphasis he said that he did not wish to have his illness affect in any way the school's activities; that he did not wish to have any change made even in the event of his death. "I want," he said, "even at my funeral that everything should be as simple as possible and that the school should be interrupted for as little time as possible"; and then he further suggested that I should arrange with Mr. Frissell's cooperation an entertainment or something, to relieve the depression which he was afraid his illness was causing.

This was in the early morning. In the middle of the afternoon of the same day he sent for me again to know what arrangements I had made. I understood General Armstrong well enough to know that if he suggested anything, even though he might say there was no hurry about it, in a very few hours he would either come into your office or call you into his and ask if you had done it, so I never put off carrying out any suggestion or request or order that he gave. So when he called me over to the house to know what had been done, I told him we had arranged for a baseball game the following afternoon with the dining-room men of the Hygeia Hotel. This game, as it was played by the waiters, always brought up a great many guests also from Old Point Comfort, officers as well as soldiers. The General was very much pleased with this arrangement and requested that it should be an afternoon holiday for teachers as well as students and that everything should be shut down. I could not understand how a man who was desperately ill—and of whom we were expecting every minute to hear that the end had come—could be thinking about such matters and going into the minutest details about all the affairs of the Institute, especially as they affected the life of the students. Also there were certain exceptional boys whom he knew, some who were not happy or satisfied about certain matters affecting their course of study and who had been in to see him. He wanted to know if these matters had been satisfactorily adjusted.

The following day, the 11th of May, 1903, the ball game was played. It was intensely interesting. Throughout the afternoon the grounds resounded with the tremendous shouts of the students. The playing was good on both sides. The cheering was equally loud from the visitors; for they, for the most part, were in sympathy with the waiters rather than with the students. In the midst of this tense situation, about the seventh inning, with the score standing "nothing to nothing," Mr. Frissell came down and called me aside and asked me what I thought of stopping the game, for General Armstrong had just died. He knew, he said, that the General would not want it stopped. I told him I felt sure the students would feel embarrassed to know that they had been playing under such circumstances, even though General Armstrong wished it so, and he and I agreed also that we owed something to the sentiment of the community and therefore decided that the game should be stopped.

General Armstrong's death was without doubt the most serious blow that the Institute had ever received. It was difficult for us to see how the school could exist without its founder. General Armstrong was a man of great force. His personality was so overwhelming that it seemed to me, as well as to others wiser than myself no doubt, that no one could carry on the work which he had founded and to which he had given the best twenty-five years of his life. Everybody at Hampton loved Mr. Frissell and had the greatest respect for him. He was in the confidence of teachers and students even more so than General Armstrong, but we seriously doubted whether he could carry forward the work of Hampton. In fact, many felt quite sure that he could not fill General Armstrong's place. And as I think of it to-day, after twenty-six years, I am convinced that we were right in feeling that neither Mr. Frissell nor any one else could be to Hampton what General Armstrong had been. General Armstrong had in a real sense completed his work, and a remarkable work it was! He had given America a new educational idea and developed a new ideal in education. He left Hampton in such condition that it could not go down, and the educational method which he worked out at Hampton could not but take a stronger hold on America and the civilized world.

I realized when I accepted the work that I would have to face difficulties, yet I also felt that if a person did his best and was honest and sympathetic in his dealings with the boys, that both Negroes and Indians would accept his decisions. During my twenty-five years in the work at Hampton I never had occasion to believe my assumption incorrect. To be sure I had to exercise discretion, especially when disputes arose between tribes or the two races; and I found that it was frequently very much better, instead of giving boys demerits for personal differences, to take the time to lead them both, if possible, to see their mistakes; and I usually found then, as I find now, that there are always two sides to a controversy. I found that it was usually worthwhile to take the time to bring them to the point where they would be willing to apologize each to the other. In consequence, I have always felt that much of the friction between races, as well as between nations and individuals, is due to misunderstanding, that if people would get one another's point of view, they would frequently find that things are not so bad as they imagine.

I had from the beginning a very strong, loyal first assistant in my work among the boys, a man who as a boy worked with me at the saw-mill along with Mr. Palmer, and who at the same time was my room-mate. This was Captain Allen Washington, now Major Allen Washington, who deserves the utmost credit for his share in any success achieved in the disciplinary work at Hampton Institute for the quarter of a century during which I was responsible for it. People even now wonder and frequently ask how the two races— the Negro and the Indian—get along together at Hampton. The truth of the matter is that at Hampton there has never been any serious manifestation of unpleasant relations between the two races. There are certain racial characteristics that are unmistakable, and the two races are in some particulars as different in temperament as they are in colour.

Types more diverse could hardly have been selected than the two thus brought together at Hampton. The Negro, as we have long known, is cheerful and buoyant, emotional and demonstrative, keen of apprehension, ambitious, persistent, responsive to authority, and deeply religious. In striking contrast stands the Indian—reserved, self-contained, self-controlled, deliberate in speech and action, sensitive, distrustful, proud, and possessed of a deep sense of personal worth and dignity.

But if the differing characteristics are evident, the similarity of the two races in condition and prospects is also striking. The Negro and the Indian have both been retarded in their development, alike in economic and social progress. They are both aspiring, the Negro with an earnestness that often outstrips his development; the Indian with a dawning realization of his needs. Both still need, as do some other races, such moral and mental discipline as will fix in them habits of obedience, order, accuracy, application, and the many other private virtues, the habitual practice of which makes the man. The very diversities of the two races under instruction at Hampton proved, in many respects, to be helps rather than hindrances to their development. Each served in many instances as a daily lesson to the other in the problems and difficulties of life. The Negro student

[51]

learned that he did not have a monopoly of the troubles incident to the effort to rise; that his is not the only race that faces a struggle in securing the rights and privileges of an advanced civilization. The Indian student saw the arts and practices of this civilization acquired and adapted by a race whose development corresponded more nearly to his own. He caught the inspiration of the manly endeavour and sturdy self-reliance that have characterized the Indian graduates of Hampton in all their subsequent endeavours among their own people. Through all my contact of thirty-one years as student and worker at Hampton it became increasingly apparent that the ground of racial adjustment lies, not in the emphasis of faults and of differences between races, but rather in the discovery of likenesses and of virtues which make possible their mutual understanding and co-operation.

After graduating at Hampton, I felt, with many of the other resident graduates, that our education was not complete, so for several years we did post-graduate work in certain advanced subjects which had not come in our regular course. The first few years we paid for this instruction ourselves, but later the school officials felt that it was proper for them to provide teachers for this work. I also continued my law studies one evening a week under the tutelage of Mr. F. S. Collier, a lawyer in the town of Hampton, a Southern gentleman who not only gave me instruction without pay but allowed me the free use of his law library.

Through the generosity of Prof. Francis G. Peabody I had the opportunity of attending several sessions of the Harvard Summer School, taking courses in gymnastics, English, and composition. For ten years I had continued my work practically without any let up, except for Summer School and Northern work and occasional visits among my own people in the South.

By this time some of my friends, among them Doctor Frissell, Mr. Robert C. Ogden, and Mr. Arthur Curtiss James, the latter two trustees of Hampton Institute, felt that I was very much in need of rest. They said I showed signs of fatigue, mental and physical which I confess I had not observed. Finally, in the summer of 1901, Doctor Frissell told me that whether I wished to go or not, he and one of the trustees had arranged for me to take a trip to Europe and that this trustee would provide the means, adding that he understood

Dr. Moton in the uniform he wore as
Commandant of Cadets at Hampton Institute

Above, Maple Cottage, the Moton residence at Hampton Institute.

Below, Major Moton's office, Hampton Institute (*Reuben V. Burrell, Hampton Inst.*)

that I was looking forward to a trip at some time. He gave me a few days to map out the route I would like to cover.

This whole conversation with Doctor Frissell afterward seemed almost a dream. The idea of actually going to Europe and going practically anywhere I wished to go was almost overwhelming. I mapped out what I would like to do and the countries that I would like especially to see, putting particular emphasis on southern Europe, because the Italian emigration was very large at that time and I was anxious to see another people who were more nearly on the plane of the majority of my own race in America; and then, too, I wanted to see Germany, and, of course, France and England. Doctor Frissell and the trustee referred to offered many suggestions when they knew exactly what I wished to accomplish.

Accompanied by a friend, I sailed from New York in May of the same year. After a day at the Azores we landed at Naples and came up through the principal cities of Italy into Switzerland and Germany, Belgium and France, England and Ireland. Before this I had been inclined to feel discouraged at times about my own race, and whatever people might say with reference to the advantages of the Negro in this country, I somehow felt that he was at the bottom of the scale of development, and of opportunities as well; but after seeing conditions in southern Europe, especially among the peasant class, my ideas regarding my race changed entirely and I realized for the first time that the Negro farmer, notwithstanding the unfairness and injustice which confront him, lives amidst surroundings much more encouraging and hopeful than is true of certain classes of the white race in Europe. While there was a striking difference in the physical surroundings and economic opportunities between the southern European peasant and the average Negro tenant farmer or renter, and while I also found a very striking difference in the wage scale which affects food, clothing, and home life in general, much to the advantage of the Southern coloured man, there was another difference even more striking, and that was the fact that the average European, to whom I have referred, was inclined to be hopeless so far as any improvement in his present condition was concerned. Few of them, moreover, had much hope of improvement for their children. They themselves were living much as their forefathers had lived, and in many cases they had lived for generations in the same house and worked on the same land with no other future before them save a desire on the part of a few of the younger ones to go either to North or South America. This was about the only ray of hope they had.

What I have said of conditions in Europe is true to some extent also of the Negro in Jamaica. While there is an absence there of the outward manifestations of racial antagonisms such as frequently obtain in this country, and while the difficulties in Jamaica, according to my observations, are due more largely to differences in character rather than in colour, nevertheless the situation so far as it concerns the Negro is in some particulars very much like that of the peasants of southern Europe.

There is this difference, however, between these countries and our own, and that is that the peasant in Europe and Jamaica has no fear for his life; he need not fear the aggressions of the lawless element of his community. If a crime has been committed he knows that the guilty will be tried by the usual legal process and punished accordingly. He knows also that there is no probability of offending persons being oppressed and terrorized by any part of the community because of the alleged misconduct of some member of their social or racial group. However, at the end of this trip I landed on American shores with the feeling that whatever may be the disadvantages and inconveniences of my race in America I would rather be a Negro in the United States than anybody else in any other country in the world. My subsequent experiences abroad have confirmed me in this conviction.

CHAPTER 4

❧ *At Hampton and Afield* ❧

BY WILLIAM ANTHONY AERY

"Welcome to Hampton, young man! Any friend of Dr. Frissell's is certainly a friend of mine." In substance these were the words with which Major Moton greeted me when, in the fall of 1906, I came to serve in the Academy of Hampton Institute as a junior instructor in the social studies.

This, in brief, was the beginning of a warm and intimate friendship which extended over a period of nearly thirty years, even to the end of his relatively brief retirement at Capahosic, Virginia. The greater portion of my story, however, relates to Major Moton's thoughts, activities and accomplishments at Hampton Institute and afield. I write of these reflectively as a man approaching seventy years of age—and not from the exuberance of youth.

In physical appearance, as I recall him, Major Moton was an impressive specimen of manhood. Tall, broad-shouldered, and very black as to his skin, he attracted admiring attention. His remarkable hands, although large, were truly beautiful—suitable to be cast in bronze. Without question, his military bearing was consistent with his assignment as Commandant of Cadets, for example is more effective than precept.

In what was known as "the bird's cage," a wooden structure glassed in at one end, the Major's office commanded a wide view of the central campus, a fact appropriately recognized by students and

[55]

workers alike. From desks in the same office Major Robert R. Moton and Captain Allen W. Washington, his assistant, administered with unusual dispatch the various rules and regulations of the Institute as they applied to five hundred young men, all members of the Cadet battalion. To my knowledge the general student verdict concerning Major Moton as a disciplinarian was somewhat as follows: "He's terribly tough to face in the bird's cage but he's fair...." "He'll let you tell your story, but you'd better be sure it's straight...." "He can spot a lie a mile off...." "When he knows you're lying he usually suggests that you come back early the following morning and tell him the truth...." "We hate to meet his severe look after we've tried to beat around the bush...." "He certainly can give you fits when you don't behave." While at first I thought the Major a bit severe in dealing with boys, I soon concluded that he believed in the value of obedience to authority as an aid to education.

As Commandant of Cadets Major Moton served as an officer on the Hampton faculty. The faculty in those days functioned as an administrative board of control responsible for the internal management of the entire school. For many years, in this capacity, the Major had an active part in the general discussion as well as in occasional debates related to special problems of the school. On such occasions he spoke rapidly and in precise terms. Although thinking quickly, he invariably exercised fine judgment when passing on the merits of the various cases introduced. He was especially skillful in getting to the crux of a complex problem and in sensing the vital issues and factors involved.

Major Moton, in dealing with the problems confronting him as Commandant of Cadets, followed Dr. Frissell's general pattern of administrative action, namely, never to bring questions to a faculty vote before there was reasonable certainty of approximate unanimity of judgments, either for or against. He, too, endeavored to have all concerned reasonably informed before any final action was taken, thereby saving himself from bringing wrath upon his own head through those who might feel themselves left out of his thinking and planning. This Frissell-Moton method was to me, in my early months at Hampton, most wearing and tearing. I soon discovered that it was wise and effective.

Serving on the Hampton faculty with Major Moton for a period of ten years, I came to know him as a keen thinker, a forceful speaker, and a courageous administrator. He was quick on the pick up and always alert to the basic issues. Thorough in his presentation of any program which he sought to develop and skillful in the clear-cut propositions calling for appropriate action, he almost invariably achieved his purpose. Fortunately, too, he well understood the working of the minds of his white associates on the Hampton faculty.

As Commandant of Cadets, Major Moton handled his students, workers, and officers, including trustees, somewhat as he did his flute or his violin, with a masterful sense of pitch and time, of sure and artistic touch, and of attainable results. At heart he was an artist who handled with consummate skill the instruments needed for the completion of his assigned tasks—the ability to reason, to speak, to write and to confer, as well as the capacity to work very long hours without showing signs of fatigue, and along with it all, an unusual ability to make friends out of potential enemies. Many times Major Moton's position was vigorously opposed. Often he won his case because he was a man who really knew the facts and was ever ready to use them for the good of others.

Between Major Moton and Dr. Frissell there existed absolute, mutual trust. Again and again Frissell told the Hampton students and workers the story of Moton's life—his association with a fine old Virginia family, his work and study experience in securing an education, and his rise, even as a student, to positions of leadership. Frissell told of the excellent record made by Moton as Assistant to the white Commandant at Hampton, and how he became the first Negro Commandant of Cadets through his own sheer merit and effort.

Major Moton, in due time, became a key man in the financial campaigns carried on by Hampton throughout the North. In this way he early obtained a knowledge of the whole country which he used in speaking and writing to bring together, for a common cause, men and women possessing a diversity of gifts and interests. Moton, like Frissell, believed in the basic goodness of common folks, although he sometimes had occasion for disappointment in little-minded men and women who worked because of their own self-interest rather than for the good of a worthy cause. He frequently displayed a remarkable degree of patience in dealing with people whose ready promise outreached their actual performance.

Major Moton's accomplishments were largely due to his intimate and cooperative relations with outstanding leaders of his time. His association with Dr. James Hardy Dillard, a distinguished Southern gentleman and scholar, began in 1908 when Dr. Dillard was made President of the Anna T. Jeanes Fund. This fund was set up to improve the Negro rural schools—first, for Virginia under the guidance of Dr. Frissell; second, for Alabama under Dr. Washington; and third, for the entire South under a Board of Directors formed by Dr. Frissell and Dr. Washington and presided over by President Taft. The Jeanes Board met regularly in the Cabinet Room of the White House at Washington. Because of his intimate knowledge of the educational problems of Virginia, Major Moton was of inestimable service to Dr. Dillard and his close associates B. C. Caldwell, Jackson Davis, W. T. B. Williams, Arthur D. Wright, Leo M. Favrot, James L. Sibley, William D. Gresham, and N. C. Newbold.

The Jeanes Fund work grew so rapidly that soon there was an educational program under way which could not be supported by the $1,000,000 fund which Miss Anna T. Jeanes, a Quaker of Philadelphia, had set up in her will. It was then that the General Education Board began paying the salaries and traveling expenses of an increasing number of state agents for Negro education. From the beginning of this important work Major Moton gave unfailing service to Dr. Dillard and his associates. While at Hampton and later he kept in close touch with the state rural school agents who, through their respective state superintendents of education, influenced the several state legislatures to make further appropriations for the Negro schools. Often the going was hard and rough for all who were engaged in revolutionizing Negro rural education.

During the year 1910 Major Moton traveled with Booker T. Washington through South Carolina, Tennessee, Delaware, North Carolina, and parts of West Virginia, studying at firsthand the actual conditions among Negroes. During the ten-day trip through North Carolina Dr. Washington spoke to thousands of people; visited Negro homes, schools, churches, and places of business; observed the relations between whites and Negroes; and presented plans for promoting interracial cooperation and good will.

For a period of six more years Major Moton was called upon by Dr. Washington—and was gladly released by Dr. Frissell—to engage in good will tours through several of the Southern States. These Washington-Moton missions opened the minds and hearts of thousands of white Southerners to thoughtful consideration of the Negro and his many pressing problems—problems which no race, either white or Negro, could possibly solve without mutual cooperation and good will.

Major Moton was a staunch and faithful supporter of Mrs. Harris Barrett of Hampton, Virginia, who, with the active cooperation of the Colored Women's Federation of Virginia and many liberal whites, both North and South, founded and developed the Industrial Home School at Peake in Hanover County, Virginia, for the care and improvement of delinquent Negro girls. By his correspondence and public addresses he helped to win for disadvantaged Negro girls the financial and moral support of many philanthropically minded Americans. Major Moton recognized that the city and county jails in Virginia and elsewhere were hotbeds of moral disease for young and old alike. This was especially true for Negro girls. Old and roughshod methods of passing sentence and inflicting punishment were in general practice. The Barrett-Moton plan, aiming at reform rather than punishment, emphasized the importance of sympathetic and intelligent guardianship for delinquents and stressed interesting work under supervision rather than revengeful abuse. This plan assumed that better girls would make better mothers, better mothers would make better homes, and better homes would certainly make a better nation.

For a period of at least eight years Major Moton worked side by side with leading Negro clubwomen of Virginia in developing Mrs. Barrett's dream into a reality. Finally, on January 19, 1915, the Industrial Home School for Negro girls was opened.

Important also was the influence of Major Moton on Negro farm life in Virginia. In cooperation with John B. Pierce, Thomas W. Patterson, and John L. Charity, as well as Miss Lizzie R. Jenkins— all Hampton graduates—he helped to improve living conditions through an extensive program of home and farm demonstration agents who worked under the States Relations Service of the United States Department of Agriculture. Year after year Dr. Frissell and Major Moton together with other Hampton workers met with these thoughtful Negro agents for consultation on ways and means of meeting local rural problems. Major Moton always vigorously stressed the importance of having the agents, who worked immediately under the direction of the Virginia Agricultural College and Polytechnic Institute at Blacksburg, build up country life as a whole rather than minister to the interests and profits of single individuals. He saw in this Federal activity the opportunity of meeting community needs and increasing cooperation between whites and Negroes. His early life on a Virginia farm in Prince Edward County had given him some basic knowledge of what Negro farmers needed and how best they could be helped.

Having heard many of Major Moton's off-the-cuff talks to these Negro agents and to the white leaders who were cooperating with them in revamping economic and social life in the Old Dominion, I learned what was really meant by the words "the Hampton idea of education in action." The Major had close to his heart the lot of the Negro farmer. He was always ready to confer with groups that aimed to give the latter better status in the American economy. His vital message to the Negro farmer everywhere was in substance as follows:

"Raise more and better crops; work more acres more days in the year; raise better stock; buy modern farming implements and machinery; save money from the sale of your crops; buy more land; have a bank account; make use of the advice given by farm demonstration agents and other experts; increase comforts in the home; conduct farming as a business venture; keep accounts showing expenditure of time, money and labor; use legumes and green cover crops instead of commercial fertilizers, and develop skill as crop producers."

The effectiveness of the Frissell-Moton type of practical wisdom was well illustrated in the origin and development of the Negro Organization Society of Virginia. For several years, beginning in 1904, a series of conferences at Hampton Institute was held every summer for the discussion of problems relating to farming, health, education and community improvement. To these conferences were attracted an increasing number of Negro leaders from far and near. Always willing to let new ideas and plans grow slowly, Dr. Frissell and his able coadjutor, Major Moton, were convinced by 1912 that the time had well arrived for the development of a super organization which would attempt to make active use of the various already existing organizations to promote a comprehensive program of community improvement among Negro citizens. To the leaders in the Hampton Negro Conference that year, Major Moton, as spokesman, proposed such an organization whose motto should be: "Better Schools, Better Health, Better Homes, Better Farms." The idea immediately captured the minds and hearts of the Negro leaders and there came into existence the Negro Organization Society of Virginia.

As President of this new group of community leaders Major Moton traveled widely over Virginia, spreading effectively the idea of achieving worthwhile results in community improvement through the active cooperation of disparate Negro organizations— for practically every Virginia Negro belonged to some lodge, club, church, or association. Major Moton proved again that he was a native-born orator and campaigner, as well as a well-disciplined thinker in the fields of economics, health, education, and sociology. He demonstrated anew that he was tireless in his effort to serve the public, both white and Negro. He gave to the Negro Organization Society, from the beginning until the time of his death, a full measure of unselfish, able and unstinting service.

At all times Major Moton impressed upon his people that they could and should help to remedy the bad conditions under which several hundred thousand Negroes lived and worked in Virginia. He pointed out how they could properly approach their white neighbors for the active support of the extensive Negro Organization Society program. From time to time he brought his associates throughout Virginia hopeful and stimulating reports of community progress, which had been made in spite of severe handicaps—lack of funds, indifference among those to be helped, lack of official support, and the prejudice of untrained men and women against all Negro progress. Major Moton stressed the important fact that from the soil of Virginia, as elsewhere, whites and Negroes must continue to get the bulk of those important products which they could sell at a profit and secure some surplus of money which, in turn, should then be used to promote community improvement work.

In this pioneer work Major Moton had the vigorous and intelligent support of John B. Pierce, who was then district agent of the United States farm-demonstration work in Virginia, and literally a host of strong Negro leaders in all walks of Virginia life. He also cultivated successfully a wide range of Southern and Northern white friends.

Major Moton, in closing the Petersburg meeting in 1915, made the following observation: "Religious, benevolent, secret and educational organizations of every character have joined in the movement fostered by the Negro Organization Society of Virginia and leading white Virginians have been most cordial in their support of the Society."

At the fifth annual meeting of the Negro Organization Society which was held in 1917 in Portsmouth, Virginia, T. C. Ervin, the Society's field agent, with headquarters at Petersburg, Virginia, reported that in a single year the Society had secured the cooperation of fifty Negro industrial supervising teachers in rural schools, eighteen farm-demonstration agents, over one thousand school teachers, two hundred county committeemen, numerous women's clubs and local Negro organizations and several hundred ministers.

Dr. Moton, then honorary president, spoke on "The Negro and Cooperation." He emphasized the importance of whites and Negroes working together in perfect harmony for important common interests and fighting together all enemies to the American nation. He urged men and women to save their wartime earnings when people in the South were so generally prosperous; to place their individual savings at the disposal of the Government; to follow in the footsteps of Dr. Frissell, who had served all men so unselfishly; and to do faithfully every assigned duty.

The Negro Organization Society at every stage of its program won the active support of Virginia state and local officials—health, charities and public welfare, education, public roads, and finance; officers of the American foundations—General Education Board, Julius Rosenwald Fund, Jeanes and Slater Funds; officials of government agencies, including the War Department and Office of Education; and Negro national organizations such as the National

Association for the Advancement of Colored People, National Urban League, National Medical Association, National Negro Business League, Federation of Colored Women's Clubs, and the National Protective League for Colored Girls.

While the Negro Organization Society owed its inception to the interest, sympathy and wisdom of Dr. Frissell, its career was started and developed successfully under the dynamic leadership and indefatigable work of Dr. Moton who, throughout his career, from the year 1912 onward, gave the Society his invaluable services in time, thought and money.

Moton was at heart a student as well as a born leader. He read widely in the fields of history, economics, anthropology, ethnology, and political science. He talked earnestly and often with visiting American and foreign research scientists on the problems of race, heredity, geopolitics, and psychology. He attended numerous technical conferences on education and sociology. He sought knowledge with avidity. He arrived at positive convictions by which he lived and for which, if necessary, he was prepared to give his life.

Indeed Moton discovered empirically and by the so-called "hard way of experience" over a generation ago what, for example, a group of UNESCO social scientists recently formulated and published (see the October 1950 issue of *Phi Delta Kappa*), namely, the lack of scientific proof that groups of mankind differ in their innate mental characteristics whether in respect of intelligence or temperament and the evidence of science that ethnic groups had much the same range of mental capacities. Moton, too, was in agreement with the modern social scientists who stress the idea that all groups of human beings had shown "capability of learning to share in a common life, to understand the nature of mutual service and reciprocity —and to respect such social obligations and contracts."

Moton, consciously or otherwise, had pledged himself to study and service—and through these weapons he won his way to valuable leadership in the Negro race—for the ultimate benefit of all Americans at a critical period of race relations, not only in the South, but also throughout the United States. He came early in his Hampton career to realize that racial discrimination—and the racial hatred which it always bred—were as unscientific as they were false and cruel. He understood, too, that cultural traits had no basic relation to racial traits.

His classroom instruction and his unending pursuit of self-education had taught Moton that men and women of all classes, creeds and colors were largely conditioned, for good or ill, by their physical, economic, political, educational and social environment. To have better men, women, and children in the American Negro population, Moton saw clearly that the entire environment of his people must be improved. Moton's study of race relations brought him to the firm personal conviction that men could be remoulded in their thinking; that they could be educated for life—in and through life; that they could be helped to higher levels of thought and action. He accepted the idea of Confucius that men have natures which are alike, but have habits which carry them far apart. He continued year after year to improve his own habits and the habits of all those whom he could influence. He taught much that was worthwhile and constructive by his own exemplary life.

Moton recognized the scientific truth that personality and character are raceless and that any group which is handled by psychological, sound and Christian methods can be vastly assisted in its uphill climb toward richness in personality, strength of character, and effectiveness in making their country a safer and better democracy for all American citizens. He further learned to distinguish in his thought and action, both private and public, between the so-called "biological fact of race" and "the myth of race superiority" due to color alone which, for example, so many white Christians of his period held tenaciously, and even still worship unduly in hundreds upon hundreds of communities,—North, South, East and West—to the disadvantage, suffering, and even death of non-whites.

Moton's philosophy of life, for him always rich and well rounded, laid definite emphasis upon relating daily experience—good, bad and otherwise—to the solution of new problems as they arise. He probably never used the educational jargon term "integration" but he nevertheless steadily adhered to the idea that thought and action, learning and doing, teaching and practice, preaching and performance should all be related to one's daily living. He insisted that education, for example, in order to be really worthwhile in the modern world, must be an instrument for finding workable answers to human problems. He sought to help all with whom he had any association find a satisfactory, even a happy, adjustment to the realities of life.

Moton was his own best exponent of a constructive philosophy of life. Seasoned, wise campaigner for sound ideas of education, for individual and group improvement of economic and social status, for the recognition of the underprivileged, disadvantaged among God's children, including whites, Mexicans, American Indians, and members of the Negro race, he sought to advance a philosophy of life and education which emphasized the importance of personal worth and the duty of the strong toward the weak.

Moton was distinctly a creative thinker in the field of American social education. While he stressed the immediate value of industrial, and then vocational education for Negroes and Indians, he definitely recognized the importance of giving Negro and Indian youth, for example, a full measure of cultural and professional education which would prepare them for the greatest possible service to their home communities and the world in which they had to live and work. He, in short, believed in the possibility of integrating so-called liberal and vocational education. With him the choice was not one or the other but rather a good balance between the two kinds of modern education. He recognized the fact that, while Negroes differed widely as to their individual traits, interests, and capacities, they as a central group represented an extremely broad range of intelligence and capacity for learning by doing, which should be fully realized in creating a new and better world both at home and abroad. In all his thinking and planning he endeavored to help his race overcome, through proper instruction and continuous education, their immediate handicap in the existing economic, political and social order. Moton agreed with the wisest thinkers of his day that for Negro youth, whom he knew best, there was real and pressing need for many different forms of education including vocational, general, liberal arts, pre-professional, professional, and graduate, if American Negroes were to come into the fruits of good democratic government. Furthermore, he believed that only healthy people—healthy in body, mind and estate—could help themselves both immediately and ultimately to climb to American freedom and win for themselves respected status. He saw the necessity for the development by Negroes of effective organizations, local and state, which would cooperate with existing health organizations to secure better health—physical, mental and emotional—for the Negro masses and their leaders. This objective of education meant to Moton, and to those who loyally followed him, the continuation of warfare against tuberculosis, social diseases and the common ailments of childhood, all of which he pointed out again everywhere faced the American Negro group.

Moton at Hampton and afield, as I knew him for over a generation, never lived just for today; he lived to make tomorrow better for all mankind, whether he was conducting the details of his office as Commandant of Cadets, or working with Dr. Frissell and others for the building and financing of Hampton, or was helping other Negro leaders do better what they had already set their minds upon doing, or was spreading the comprehensive program of the Negro Organization Society, or was preparing and delivering public addresses, or was studying difficult situations abroad such as the status of Negro troops in France during World War I, or was writing out very carefully for publication his interpretation of Negro thought and feeling, or was following the common round of daily work as a plain American citizen.

Moton's message for tomorrow lay in today's work and was expressed in terms of faith, hope, and love. He clearly saw a better day coming for the American Negro population of 14 million citizens and all their white neighbors but he was fully aware that the fundamental American institutions such as the home, the school, the church and the vocation must carry a fair share of the responsibility for bringing this to pass.

CHAPTER 5

❧ *The Major* ❧

BY WALTER R. BROWN

My interest in Robert Russa Moton began when I was a small boy living in Prince Edward County, Virginia. Although he was born in Amelia County, he and his parents soon moved to Rice in Prince Edward County, only a few miles east of Farmville, the county seat. Our own home was a few miles southwest of Farmville where I was born and reared. Being the largest tobacco market between Petersburg and Lynchburg, Farmville had become the business and social center for the rural people in three or four of the surrounding counties. This was especially true on Saturdays and during the tobacco marketing season. Through parents' attendance at the town gatherings and occasional visits by townspeople to Sunday church services in the surrounding rural areas, even the children learned the names of many people whose faces they seldom or never actually saw in person.

It was in this way that at an early age I heard of the Moton family. Somewhat later I began to hear the name of "Captain Moton" at Hampton and still later "Major Moton." An older brother and sister of mine, who were students at Hampton during those years, frequently mentioned Major Moton. He had become well known at the Institute because of his various interests and activities. Also, through conversations of Hampton graduates in our community, we heard more and more about Major Moton. My first contact with him, however, was in the spring of 1907, the year of the opening of the Jamestown Exposition at Pine Beach near Norfolk.

The records show that General Armstrong discovered in Robert Moton, even during his student days, the budding characteristics of a successful leader and executive. He was a young man of strong will, moral integrity, and possessed of a happy combination of traits of personality essential to the creation of respect and good will. Because of these and other qualifications Robert Moton, immediately following his graduation in 1890, was invited to join the Institute staff. Within a year of the date of his appointment he became Commandant of Cadets, a position which he held for a full period of twenty-five years. During all this time and until his acceptance of the principalship at Tuskegee, he was ably assisted by his associate, the late Major Allen Washington. The two, Moton and Washington, throughout the years were an inseparable pair in the work of the department. In size and general appearance they could easily have been taken for brothers.

About three years after Major Moton had received his appointment to the staff, General Armstrong, following a long period of illness, was claimed by death. Immediately the Rev. Hollis Burke Frissell, beloved Chaplain of the Institute, took on the head administrative responsibilities of the institution. Having been associated as colleagues under General Armstrong and having seen eye to eye on almost all of the important issues pertaining to the Institute and its future, Frissell and Moton became a powerful team, working together for more than twenty years in the development and administration of Hampton Institute. They were ably supported by such persons as Albert Howe, Elizabeth Hyde, Alexander Purves, Frank K. Rogers, Francis C. Briggs, Dr. Herbert B. Turner, Dr. Thomas Jesse Jones and many other loyal and conscientious workers whose names are well and favorably known in the history of Hampton Institute.

I remember my first visit to Major Moton's office. It was in the summer of 1907. I went to inquire as to the possibility of my entering school the following September. From the first I had the feeling that the Major was my personal friend. Having secured from Miss Louise M. Goodrich, Secretary of Admissions, the application form, I proceeded to apply for entrance on the Work-Study Plan. I had

Above, Marshall Hall, Hampton Institute (*Reuben V. Burrell,
Hampton Inst.*)

Below, Academy Building, Hampton Institute (*Reuben V.
Burrell, Hampton Inst.*)

Dr. Moton at a dedication of a Rosenwald school, around 1925

already obtained work at one of the nearby hotels for the purpose of earning money with which to pay my entrance fees, should I be permitted to enroll.

Within a few days I was instructed to report for the examination. Arithmetic and composition were the tests required. I was somewhat surprised when Miss Goodrich, having looked over my papers said, "You did very well in your English but not so well in your fractions." She then presented me with an admission card.

If tact is, as someone has defined it, "the happy art of making others feel at ease," Major Moton was tactful in unusual degree. Even in asking questions he knew how to avoid embarrassment. When I informed him of having received my admission card, he asked—evidently noticing that I was well grown—"How long have you been out of school?" "At thirteen years of age," I replied, "I stopped school and have worked on the farm ever since." "Well," he remarked, "one can get pretty rusty over a period of five or six years."

After asking several other questions the Major said, "Mr. Williams [the late W. T. B. Williams who left Hampton to join the faculty at Tuskegee shortly after Major Moton became Principal there] is conducting a night class in arithmetic for the benefit of students whose grades were low during the past year. I am suggesting that you come into his summer class and prepare yourself for entering school in September."

Accepting his advice, I reported for the summer study early in August, 1907. While carrying on the work in arithmetic with Mr. Williams, I worked as orderly in the executive building, which included the offices of the Principal, the Commandant, the Secretary, and the Business Manager. The combined work as student and orderly was a most valuable, orienting experience for me. All of this, on the campus of the school I was to enter in the fall, was truly educative in its effect on me, a rural youth just from the farm.

In those days the regular term opened about the first of October. This gave me approximately nine weeks of intensive study with Mr. Williams in a class of twenty-five or thirty boys. Soon I learned from other students that our teacher was a graduate of Andover Academy and Harvard University and of course that, we thought, made him the last word in everything. He was truly a teacher of the first order—interesting, thorough and patient. Happily, near the end of September I received credentials for admission to the regular term. To Major Moton I have always given credit for advising me what to do in order to prepare for admission to Hampton; to Mr. Williams credit for preparing me.

While my assignment as orderly was in the executive building, my duties were centered largely in the Commandant's area, thus placing me in close contact with the Major. Some of the older students delighted in giving the new students their personal appraisals of the various members of the administrative staff. All were aware of the intimate cooperative relationship between the Major and Dr. Frissell in matters of policy making and administration. They were also unanimous in the judgment that if Major Moton considered you an undesirable citizen it would be well for you to change your way of life or be prepared to leave Hampton on short notice. Needless to say those of us who were students at that time can testify to the fact that the Major was positive and consistently unwilling to accept low standards either of conduct or of performance in general.

Whenever the need arose for a frank "family lecture" the Major was thoroughly prepared to give it. He could do this in an appropriate, but effective, manner to any group under his supervision. Many of us remember occasions when the Major found it necessary to deliver sharp and positive "lectures." When, for example, misunderstandings arose between individuals or among groups of individuals the Major not only knew the appropriate method for resolving the differences but he knew how to command the confidence and respect of all concerned. On one occasion calling for reproof the Major said: "Never lose your head. If you do you are likely to lose your fist. You cannot always settle differences in this manner. Remember, a mule can kick harder than any man among you, yet he is just a mule. After all, the mule can be bridled and led around most of the time."

Military drill, under the supervision of the Commandant and his staff, was required of all able-bodied men. There was no special concern about ages for, in those days, scarcely any married persons were admitted to the Institute, and students over twenty-four years of age were seldom encouraged to enter. Many changes, however, came about later when the educational offerings were extended to the college level. There were daily formations at noontime when the men of six companies answered the roll and marched to dinner. One hour each week was regularly set aside for special military drill. On this occasion an army officer from Fort Monroe participated. Every Sunday morning at 10:30, weather permitting, the battalion formed on the church lawn, at which time Dr. Frissell, accompanied by Major Moton and Captain Washington, inspected the men. The appearance of this trio, averaging more than six feet in height and two hundred pounds in weight, passing down the lines inspecting the men and then observing the companies as they passed in review, was very impressive. Led by the band the battalion passed in review and marched into church.

The Major was possessed of a persuasive and penetrating personality, generally recognized at sight, and supported by a voice and mode of expression equally forceful and effective. These qualities, combined with his courage to stand by his convictions, to put into practice the prescribed regulations and to carry out the general policies of the institution—difficult as they frequently were—won for him a substantial reputation. In matters of discipline he believed in quick action; there was no place in his program for unnecessary delay. Failure to live up to moral obligations and to disregard community requirements were, in his philosophy of life, inexcusable.

Some of the boys, as could be expected, felt that he was rigid in the enforcement of regulations and many times experienced a feeling of fear when called to his office. In most cases, however, even those most critical and fearful at first, were gradually changed through their conferences with the Major and eventually developed a deep respect and reverence for him.

Strict institutional requirements in those days were looked upon as aids to character building. Not only Major Moton but most of the other members of the staff were agreed in this matter. Keeping accurate attendance records and immediately following up any absentees not accounted for was a part of the system. To Major Moton and his assistants belonged the responsibility of checking, following up, advising and counselling the men, and the effectiveness of their work in these areas has been acknowledged through the years by those who attended Hampton in those days.

[71]

Perhaps the most enjoyable assembly in the campus life of Hampton was the Sunday evening service in Cleveland Hall Chapel. The program usually consisted of an opening hymn, a group of spirituals led by the Major, and a short address by Dr. Frissell, Dr. Herbert B. Turner or Major Moton. Visitors from many parts of the world stopping over at the local hotels, people from neighboring communities, personnel of the Army and Navy stationed at nearby posts and bases, together with the campus population of the Institute usually filled all available seats in the chapel. The Major was widely known for his ability to lead large audiences in the singing of Negro spirituals.

At a much later date, and long after the Major had become Dr. Moton of Tuskegee, he said on one occasion when addressing a Hampton chapel service: "I have no memories of Hampton Institute more pleasant than the privilege that was mine, so many times, to lead the singing of these songs at prayers and on other occasions. Nothing in all my religious experience has been more inspiring than these melodies, and tonight I feel again something of the old thrill as I listen to your voices in the songs that meant so much to our fathers and mothers and that, I trust, will always mean much to us."

Although official duties and responsibilities at the Institute claimed for Major Moton priority over all others, he still found time during evenings, Sundays, and other off-schedule periods to help in the promotion of various activities in the nearby communities—chiefly in churches, schools, business and fraternal organizations. He was in constant demand as a speaker on important occasions throughout Virginia and beyond. Such sharing in the promotion of community activities carried on by scores of Hampton's staff members over the years, was the continuing process of extension service as conceived and initiated by General Armstrong and enlarged by Dr. Frissell, Major Moton, Booker T. Washington, W. T. B. Williams, Thomas C. Walker, Allen Washington, and others.

Major Moton, in many respects, was an unusual personality. He never appeared to seek recognition and honor. He was, however, something of an individualist. In the varied experiences of his life he had acquired an almost uncanny ability to meet, seemingly without special preparation, whatever situation arose. Being called upon by Dr. Frissell to fill important speaking engagements away from the campus became one of the more or less expected duties of the Major in the common effort to keep Hampton's needs before the public. He not only performed these services to the satisfaction of Dr. Frissell and the communities where he spoke, but he was versatile to the extent of filling the pulpit on Sundays and other occasions in the absence of the Chaplain.

Sometimes in his jovial moments with friends he would relate the story of a Sunday when it had fallen his lot to take charge of the chapel service. Meanwhile a very prominent visitor, a Quaker minister, arrived on the campus and Dr. Moton invited him to preach. The minister replied, "I cannot tell, but if the spirit moves me, I'll preach." Sunday morning came. The Major called for the guest and, while escorting him to the chapel, said, "Well, Dr. ——, we are glad to have you speak to our staff and students this morning." The minister replied, "I cannot tell at all, but if the spirit moves me, I'll preach."

Before proceeding to the platform the Major again repeated his question only to receive the same reply. When it came time for the sermon, knowing that if the visitor was not moved by the spirit he himself would have to preach, the Major took no further chance but rose and said: "We are very fortunate in having Dr. —— of —— as our guest this weekend. I am especially glad to have him worship with us, and I take pleasure in presenting him and asking him to preach today." The spirit, fortunately, did move. The visitor, without hesitation, went over to the pulpit and delivered an extraordinary sermon.

To usher his many distinguished guests into Major Moton's office and to introduce them seemed one of Dr. Frissell's greatest pleasures. Hampton, in those days, was blessed almost beyond description by visits of celebrated people from distant parts of the world. Many came to study Hampton's educational program for the dramatic story of Booker Washington—how he had struggled to obtain his education here and how he, almost miraculously, founded Tuskegee Institute—had practically encircled the globe. Washington's story, added to that of the founding of Hampton Institute by General Armstrong, was of special interest to educators not only in

Virginia and the neighboring states but in many places beyond the seas.

No one was better informed concerning the early history of Hampton, nor more deeply imbued with the spirit of its founder and successor, than Major Moton. He was ever ready and at ease in the presence of distinguished visitors, including several presidents of the United States. On good authority we have it that he was equally at ease in their homes. When travelling abroad he was cordially received and entertained in the homes of noblemen; yet he found time to visit among persons of the lower economic classes. From all, the high and the low, the rich and the poor, he gained invaluable ideas which made him more effective in dealing with the problems of his own people.

The Major loved his friends, Negro and white, Northern and Southern; enjoyed entertaining and being entertained. He was appreciative of music and art, enjoyed dancing, was interested in athletics, played tennis, practiced on the violin, enjoyed storytelling and good jokes; he was a versatile and entertaining conversationalist; and he added constantly to his store of knowledge by extensive reading. The Major often related that, having to fill many speaking engagements for Dr. Frissell, he had sometimes been mistaken for him. At other times, during the period when Jack Johnson was the world's champion prize-fighter, the Major was mistaken for the pugilist.

The Major was fond of good plays. He especially enjoyed Williams and Walker and Cole and Johnson in their heyday on the stage. Perhaps his favorite among the dramatic readers was Richard Harrison. This was certainly true during the years when Harrison played the role of "De Lawd" in "The Green Pastures." There were some doubts and concern as to how the play would be accepted, and the producer knew that its success depended largely on the type of man chosen for the leading role. When Harrison accepted the assignment he did so with the understanding that it would not be a burlesque of the Negro but rather a revelation of his religious background.

Before the initial staging of "The Green Pastures," Mr. Harrison consulted friends, including Major Moton, inviting them to see the show and to give their appraisal of its worth. Again and again during its long run in New York the Major saw the play and considered it one of the greatest he had ever witnessed. I recall one of the Major's visits to Hampton when he was invited by President Howe to speak at the chapel services on a Sunday evening. He told the story of the production of "The Green Pastures" by Mr. Connolly, with special emphasis on the acting of Richard Harrison as "De Lawd." Later, after the great drama had completed its long run in New York, we had the pleasure of seeing it in Ogden Hall. The show ran both afternoon and evening performances in order to accommodate the large number of people who clamored for admission. Having to share in controlling the door at the two performances, I had the great satisfaction of seeing the play twice. Even if I had never seen it, the dramatic description given by Major Moton would never have been forgotten. About the only difference for me was that in the one case I saw it with the physical eye, whereas in the other I saw it with the mental eye.

Looking back to the days when I knew the Major at Hampton, I feel quite certain that he seemed at his best when leading in the singing of the spirituals. In later years I heard him say that sometimes, when he was feeling elated before the Sunday evening service, he would remark to his close friend, Captain Washington, "Wash, I'm going to whoop 'em up tonight." And there are those of us who can remember his rising and giving the pitch. A soft hum would go up from the student body in response, followed by such songs as "We Are Climbing Jacob's Ladder," "In Dat Great Gittin'-Up Mornin'," "Rise and Shine an' Give God De Glory," "Who'll Jine De Union?" "My Lord What a Mornin'!" "Go Down, Moses," "Ev'ry Time I Feel the Spirit," etc.

There was one important part of these services that faded somewhat after Major Moton left Hampton. At the opening of each school year, and especially for the benefit of new students, it was his custom to tell the origin of the spirituals—how they came into being and the conditions from which they sprang—and why the spirituals should be cherished. He would remind the students that Fisk University, Hampton Institute, Tuskegee Institute, Calhoun and a few other schools had done more than any other agencies to collect, record and set to music the characteristic songs of the Negro. One may be sure that after such an initial explanation music would burst forth from the throats of every person in the audience.

The versatility of the Major was marvelous. He was unusually quick in sizing up a situation; but the more weighty matters he would often take under long and serious consideration. He was proud and sensitive and quick-tempered; but he maintained such control of his emotions that only careful observers could discern them.

During the Major's professional service at Hampton only one department, the Major's, was headed by a Negro. As a result Major Moton was the only Negro representative on the executive staff of the Institute during that period. The more mature and thoughtful students of the Institute were conscious of the great responsibility that was his. Sincere reverence for the statesmanlike manner in which he dealt with all kinds of issues was everywhere in evidence.

There are those who recall the customary practice of Dr. Frissell, Major Moton and others of reviewing their off-campus trips at the Sunday evening services. It is highly probable that the information we received on these occasions concerning Hampton and its relationship with the outside world was as important as that received in the regular classrooms and textbooks. How Hampton received its support and why Hampton men and women should make the best use of their time in order to be prepared for lives of service was impressed deeply upon our minds. Major Moton's part on these occasions was very effective.

Robert Moton and his mother were mutually intimate and even chummy. Every summer he would have her visit him and his family. Frequently he and his mother would sit under the big shade trees on the lawn and chat for hours. Sometimes, when she was not present, he would tell amusing stories about her.

Although very active in her old age, and remarkably young in spirit, Mrs. Jeter believed in the morals of the "old school." One day, for example, as the story goes, the two, mother and son, were sitting on the lawn talking together when a next-door neighbor came out on her lawn, sat down, and began smoking a cigarette. Moton's mother looked on for a moment, and then turning to her son remarked with some feeling: "My God, Robert, what are we coming to? Look at that woman sitting there with her legs crossed and smoking a cigarette." "Well, Mother," the son replied, "many women feel they have a right to smoke." The mother's only reply was, "My God." Within a few minutes, according to the story, the mother reached into her handbag, pulled out her long-stemmed pipe, turned to her son and said, "Give me a match, Robert."

A few weeks after my graduation from Hampton in 1913, I received an unexpected invitation from the late John Hope, President of Morehouse College, to join his staff and work with the boys in the preparatory division of that institution. Without my knowledge I had been recommended by Major Moton and other members of the Hampton staff. The Major had a way of bringing about such invitations as surprises to the recipients. After two interesting years at Morehouse I was released, at Major Moton's request, to return to Hampton and there to enter upon my work as assistant in the Commandant's office.

Shortly after this, in November 1915, we received a telegram from Tuskegee Institute telling of the death of Booker Washington, and a request from Mrs. Washington that Major Moton come to Tuskegee immediately. Needless to say, the decision to give up his work at Hampton and to accept the administrative responsibility at Tuskegee was the most serious of his life. The Major had been happy at Hampton and had fully intended to spend the rest of his professional life there.

We shall leave to others the story of his remarkable accomplishments at Tuskegee, where he spent two eventful decades of his life, serving his people, the South and, in a very real sense, the nation. In his new position the field of his activities was broadened, his responsibilities multiplied and his opportunities correspondingly increased. In a true sense Major Moton's Tuskegee achievements were a continuation and enlargement of all that he had accomplished before, but on an ever increasing scale.

CHAPTER 6

❧ *To Tuskegee* ❧

BY G. LAKE IMES

The death of Booker T. Washington on November 14, 1915, was as sudden as it was unexpected. The general public had not suspected any decline in his health. After many years of vigorous activity there was no suspicion of failing strength. In fact, just the week before, he had addressed a large gathering of Congregationalists in New Haven, Connecticut, with all his wonted vigor and forcefulness. Returning to New York City the next day he met with a small group of the trustees of Tuskegee Institute to decide certain important questions. To them it was apparent that Dr. Washington was not in his usual good health. He was counselled then and there to take time off for rest. His reply was that he had a speaking engagement at Roanoke, Virginia, and did not wish to disappoint the people, his own people, who had planned his coming and arranged for a large attendance of both races to hear his address. Accordingly, he went to the station to take the train for Roanoke.

The trustees, unable to shake off their uneasiness, followed him to the train and insisted that he return with them to St. Luke's Hospital for an examination. After several days a report was made to the effect that "not a single organ of his body was functioning more than five percent of normal." It was manifest that the end had come. Mrs. Washington was hurriedly summoned to his bedside.

[78]

It was apparent to Dr. Washington that he could carry on no longer. He requested that he be returned to Tuskegee, to the South where he had lived and labored, where he wanted to pass his last moments. The newspapers of November 15th startled the world with the announcement that Booker Washington was dead.

There was immediate speculation as to his successor. There were those who thought that no man alive could qualify to carry on the work of Booker T. Washington. He was so unique, both in his personality and in his program for the advancement of his people, that they thought finding a worthy successor was almost out of the question. Tuskegee, they feared, would decline and finally pass out of existence.

It was known that several members of the faculty of Tuskegee had aspirations to succeed Dr. Washington, men who had been associated with him for many years in the development of the institution. They had never expressed themselves in this wise, but their reticence in discussing the subject was to many an unfailing indication of their thinking. The situation called for tact and judgment on the part of the trustees of the institution. Ex-president Theodore Roosevelt, a member of Tuskegee's Board of Trustees, was heard to say that the selection of a principal for Tuskegee Institute was as important a matter as the election of the president of the United States.

After careful deliberation the announcement was made that Major R. R. Moton, Commandant of Cadets at Hampton Institute, had been selected by the Board of Trustees to be the next principal of Tuskegee Institute. It was not wholly a surprise. In one of his books Dr. Washington had devoted an entire chapter to an appraisal of the character and qualifications of Major Moton as a member of the executive staff of Hampton Institute. "It always seemed to me very fortunate," he said, "that Hampton Institute should have in the position which Major Moton occupies a man of such kindly good humor, thorough self-control, and sympathetic disposition.... I have learned from Major Moton that one need not belong to a "superior" race to be a gentleman.... It has been through contact with men like Major Moton—clean, high-souled gentlemen—that I have received a kind of education that books could not impart." Later on it became known that when Dr. Washington realized the end was near he sent for Major Moton. What passed between them has never been revealed except that Dr. Washington said, "Major, I want you to stand by Tuskegee Institute." It is known that Mrs. Washington indicated that Major Moton was Dr. Washington's choice for a successor, though he had never been heard to say as much officially or perhaps even directly.

Another factor in making the choice was undoubtedly the situation at Hampton Institute. Dr. Frissell, Principal and successor to General Armstrong, was known to be in poor health. Already the matter of his successor had been under advisement. Among the students and colored members of the staff at Hampton there was a large group that felt that Major Moton was the logical successor to Dr. Frissell. His intimate association with General Armstrong, both as a student and subsequently as Commandant of Cadets, his effective collaboration with Dr. Frissell in promoting the program of Hampton Institute for the welfare of the Negro people of this country, his wise counsel in administrative matters within the Institute, his tact and effectiveness in representing the school in public relations North and South, all combined to make him the strongest man on the Hampton staff, next to Dr. Frissell. His own people, therefore, thought that it was only fair and just, as well as logical, that Major Moton should succeed Dr. Frissell as the Principal of Hampton Institute.

There was another strong and influential group who felt that to choose a Negro as successor to Dr. Frissell would be too radical a departure from the traditions of Hampton where its management and control were the responsibility of white people. There was some doubt whether Major Moton would be acceptable to the entire staff at Hampton Institute which was predominantly white. Those who favored Major Moton felt that it would be a breach of faith if the succession should be denied him because of his race and color. There were some grounds for thinking that such a decision would be received by Negroes, both in the school and outside, with grave misgivings.

The death of Booker Washington solved this problem in a way which no human wisdom could dictate. It was fair and logical that the successor of Booker Washington should be a Negro. Moreover, it was appropriate that he should be a graduate of Hampton. To transfer Major Moton to Tuskegee Institute as principal not only would give recognition to his labors at Hampton Institute but would, at the same time, leave the way open for the selection of a white man to succeed Dr. Frissell. Such a course would give no ground for offence to Negroes and would relieve the misgivings of those who felt that it was not the right time to break the tradition of Hampton Institute as cherished by a large contingent of the white members of its staff.

When, in addition, it is considered that there was an interlocking membership on the board of trustees of the two institutions, it is easy to understand how these gentlemen would turn toward Hampton for the successor to Booker T. Washington. Dr. Frissell died within a year or two after Major Moton came to Tuskegee and a white man was chosen as his successor without the slightest suggestion of controversy or dissatisfaction.

That matter was settled. Some time later a member of the Board of Trustees of Hampton Institute was heard to say that in selecting Major Moton to be the successor of Dr. Washington the policy had been established that Hampton Institute was a school founded by white people for the benefit of Negroes while Tuskegee Institute was a school founded by Negroes and managed by Negroes for the benefit of Negroes. It was both logical and appropriate that the Institute established by a graduate of Hampton should have as his successor another graduate of Hampton trained in the same tradition and motivated by the same spirit. Hampton was delighted by the arrangement. At the same time it was loath to give up Major Moton. One of its officers put it in this way, speaking for the Hampton administration, "We gave you Booker T. Washington, but we are only lending you Major Moton."

Shortly after the announcement of the election of the successor to the founder, Major Moton made a visit to the campus for an informal meeting with the faculty of the Institute. He was no stranger to teachers or students, having frequently visited the campus as the guest of Dr. Washington. There were many graduates of Hampton on the faculty at Tuskegee, among them a classmate of Major Moton's, Mr. John H. Palmer, for many years the registrar at Tuskegee Institute. With exquisite tact the new principal gave the assurance that there would be no change in the policies of the Institute. He invited the cooperation of all members of the faculty, and echoed the theme of Dr. Washington's last address to students and teachers calling for teamwork among all the workers. He formally designated Warren Logan, Treasurer of the Institute, as Acting Principal, and insisted upon his presiding at meetings of the executive council and faculty for the rest of the school year.

Having many personal friends among the members of the staff, the adjustment to a new administration was made without friction or confusion. For the rest of the year the new principal devoted himself to becoming familiar with the details of administration and cultivating personal acquaintance with all the workers, those of humble position as well as those holding executive posts.

The trustees had already authorized a campaign to raise a Million Dollar Fund as a memorial to the Founder which would stabilize the financial situation of the Institute, the proceeds to be used for needed repairs and operational expenses, besides increasing the school's endowment. In this effort the task was lightened by a gift of $250,000 from Mr. George Eastman, of Kodak fame, who had promised that sum to Dr. Washington sometime before his death for a program of definite expansion of the school's equipment.

With this campaign in progress the new principal spent most of his time away from the campus, leaving the operation of the school in the capable hands of those who had already played a considerable part in shaping the school's program. Very early Principal Moton was confronted with a new and grave problem. A disastrous fire practically destroyed the Trade School, housed in one large, sprawling building which was the result of successive additions to the original made over a period of years to accommodate new trades in the Department of Mechanical Industries, familiarly designated as Boys' Trades.

Thus the Institute was visited with two calamities within a single year; first, the passing of the Founder; and, second, the loss by a major unit of its equipment for the vital function of the school, the training of Negro youth in the techniques of mechanical trades.

Principal Moton did not return to the campus at once. A prompt report of the nature of the calamity and the extent of the loss was conveyed to him by telephone and letter. With characteristic wisdom he concluded that there was nothing for him to do at that moment on the campus, but there was much that he could do in the field to replace the building.

At a hurried conference of trustees, of whom there were eight or ten in the vicinity of New York, it took little time to decide upon the replacement of the building and equipment that had been destroyed. Dr. Moton realized, as never before, the weight of responsibility that rested on the shoulders of the head of a great educational institution, especially the unique educational enterprise which Tuskegee Institute had become under the dynamic leadership of Dr. Washington.

Before the end of the year, operations had begun to replace the old structure with a group of five buildings with better arrangements, added facilities, and increased equipment for instruction in the twenty-seven trades included in the program of the Department of Mechanical Industries. The design and plans for these buildings were the work of the Department's Architectural Division which supervised the construction of the buildings by students of the Department.

Entering upon his new duties, Dr. Moton had the assistance and cooperation of a staff of able workers who had been assembled by Dr. Washington over a long period of years and without whom, of course, the work of such an institution would not have been possible. From the very beginning he was assured of the counsel and advice of Mrs. Booker T. Washington who continued to serve as the Director of Women's Industries. In addition there was Mr. Emmett J. Scott, who had been in charge of the Principal's office as administrator for a period of about eighteen years, and upon whom Dr. Washington had leaned for much of the detail of the operations of the institution as they centered in the Principal's office.

There were others, not members of the staff, whose services contributed greatly to the effectiveness of the work of the school. Among these was Thomas M. Campbell, District Supervisor for the Extension Service of the United States Department of Agriculture. "Tom" Campbell was the first Negro member of the staff of the Extension Service, receiving his appointment from Dr. Seamon A. Knapp, the Secretary of the Department of Agriculture at that time, and supervising the work in fifteen southern states. Mr. Campbell had already become widely known among both races throughout the South. His headquarters were on the campus of Tuskegee, where he was thus available for counsel and contacts in the Institute's program of service to the South. Few men among the Negro people of the South have rendered more valuable service to this section and to the country than has Mr. Campbell.

Another valuable assistant to the Principal was Colonel B. O. Davis, of the United States Army, appointed to Tuskegee by the Secretary of War as Professor of Military Science and Tactics in charge of the ROTC. Colonel Davis was later designated as Commandant of Cadets in charge of the Institute regiment of the ROTC. He was subsequently raised to the grade of Brigadier General during World War II, while serving in Washington, the first Negro to attain the rank of a general in the U.S. Army.

It was no easy task that confronted the new principal. Beginning with an appropriation of two thousand dollars by the Alabama Legislature in 1881, without buildings, land or equipment, the school had grown within thirty-four years into a great institution of more than two thousand five hundred acres, nearly one hundred buildings, a staff of nearly three hundred teachers and workers, about one thousand five hundred students, and a yearly budget of nearly three hundred thousand dollars and was still growing. Located in a remote area of a section that was not too sympathetic toward education for Negroes, it was nothing short of genius which had enabled its Founder to develop a program of education which, at the time, was a wide departure from accepted educational practice, to assemble the needed equipment, financial resources and a staff of workers from among his own people, most of them trained in the methods of education that had little in common with the new program which the Founder was setting up for his school. At the twenty-fifth anniversary of the founding of the Institute in 1896, President Charles Eliot of Harvard University, in paying tribute to Dr. Washington, said Tuskegee had made more progress in the first twenty-five years of its history than Harvard University had made in its first hundred years.

In the management of any school dependent for its support on contributions from the general public, the problem of financing is of major importance. Though Tuskegee had begun as a public institution, in the early years of its development Dr. Washington secured from the legislature a change in its charter, making it a private institution with an independent Board of Trustees. It was no longer the state's obligation to maintain the institution. The principal, from the very beginning, had looked to the general public for the funds necessary to operate the school. His task was to interpret the program of the school in such a way as to win public confidence and secure from private sources donations with which to supplement the small annual appropriation received from the state and the meager fees received from the students. In this latter phase Dr. Washington had inaugurated a program that would make it possible for deserving students to work their way through school. This meant that in the early years practically all the funds for the operation of the Institute had to be secured from private sources. With the passing of the Founder this task fell upon the shoulders of his successor.

There was another phase to the problem of financing the institution that was equally as important as securing the necessary funds. The other phase was seeing to it that these funds were judiciously and effectively disbursed. This work became more important as the school expanded. The preparation of the annual budget and the careful supervision of its provisions were as great a responsibility as securing the funds from the public. In such operations all sorts of exigencies arise, such as underestimating costs, unexpected increases in the price of materials, making allowance for unavoidable wastes in the process of training, and the use of unskilled student labor in operations generally performed by skilled hands. In consequence it was as much of a problem to the Principal to see that funds were properly expended as it was to raise them.

The curriculum of this new program of education was the next problem with which the Principal had to deal. Industrial education, as Tuskegee developed it, was not simply a matter of training in trade techniques. It involved also the elements of what is frequently described as a common school education, and the combination of these two types of education in equipping the student to take his place in the work-a-day world. It was a part of the policy of this type of education to use student labor for as many of the operations of the school as was possible, even though it might mean a certain lowering of the standards of achievement. The justification of this was found in the training and development of the student. The mere maintenance of the institution was a secondary consideration. It involved such things as the repair and maintenance of buildings, the care and upkeep of the grounds, providing light, heat, water and power, the maintenance of roads, the raising of food and food stuffs, the care of animals as well as human beings, and a hundred and one other operations necessary in a self-sustaining community of some twenty-five hundred souls. All of this was subject to interruptions, at one time or another, by the educational program of the student—general exercises of one sort or another, especially those connected with the presence of distinguished visitors, the observance of holidays and numerous other events, the incidence of sports and recreational activities, all of which were made a part of the student's education. Added to that was the fact that the institution was located on a tract of land that was really submarginal in character, greatly increasing the cost of production as well as lowering efficiency. All this was further complicated by the demands of a constantly expanding program.

All these activities pertained more or less directly to the student. But there were other demands made upon the time and energies of the Principal that lay outside the program of the usual school. For example, Tuskegee maintained a hospital of seventy-five beds, a bank, a commissary, a farm, a dairy, a truck garden, a greenhouse, a garage service, a power plant, all of which ministered to the needs of the adjacent community as well as to the students and staff of the school. While all these operations came under the direction of a Business Committee representing the departments most heavily involved, the principal had the final responsibility. It was this wide range of activities that lay behind the task of the Principal in securing the funds necessary to keep the school going.

Dr. Washington's phenomenal success in this undertaking made many people think there was some magic, some trick, by which he was able to secure the results that were apparent. That was far from the truth. There was a time when Tuskegee had few friends, a time when the Principal faced a heartbreaking struggle in his efforts to keep the school alive. In the early days there were times when there was not sufficient food for the students, when he was not able to pay salaries to his teachers, as had been promised, when buildings and equipment deteriorated for lack of funds to make the necessary repairs, when bills were unavoidably left unpaid.

By the time Major Moton came upon the scene that situation no longer obtained. There had accumulated an endowment of nearly two million dollars; but the returns from the investments at no time yielded more than a minor fraction of what was needed to keep the school in operation. At all times it was necessary to turn away hundreds of young people who were seeking an opportunity to get an education, because of the lack of resources necessary to give them that opportunity. There was a time, however, when it could be said truthfully of Tuskegee that no worthy student was turned away for lack of funds with which to pay his way. But those days have passed. By the time Dr. Moton came to the Institute, the number of friends and donors of the school had considerably increased; but the appropriation from the state at no time exceeded five thousand dollars annually during the lifetime of Dr. Washington or of Dr. Moton, even after the budget had increased to hundreds of thousands of dollars.

The task of the new Principal was to keep this organization in operation, to continue public appeals for support, to make new friends, and to replace old friends who had died or had discontinued their gifts to the institution. In other words, it was necessary to sell Tuskegee continuously to the American public and to win their support for this outstanding enterprise for the development of the Negro.

In this effort, the momentum of Tuskegee contributed greatly to the success of Dr. Moton's labors. The American public had been fully informed of the nature of the work of the school and the cost of its operation. The great problem was to reach new donors. It is not possible to barge into a man's office and secure a gift of several thousand dollars at the first interview. Such plans must be laid very carefully and ofttimes call for the most circuitous approaches. It is said of Dr. Washington that in one instance it took ten years for him to reach a man who afterwards became one of the most substantial contributors to the work of the school.

In this phase of his efforts Dr. Moton was eminently successful. In 1925 the trustees of Hampton Institute and of Tuskegee Institute decided upon a joint campaign to raise five million dollars for the support of both institutions. The principal of Tuskegee and the principal of Hampton were to head up this campaign. At the outset several of the philanthropic foundations made generous pledges toward the goal. Then individuals added their pledges until, at the close of the campaign, not only was the goal of five million dollars reached but a total closely approximating ten million dollars.*

This successful campaign went a long way toward solving the financial problems of these two institutions. In the end Tuskegee received a large sum for its new building program necessitated by the plans for training on the college level; but at the same time practically trebled its endowment fund, while Hampton's endowment, originally larger than Tuskegee's, was doubled. This did not mean that there would be no further need of contributions; there still is. But from this time on it was possible to make plans and carry them into effect with reasonable prospect of being able to finance them. It is no longer a secret that the labors of this campaign, which fell largely upon the shoulders of Dr. Moton, drew heavily upon his physical resources, the effects of which were to remain with him until his retirement in 1935, and, coupled with a series of tragedies on the campus of the school, led ultimately to his death in 1940.

When Dr. Moton came to Tuskegee its courses of study were being operated on the high school level. There was a continuous expansion in educational standards throughout the country, particularly in the South. State departments of education had adopted the policy of employing only teachers who held degrees from recognized colleges. The effect of this was to impair the opportunities for Tuskegee graduates to secure employment in the public school systems in the South. It was decided to advance the curriculum of

* "... reference should certainly be made to the fact that Major Moton secured a five million dollar gift single handed. Of course it had been prepared for by Booker Washington earlier interesting Mr. Eastman in Tuskegee. I happened to be Chairman of the Special Gifts Committee, and knew a good deal about the campaign, and there was no question but that Major Moton was the leading factor in it. My own work was mainly with a few foundations and men of large means. When the campaign was over Mr. Eastman invited Dr. William Jay Schieffelin and myself to Rochester to tell his friends about Hampton and Tuskegee, and he said he wanted them to know why he had singled out these two institutions for such large gifts." (Letter of May 11, 1954 from Dr. Anson Phelps Stokes)

Tuskegee Institute to the college level in order to meet this requirement.

At the time there was widespread misunderstanding of the purpose of Tuskegee in taking this step. Some of Tuskegee's own trustees thought that the school was departing from its original policies and program by entering the field of the liberal arts colleges. In a special report to the Board of Trustees, made in 1930 in anticipation of the Fiftieth Anniversary of the founding of the school, Dr. Moton dissipated this idea quite effectively in an analysis of the original aims and purposes of the institution and of the relation of the new courses of study to the accomplishment of those objectives. In the course of a few years, it became an accepted fact that Tuskegee was making rapid strides toward raising vocational education to the college level.

This meant that additions had to be made to the school's equipment and teachers secured with advanced qualifications. It was necessary to secure men and women who understood and sympathized with Tuskegee's aims and policies of education. Even under Dr. Washington there was a need for the principal to indoctrinate the teachers in his philosophy of education and the significance and value of industrial education. It frequently happened that there were teachers on the staff of the school who openly expressed their lack of sympathy with its methods and objectives and encouraged their students to go elsewhere to further their education. The raising of vocational education to the college level was not an easy thing to do. To chart out the areas of knowledge and adapt them to the requirements of vocational training was something that had not yet been done. There are still problems in this field which have not been solved.

All of this was complicated by the problem of offering adequate salaries. After World War I private schools all over the land were faced with actual competition from government-supported schools and other public agencies where salaries had been raised beyond the level of successful competition from privately supported institutions. This situation added greatly to the load already carried by the Principal. Somehow the problems were solved as they occurred and the school continued to make progress in the areas to which it had been dedicated.

It does not take long for the administrative head of an educational institution to discover that the problems of personnel are as large, as important, and often as troublesome as any other problems. One of the major problems encountered by Dr. Moton was housing for teachers as well as students. For unmarried teachers the solution was comparatively simple; they were housed in the school's dormitories along with the students. But this sort of arrangement makes it too easy for teachers to leave the service of the school. For the institution's sake it is better to have married couples, young people who want to settle down, to establish a home and rear a family. This requires the building of new homes and progressive increases in salary to meet the needs of the growing family.

All this is accentuated sooner or later when domestic problems arise, situations which affect the morale of the campus and which the principal cannot ignore. In the same category are the relations between families, common to every school campus. Advantages enjoyed by one family are compared with those enjoyed by another. Seniority of teachers who have been a long time on the staff of the school and have endured the hardships and privations encountered in its establishment is placed over against the qualifications of younger teachers who have but recently graduated with advanced degrees. To keep tranquility, harmony and good will among the members of the staff and to achieve coordination and cooperation of effort are no less a problem than that of providing their salaries. Along with this is the relation between teachers and students. This applies to grades and marks as well as to social contacts. And let no one think that these are not real problems, delicate and sometimes highly disturbing. They are found in all educational institutions and there is no one formula for their solution. Then there are the problems between students, especially in co-educational institutions. In the last analysis a large proportion of these problems come to the attention of the principal, especially those that call for severe measures of discipline and sometimes even dismissal, in which case parents often enter into the equation. Here, once more, the student is the major consideration and his development in character by systematic training must be the ultimate objective. Such matters call for tact, for sympathy, for understanding, and wise judgment. In all these matters Dr. Moton exhibited characteristic tolerance and patience, and won a full measure of the confidence of both teachers and students. Many are the students who, in after years, have felt a deep sense of gratitude toward their alma mater for the patience with which they were treated in matters of discipline. Dr. Moton was notably kind and helpful in dealing both with teachers and with students. He was not severe in his judgments. He was never too busy to listen to all that they had to say, and no one could ever accuse him either of harshness in his decisions or laxity in his standards.

In a community like Tuskegee recreation for teachers and students was a major responsibility. Tuskegee is isolated. The nearest city of any size—Montgomery, Alabama—is forty miles away. Such facilities as were found in the local town were, of course, not available to either teachers or students. Save in business matters there is practically no contact between the school and the town of Tuskegee, except that whatever facilities are available at the school are accessible to townspeople without discrimination. In most matters Tuskegee Institute is a self-sustaining community. It was the aim of the founder to create at least one place in the world where his people could move about with perfect freedom and have access to whatever privileges they could afford.

It was a help in these matters that the school maintained a full program for its students beginning at 6:30 A.M. and continuing until 9:30 at night. This was required by its dual system of education which assigned trade work for one day and academic studies for the next. The student is kept busy at the main purposes of his education. This does not deny him time for relaxation and recreation. Much is made of sports at Tuskegee. Basketball, baseball and football, along with track sports, are as popular at Tuskegee as at other institutions, with the usual schedule of intercollegiate competition. The new principal encouraged participation in sports of every kind by the students, and regularly insisted that the whole school get behind the teams which represented the institution. In consequence, during the administration of Dr. Moton, the Tuskegee football team was for many years the ranking team among Negro colleges and achieved the enviable record of fifty straight games without a defeat, forty-nine of which it won, and was tied on the very last of the string. This was accomplished under the capable guidance of Coach Cleve

L. Abbott, a former football star of South Dakota State College. A site was chosen for the construction of an Alumni Bowl adjacent to the new auditorium-gymnasium which was equipped with all the necessary facilities for sports events.

Dr. Moton inaugurated an Entertainment course which, besides maintaining a regular schedule of movies, brought to the Institute each season some of the outstanding musical attractions of the American concert stage. In time this course came to be one of the best concert series in the South. Among the artists who appeared through the years were Roland Hayes, Marian Anderson, Percy Grainger, and many others of like distinction. Included also in the list of attractions were the Russian Symphony Orchestra, the St. Louis Symphony Orchestra, the Minneapolis Symphony Orchestra, Sousa and his Band, and "Roxy and his Gang." Along with these were the Hinshaw Opera Company, Martha Graham and her Dance Ensemble, the Dennishawn Dancers, the Abbey Theatre Irish Players and Andre Segovia, the Spanish guitarist. In due course Duke Ellington appeared with his band, William Handy and his orchestra, Noble Sissle and his band. The climax was reached with the appearance on the stage of the auditorium of Richard Harrison and the original company in "The Green Pastures." For a season ticket, priced within the reach of every student, the school provided not only recreation in these entertainments but culture in the finest American tradition.

Still another part of Tuskegee's work that called for careful organization and planning was the entertaining of visitors who came to Tuskegee in great numbers, following the national acclaim which greeted the memorable address delivered by Booker T. Washington at the Cotton States Exposition in Atlanta, Georgia, in 1895. From every section of our country and from all parts of the world visitors came to see the school, to study its methods, to confer with its principal and to learn how they might adapt the program and policies of the Institute to the needs of their own people and the solution of their own problems. The entertaining of such groups soon became a major undertaking. As in all schools, commencement time brought great numbers of visitors to the campus, including returning alumni and the parents and friends of the graduating class. Sports events also brought their quota. In due time Tuskegee became a meeting place for annual conventions and conferences of various organizations, brought thither by the repute of the school.

Another event which brought many visitors to the Institute was the Annual Farmers and Workers Conference held in December of each year. This was a forum for the propagation of Dr. Washington's policies for the advancement of the Negro and brought literally thousands of his people from all parts of the South as well as other sections of the country. In later years neighboring institutions brought groups of their students, ranging from children in the grade schools to classes in the social sciences from colleges and universities, under the guidance of teachers, to see this great institution. Following the practice of his predecessor, Dr. Moton took great pains to see that all these people were received with courteous attention and made comfortable during their stay. This, too, called for tact and judgment to say nothing of the expense involved. Dr. Moton always felt that this policy amply paid in good will and in the generosity of the public for all that was spent in this direction.

Still another event of major importance in the life of Tuskegee was the annual meeting of the Board of Trustees held on the campus. After the death of Dr. Washington the observance of Founder's Day was instituted and thereafter this meeting was held in connection with that occasion. Advantage was taken of this gathering to give the trustees and the friends who invariably came with them a first hand knowledge of the workings of the school. An alumnus returning for his class reunion would be asked to tell the story of his accomplishments since graduation. The Founder's Day address became a notable feature of the occasion, delivered by some outstanding leader in American life who offered an appraisal of the Founder's life and work. It was on such an occasion in 1922 that the Booker T. Washington monument was unveiled on a site adjacent to the Institute Chapel. This monument was the work of Charles Keck, a distinguished American sculptor who had been a student of Saint Gaudens. It represented Dr. Washington as "lifting the veil of ignorance from his people and pointing the way to progress through education and industry." Dr. Moton left the task of raising the necessary funds for this memorial to Mr. Emmett J. Scott, the efficient and devoted secretary to Dr. Washington for eighteen of the climactic years of his career. The funds for this undertaking were raised, in greater part, among Dr. Washington's own people as a testimonial of their esteem and appreciation for the great work which he had accomplished in their behalf.

Another feature of this meeting was a pilgrimage of the trustees' party to some school or church in the outlying rural districts which reflected the application of the school's methods in promoting rural progress. After the inauguration of the Rosenwald School program, the party was usually taken to one or another of the schools erected in Macon County as one of these projects, stopping en route to inspect the home and land of some successful Negro farmer who had been helped by the extension activities of the Institute. They returned with a better understanding of the people who lived in these rural areas, of their problems, their progress and their aspirations.

The prestige of the school continued to grow under the leadership of Dr. Moton. During his administration as principal certain outstanding events in the history of the school testified to the far-reaching influence of the Institute and its relation to American life in other than strictly educational matters. Perhaps the most important single event on the campus of the Institute was the observance of the Fiftieth Anniversary of the founding of the school. This event paid tribute to the Founder and the phenomenal growth of the institution under his leadership and its continued progress under his successor. Booker Washington was the central theme of all the programs during the three day observance of this milestone in the history of the school, which brought to the campus, among others, Booker T. Washington's first teacher in West Virginia, an Indian pastor from Montana who was under Dr. Washington's guidance as house father at Hampton, a special delegation from Hampton Institute led by its Principal, Dr. James E. Gregg, and other distinguished friends and associates of Dr. Washington.

The climax of this occasion was the address by President Herbert Hoover, delivered from the White House on the last day of the celebration by direct wire to the assembled audience in the Institute Chapel and at the same time broadcast over the entire nation by the National and Columbia Broadcasting Systems. It happened that President Hoover was attending the opening game of the major league baseball season in Griffith Stadium in Washington and left the game in the ninth inning with the score tied to keep his appointment with Tuskegee Institute. It was a unique event in educational circles, and thereafter the President received numerous requests to repeat the arrangement for other educational institutions in the South.

For Dr. Moton the event was particularly meaningful because of the presence on the platform that afternoon, as a guest and a speaker, of a childhood companion, known then to each other as "Bob" and "Little George," the latter at that moment President of the University of Alabama, Dr. George Denny, another son of Virginia.

Another significant event in Dr. Moton's administration was the unveiling of the Lincoln Memorial in Washington. The committee charged with the work of erecting this memorial, of which the chairman was Chief Justice William Howard Taft, decided that it was appropriate that the principal address on this occasion should be delivered by a member of the race which was the chief beneficiary of the Emancipation Proclamation. It was unanimously voted to extend the invitation to deliver that address to Dr. Robert R. Moton, the Principal of Tuskegee Institute. The comment of the press on the following day was that the address was worthy of the man whom it was intended to honor, worthy of the occasion, and worthy of the man who delivered it.

Still another auspicious event during the administration of Dr. Moton was the dedication, in 1923, of the U. S. Veterans Administration Hospital, erected at Tuskegee on a site of some three hundred acres of land given to the Government for that purpose by the Trustees of the school. This occurred during the administration of President Warren G. Harding. Being unable to attend in person he designated the Vice-President, afterwards President Coolidge, to represent the President on this occasion.

An event which projected Tuskegee Institute into a new field of distinction was the opening of Radio City in 1932. For this occasion the Tuskegee Institute Choir of 100 voices under the direction of William L. Dawson, a member of the Choir in his student days, now its director and head of the Institute's School of Music, was brought to New York for a series of performances in the great Music Hall. Thereafter the organization was in constant demand for concerts and radio programs. Mr. Dawson was to win further distinction at a later time as the composer of the first symphonic work based entirely on Negro spirituals, subsequently performed by Leopold Stokowski and the Philadelphia Symphony Orchestra in the Academy of Music in Philadelphia and Carnegie Hall in New York.

While the Choir was in New York, the work of renovating the Institute Chapel was completed. The major features were the installation of a pipe organ previously refused the school by Andrew Carnegie with the comment that the singing of the Choir was of such extraordinary quality that it would only be marred by the introduction of a mechanical instrument that could in no way compare with human voices, and of new chancel windows in which eleven Negro spirituals were depicted in art glass. The latter are frequently referred to as "The Singing Windows of Tuskegee." On the return of the Choir to the campus, the Chapel and these windows were dedicated with appropriate exercises. An interesting detail of the design of these windows is that, on the suggestion of others, Dr. Moton was used as a model for the figure representing Africa in the group of "Three Wise Men" worshipping the Christ Child.

The success of Dr. Moton's administration was due in no small part to the confidence and support of his Board of Trustees. The Chairman at the time of Dr. Moton's induction into office was Mr. William G. Willcox, a member of the Board of Education of New York City. On his demise his place on the Tuskegee Board was filled by Mrs. Willcox, who continued her husband's interest and support of the work of the Institute. Mr. Willcox was succeeded as Chairman of the Board by Dr. William Jay Schieffelin, of New York, who was at the same time a member of the Board of Trustees of Hampton Institute. No member of the Board was more deeply concerned about the progress of the institution and the success of Dr. Moton's administration. Altogether he gave fifty years of service to the cause of Negro education as a member of the Boards of Trustees of Tuskegee and of Hampton.

Another member of the Board who gave his time and services freely to the Institute was Mr. William J. Scott of Philadelphia. Mr. Scott was an engineer, a graduate of the Massachusetts Institute of Technology, besides being a successful businessman. He gave the school the full benefit of his knowledge and experience in all the mechanical operations of the campus. Another name to be inseparably linked with the Board of Trustees was that of Julius Rosenwald, whose munificent generosity of more than seven million dollars made possible the building of at least 5,670 school buildings in the rural districts of the South for Negro children, involving the expenditure of more than twenty-one million dollars. They are part of the public school system of the South and are known throughout the section as Rosenwald Schools. The first of them, erected in 1913 during the administration of Dr. Washington cost $900; the four thousand erected during the administration of Dr. Moton cost approximately $40,000 each. At his passing Mr. Rosenwald was succeeded on the Board of Trustees by his son-in-law, Mr. Alfred K. Stearn, of New Orleans, who brought to the Board a wide range of experience in the commercial world and a fund of energy which were to prove of valuable service to the Institute. Without the support and help of men like these, of whom there were many on the Board of Trustees at one time or another, the work of Tuskegee would not have been possible either for Dr. Washington or his successor.

Amid these activities Dr. Moton found time to respond to calls for newspaper articles, addresses at various colleges, conferences, conventions, seminars, and other special groups and gatherings— both Negro and white. The general theme at most of these was some aspect of race relations. Typical among these was an intensive article under the caption, "The Status of the Negro in America," which appeared in *Current History*, May 1922. Just before this in 1921 Dr. Moton had contributed to *The London Times* an historical essay entitled "Fifty Years of Negro Progress in America." Both contributions were praised for their quality and interest both at home and abroad. In the November 1924, issue of *The Manufacturer's Record* appeared another article by Dr. Moton under the caption, "The Negro in the South." It is certain that he enjoyed excellent relations with the press in all parts of the country—a relation which had immeasurable value for Tuskegee Institute.

Besides such literary contributions as those referred to above, two books, both of them dealing with race relations, were written by Dr. Moton. Tuskegee Institute had become recognized as an authority on such matters in all parts of the country and throughout the world. The first volume, published in 1920, bore the title *Finding a Way Out* and was, in effect, autobiographical. He recounted in some detail the story of his life, of his progress through school, and his activities subsequent to his officership at Hampton Institute. In addition he recorded his experiences in race relations and his observations covering the period up to his coming to Tuskegee.

Years later, in 1929, he took time out to write another book, *What the Negro Thinks*. This volume was chiefly significant for the candor of his discussion of the various aspects of the race problem in America. It was widely quoted in newspapers, magazines, and by authors of other books, especially by Gunnar Myrdal in his study of the race problem in this country under the title *An American Dilemma*.

Dr. Moton's influence and activity was not confined to the campus or interests of Tuskegee Institute. Following the example of his predecessor, he gave his time and his energies in movements affecting the wider welfare of his people. Dr. Moton had already become a national figure. It was natural that he should become a Trustee of Hampton Institute; he was also a trustee of several offshoots of Hampton, among them the Calhoun School in Alabama, Penn School on St. Helena Island, South Carolina, and the Voorhees School at Denmark, South Carolina. Later on he became a trustee of Lincoln University, in Pennsylvania, of Fisk University, of Howard University and of Bethune-Cookman College. He was a trustee and also the secretary of the Anna T. Jeanes Fund; a trustee and a vice president of the American Bible Society; a chairman of the Committee on Colored Work of the National Council of the YMCA; chairman of the Tuskegee chapter of the American Red Cross, the only chapter among Negroes in the country; a trustee of the Phelps-Stokes Fund; and one of the organizers of the Interracial Commission of Atlanta.

From time to time he was called upon to serve the nation by various Presidents of the United States. He was a member of the Hoover Commission on the Mississippi Valley Flood Disaster, and afterwards designated by President Hoover to serve as Chairman of the U. S. Commission on Education in Haiti. In the field of business he served as President of the Tuskegee Institute Savings Bank; he

[98]

was a director of the Dunbar National Bank in Harlem; and President of the National Negro Business League, an organization for the promotion of business enterprises owned and operated by Negroes, that had been organized and sedulously fostered by Dr. Washington. Before coming to Tuskegee he had been the leading spirit and President of the Virginia Organization Society created to coordinate the activities in the State designed to assist the progress of Negroes in that Commonwealth.

Near the end of World War I he was commissioned by President Wilson to go to France in the interest of Negro troops who were awaiting their return home to America. In one way or another, five Presidents called upon Dr. Moton for service on a national scale—Presidents Wilson, Harding, Coolidge, Hoover and Franklin Delano Roosevelt. And at the time of his retirement he was offered an official position in the Roosevelt administration which would place his services at the disposal of the Government on call.

In recognition of his achievements in the development of Tuskegee Institute, Dr. Moton was honored with the degree of Master of Arts by Harvard University; and with the degree of Doctor of Laws conferred upon him successively by Williams College in Massachusetts, Wilberforce University in Ohio, Virginia Union University in Richmond, Virginia, Lincoln University in Pennsylvania and Howard University in Washington, D. C. In addition to these honors he was a recipient of the Harmon Award and the Spingarn Medal for conspicuous service to his race.

During his administration Dr. Moton made several trips outside the country. Shortly after coming to the school he made a vacation trip with Mrs. Moton to Bermuda; in 1922 he was invited to be the chief speaker at the Scottish Churches Missionary Congress in Glasgow. On this trip he was accompanied by Mrs. Moton and his lifelong friend and associate on the staff at Hampton, Major Allen Washington. In 1930 he went as Chairman of the U. S. Commission on Education in Haiti. Just before his retirement he made a trip around the world with Mrs. Moton and his personal physician, Director of the Institute Hospital, Dr. Eugene H. Dibble and Mrs. Dibble. On all of these trips Dr. Moton moved about with modesty but was received wherever he went with distinguished attention and consideration. He was a careful observer and gathered for himself stores of wisdom which were subsequently applied in the interests of his own people in America and other parts of the world.

More impressive than any record of his achievements was the personality of the man. In size he was large without being massive. His six feet three inches made him a conspicuous figure in any crowd. In color he was dark. In general appearance he was frequently mistaken for other prominent members of his race. He liked to tell the story of an incident in Memphis, Tennessee, which occurred shortly after he became the principal of Tuskegee. Walking along the street, he was accosted by a colored newsboy. He reached out for the paper and, having received a copy, offered the lad a dime. "No Sir," the newsy shot back. "I wouldn't take any money from Jack Johnson."

Because of his color and certain characteristically Negroid features, it was often asserted that Robert R. Moton was of unmixed Negro blood. This was not correct. To his intimates he had disclosed the fact that on his mother's side there was white blood in his veins. This was so far removed that perhaps the only characteristic in which it appeared was his hands, slender and delicate, with the refinement of a woman's hands. He was always easy of approach, considerate, thoughtful and kind. In race relations his attitude was conciliatory, no less toward whites than toward his own people. He was never contentious, but when occasion required he could stand up with unmistakable resolution and express himself with candor and vigor.

The combination of courage and consideration in his nature was strikingly exhibited at a public meeting in New York at which the late General Jan Christian Smuts was the principal speaker. The meeting was held in Town Hall. Dr. Moton was invited to be present. This occasion brought together leaders of both races who were interested in the welfare of the Negro, especially in South Africa. General Smuts was programmed to give a presentation of the progress of the native in South Africa and the attitude of the white elements of the population toward the native peoples. The Hampton Quartet furnished music. After their singing General Smuts was introduced by General Ely. He began with a comment on the singing of the Hampton Quartet which, he said, reminded him of the singing of South African natives which he had often heard. He next expressed his admiration for the patience of the native peoples say-ing that it was "like the patience of the ass." With that expression a gasp rose from the audience. General Smuts continued his discus-sion of conditions in South Africa.

At the close of his address the meeting was thrown open for questions. Members of the audience challenged the statements of General Smuts and asked pointed questions about the treatment of the natives by the whites. It happened that the phrasing of most of the questions was such that General Smuts could answer with a simple "yes" or "no." The audience could not elicit much from the General by way of admission that the natives were being mistreated. Just before the close of the meeting General Ely rose and said that there was a gentleman on the platform from whom nothing had been heard up to that time and that he felt the meeting would be incomplete without some expression from Dr. Moton.

Rising from his seat on the platform, Dr. Moton proceeded to pay tribute to General Smuts as a liberal in South Africa and to ac-knowledge his activities in sympathetic handling of the native prob-lem when he was Prime Minister. However, he said he wished to ask the General a question. He continued, "You referred to the natives as being 'patient like the ass.' Whether or not you know it, General, that expression shot a pang through the hearts of my peo-ple in this audience and many others who are kindly disposed to-ward us. I wish you would explain to these people what you meant when you compared the Negro with the ass." General Smuts was visibly perturbed and quickly apologized for the allusion, protesting that he had no intention of speaking disparagingly of the native people. He thanked Dr. Moton for calling it to his attention. The next morning headlines appeared on the front page of metropolitan dailies with the words "Moton rebukes General Smuts."

It was all done in such a tactful way that the General could not be offended by Dr. Moton's reference to his words. Afterwards, on his way back to England, General Smuts wrote Dr. Moton a letter in which he thanked him once again for his thoughtful considera-tion and closing with the words, "I think you are one of God's own children." By many of his own people this tolerance and patience and consideration were misinterpreted. There were those who thought that the Principal of Tuskegee Institute should be more belligerent, should be more militant and aggressive in protesting abuse against his people.

On the other hand most of the country, North and South, white and colored, supported him. The South took Major Moton to its heart, not because he excused its failures, not because he ignored wrongs and abuse, but because of his loyalty to those elements of the South which were striving with sincerity and with success to correct the admitted abuses to which the Negro was frequently subjected. He did not use the public platform as an opportunity to denounce the South, to discredit its people or to expose the faults and weaknesses of that section. He used it to promote goodwill and understanding, to allay suspicion and hatred, to bring the two races together in constructive efforts to make the South a better place to live for both races, but at the same time, speaking frankly about the wrongs of which Negroes justly complained.

Dr. Moton was a man of great personal courage as reflected in two incidents of which the public knows little or nothing. On one occasion in New York he was about to cross the street when the light changed for pedestrians to go forward. A white woman stepped down from the curb on the opposite side of the street directly in the path of an onrushing truck which had rounded the corner at considerable speed. The woman herself had not noticed the truck. It all happened so suddenly that there was no chance for the driver to check the speed of his truck or for the woman to get out of its way. Dr. Moton was in the middle of the thoroughfare approaching from the other direction. Sensing the woman's danger he sprang forward, clutched her in his arms and bore her in safety to the sidewalk. Without waiting for any acknowledgement from the woman he went on his way. Spectators had noticed what had occurred and presently he was overtaken by a newshawk who asked his name, commented that undoubtedly he had saved the woman's life, and asked for an interview. Dr. Moton declined to give his name but said to the reporter, "Just tell them that a black man did it." Returning to his room in the hotel he found that in the stress of the action several buttons had been torn from his coat and otherwise had damaged his clothing. With that the incident was dismissed.

At another time he was a guest of a friend in Little Rock, Arkansas, a graduate of Tuskegee Institute, who had achieved considerable success as the leader of a national fraternal organization. There was a pond on the estate which was used for recreational purposes by the family and their friends. Dr. Moton was sitting under a tree when he heard a cry of alarm and saw the little daughter of his host on the verge of drowning. The pond was only a few yards away. Without stopping to shed his coat or other garments Dr. Moton plunged in, for he was a good swimmer, and brought the child to safety. His host never ceased to express his gratitude.

Family ties had a very strong hold on Dr. Moton's life. He was devoted to his mother and throughout her life gave her thoughtful attention and care. For years after her son Robert had gone off to school she continued to live at the home place in Prince Edward County, Virginia, back in the country beyond the railroads. Whenever he went from Tuskegee to Hampton he made it a point to stop off en route at Burkeville to see her. A fishing expedition was a routine part of these visits. Both he and his mother loved to fish. Dr. Moton himself enjoyed the reputation of being one of the best fishermen on the York River in Tidewater, Virginia. Fishing was not the primary purpose of these visits. On these occasions mother and son engaged in long conversations concerning matters that were closest to their hearts. In this way they could be alone, free from all interruptions. When the visit was over his mother frequently accompanied him to the train. It was touching when they parted to hear her say as he boarded the train, "Goodbye, Robert. Be a good boy."

In later years he arranged that she should live in Philadelphia where she could make her home with others of her children and where he could see her more often and more conveniently on his trips to the North. The fishing expeditions were over. Instead he made it a point to go with her to church. She was devoutly religious, a member of the Baptist Church, as was her son. Her religion was simple, clear-headed, without demonstrativeness. Dr. Moton used to enjoy telling how, at a time when the game of checkers was commonly regarded as sinful, his mother had encouraged her children to play checkers, but always at home under her watchful care.

Dr. Moton's own religious life was as simple as his mother's, from whom he inherited it. When on the campus he attended Chapel

Services with consistent regularity. For the students attendance at
Chapel exercises was required, but with no more thought of com-
pulsion than attendance at classes and other school exercises. It was
part of the training provided for all, no less important than the trade
or academic schedule. In this the Principal set the example.

The Vesper Service on Sunday evening was traditionally led by
the Principal, a custom inaugurated by Dr. Washington and faithfully observed by Dr. Moton. This was the opportunity for the
Principal to make his impress on the minds and hearts of students
and teachers alike. His Sunday evening talks were a guide in shaping the ideals and character of the young people under his care and
maintained the high standards set by the Founder.

His personal religious convictions are best indicated in his own
words, expressed in a Christmas message dated 1923 and sent to
members of the staff and friends of the school with whom he had
personal acquaintance:

CREDO

I BELIEVE in my own people—in their native worth—in their at-
tainments of character, accomplishment and service—and their ultimate high destiny in the progress of mankind.

I BELIEVE in my fellow-men of all races—in their right to an equal
chance to share in all the good of this world—and my obligation to
respect to the full their person and their personality.

I BELIEVE in the essential goodness of human impulses—in the in-
stinctive desire to do what is just and right—and the will to respond
to the noblest appeals.

I BELIEVE in the power of good over evil—the power of love over
hate—the power of truth over error—and the final and complete
triumph of right over wrong.

I BELIEVE in freedom—in freedom to live one's life to the full—to
serve wherever there is need—to achieve the limit of divine endowment.

I BELIEVE in patience—in the beneficent workings of time—that a
Providence, wise and good, will with the years bring fruition to
earnest hopes and honest strivings.

I BELIEVE in the fellowship of men of good will—in their ability to live together in peace—and to cooperate in service and in the pursuit of truth.

I BELIEVE in my friends—who know my strength and my weakness—their confidence is my inspiration—their loyalty my comfort —and their approbation my greatest earthly satisfaction.

I BELIEVE in God—in his purposes of good toward all men—and the ultimate triumph of His justice and righteousness in all the earth.

Home life played a great part in Dr. Moton's career. He was twice married. His first wife, Miss Elizabeth Harris of Williamsburg, Virginia, died within a year after their marriage—in 1906. In July, 1908, he was united in marriage to Miss Jennie D. Booth of Gloucester County, Virginia, also a graduate of Hampton, to which union five children were born, three girls and two boys. They were all young when the family went to Tuskegee, where each in turn finished one or another of the courses offered there, save the younger boy who went to study elsewhere. The oldest, Catherine, graduated from the Conservatory of Music at Oberlin, specializing in the harp, and later became the wife of Dr. Frederick D. Patterson, who succeeded Dr. Moton as President of Tuskegee Institute in 1935. The next daughter, Charlotte, finished the course in physical education at the Sargent School in Boston. The third daughter, Jennie, graduated from Tuskegee, later did graduate work at Hampton Institute and then became a teacher of music in the public schools of Indianapolis. The older of the two boys, Robert, who bears his father's name and strongly resembles him in both face and figure, finished the business course at Tuskegee and subsequently became the business agent of the school, and later assistant to the President and Secretary of the Institute. The younger of the two boys had a strong bent toward music and later attended the New England Conservatory in Boston.

At Tuskegee Dr. Moton knew no other recreation than such as he found in his home and an occasional fishing trip. It is needless to say that his children received every care and attention that wise, considerate and thoughtful parents could give them. Mrs. Moton was a vigilant mother and painstaking housekeeper, but she also shared the labors of her husband as Director of Women's Industries, which gave her large opportunities for influencing the character and development of the young women of the Institute. Her personality and character are epitomized in the citation with which the degree of Master of Arts was conferred upon her by Bennett College in Greensboro, North Carolina, at its annual commencement exercises in June of 1931:

"Director of Women's Industries and the School of Home Economics at Tuskegee Institute; native of Virginia; loyal daughter of Hampton; teacher and worker with girls; leader and helper of women of high degree and lowly estate; strong factor for interracial understanding and good will; staunch and intrepid helpmeet amid threatening dangers; faithful and vigilant mother."

When the family was on the campus the Moton home was open to visitors and members of the faculty for informal contact as well as for formal entertainment. The Principal and his wife made it a point on holidays to invite into the family circle teachers who were at considerable distance from their homes without opportunity for joining their own families. Sunday nights after chapel were devoted to informal gatherings of intimate fellowship. When distinguished guests visited the institution, the Principal made it a point to open his home for the opportunity it afforded for visitors to meet members of the faculty, and for the faculty to make personal contacts on more intimate terms with distinguished people from the outside. Even formal occasions were delightfully informal in mood and atmosphere. It was on these occasions that the staff met the members of the Board of Trustees on their annual visits to Tuskegee, which in many instances resulted in personal friendships that lasted through many years.

But family life for the Motons was at its best when they left the campus for the summer and went up into Virginia to their haven of rest on the banks of the York River at Capahosic, where they occupied a rambling old country house. Here everything was informal. The furnishings were of the simplest. Leisure and comfort were the major objectives. Food was abundant and wholesome, and much time was spent out-of-doors. Only necessary business was allowed to interrupt the day's activities. For Dr. Moton the chief diversion was fishing. He was admired, respected and, in some quarters, envied for his skill in the art of angling. He loved to go out on the broad reaches of the York River in a rowboat with such equipment only as the local fishermen used. He preferred a line with hooks and sinkers to rod and reel. In fact a rod was not among his possessions. It was seldom that he returned without a goodly catch, even when the fish were not biting well. When his friends came to see him he took them fishing, too. Many were the contests he enjoyed with them in which he was almost always the winner. Aside from the fun it provided, it also supplied the table of a household of never less than ten people.

On the point of retirement, Dr. Moton built a more substantial home on the same site. This time he took pains to make his home, only a few yards from the York River, commodious as well as attractive and comfortable. The building of this new home was a necessity. The simple fact is that the old home was not adapted for year-round living. A frame structure, it had no facilities for heating. There was not room enough to accommodate the Moton family, and besides there were no accommodations for inescapable office work. Plumbing was of the crudest sort. Nothing about the place was adapted for winter comfort.

When Dr. Moton began to make plans for the needed structure, a Negro contractor in Alabama who had benefited by the new building program at Tuskegee, in acknowledgement of the consideration shown him in these matters, offered to build the home without charge of any kind for overhead. When his friends learned that Dr. Moton was about to retire and inquired about his plans for the future, he told them that he wished to return to Virginia where he was born and had spent the greater part of his life.

He said that in retiring he was not surrendering his interest in Tuskegee Institute. He hoped to devote a large part of his time to continued efforts in behalf of the school, besides doing a great deal of writing that he had not previously had the opportunity to indulge in. Quietly a movement was set on foot among these friends to provide him with an adequate home, in recognition of the devoted service which he had rendered to the cause of Negro education and race relations. As often happens in such cases it was not long before knowledge of this generous interest in his welfare reached Dr. Moton. Coming as it did from authentic sources, he made his plans accordingly.

While he was in Gloucester County in the summer for rest and relaxation, it was nevertheless true that he received many callers on various missions. This he knew would continue after he retired. Since Gloucester County is in a remote section of Tidewater Virginia, he knew that his visitors would often be put to great inconvenience to find accommodations while in the neighborhood. Accordingly, his plans for his new home included provisions for the entertaining of guests over night or over the weekend. When completed, the building was not only commodious but, in comparison with many other structures along the river, imposing. Mrs. Moton promptly christened it Holly Knoll, the name suggested by a group of holly trees just beside the walk that led down to the river and the boat landing. Here Dr. Moton continued to live and work after he left Tuskegee. But his enjoyment of the place was relatively short-lived. The strenuous work of the Hampton-Tuskegee campaign coupled with a series of tragedies on the campus of Tuskegee took their toll of his strength and vitality. He was never able to carry out his plan for work and writing. The next few years were passed in reading, in fishing and in receiving friends who, solicitous for his welfare, continued to visit him in his retirement.

CHAPTER 7

❧ *The First Six Years* ❧

BY ALVIN J. NEELY

The successes of the "New Principal" at Tuskegee Institute can best be understood and appreciated in light of the peculiar nature and requirements of the institution itself. Viewed from every angle the educational and administrative capacities of Major Moton matched, in extraordinary degree, the varied requirements of the institution which he was called to serve.

Tuskegee Institute is, first of all, a great educational institution, planned and developed along original and characteristic lines. Its policies and methods are the product, not of educational theory, but of practical necessity. It is in itself a challenge to much of the educational philosophy that has been accepted throughout our country for several generations. Its founder constantly questioned every detail of educational practice, insisting that education justify itself in practical results manifest in the enhanced ability and increased efficiency of those whom it sought to train. Tuskegee has undertaken the task of educating the youth of the race in the essentials of modern civilization in order to prepare them for intelligent, efficient, self-supporting service along lines of practical and immediate usefulness to the communities in which they must ultimately live. This work it does on a large scale for a group of people who, without generous public support, would be unable to obtain its peculiar advantages.

Again, Tuskegee Institute is a great social force which not only educates the individual student, but at the same time extends its activities to the great body of Negro people and stimulates its various classes to such economic, educational, commercial, social, and moral effort as would lift the whole body of the race to higher standards of living and to higher levels of American citizenship. From these considerations it follows that the institution is much more than a school in the generally accepted sense. The general public itself has come to recognize Tuskegee Institute as a highly organized social agency for the development and improvement of the Negro race that is not equaled in influence and effectiveness by any other force operating either from within or without the race.

In addition to these functions Tuskegee Institute has, for many years, occupied a distinctive place as the leading factor in promoting harmonious relations between the two races in the South, a service both difficult and delicate to render. In a way that can hardly be defined, this function became, in the public mind, the outstanding service of the Founder of the institution to the South and to the nation. It becomes inevitably and unavoidably a part of the duties of a new Principal of such an institution, therefore, to undertake these same and most responsible activities, a responsibility which not only bulks large in the duties of the Principal himself but which, at the same time, exerts a determining influence upon the methods and policies of the institution. Tuskegee was conceived by its Founder to be a great instrumentality for promoting mutual understanding and good will between the white people and the black people of the South, a service which time and events themselves enlarged to constitute a similar service between white men of the North and white men of the South.

For all these purposes Tuskegee Institute has, through the years, evolved from a modest group of three or four teachers into a highly organized staff of several hundred workers, both inside and outside of the class room, whose duty it is to sustain its varied activities in education and public service to the point of efficiency which justifies the large and generous contributions for its support which come from every section of the American public. These workers, coming as they do from all parts of our country, have received their training in many different schools, and have directed their efforts for years along special lines of educational, industrial, social and professional work. By his strong personality Dr. Washington was able to gather about him a group of some of the most capable and accomplished men and women of the Negro race, persons capable of independent thinking and strong initiative, all of whom found inspiration and satisfaction in his leadership. This force of workers carried forward the details of the Institute's activities during the life time of its Founder while he was engaged in the many necessary public duties which required him to spend a great part of his time away from the school—a force that remained to continue the work which he inaugurated and developed, giving attention to details in such a way as must always be impossible to the Principal himself.

With such ideas in mind those persons who thought first of the future of the Institute, rather than of the interest of any individual candidate, felt that the successor of Dr. Washington at Tuskegee must carry a four-fold task: that, first, of directing a unique educational institution; second, of promoting the substantial progress and development of the Negro race; third, of helping forward the establishment of just and harmonious relations between the races in the South; and, fourth, of holding together and leading in harmonious and effective cooperation the personnel of one of the most unique social agencies that has been developed anywhere in the world. Such a task required that the new Principal of Tuskegee Institute should be a man of sober sense, of practical efficiency, of wise forebearance, of sympathetic understanding and of broad and generous impulses. In brief, the new Principal should be one who would appreciate the significance of the outstanding characteristics of the work of the Institute.

After careful investigation and consideration of all aspects of this difficult and delicate question, Major Robert Russa Moton, for twenty-five years Commandant of Cadets at Hampton Institute, Virginia, was elected by the Board of Trustees as the successor of Dr. Washington to be Principal of Tuskegee Institute.

Accordingly, on May 25, 1916, Major Moton was to be inaugurated Principal of Tuskegee Institute. The occasion was particularly interesting and significant, being the first formal inauguration of a Principal in the history of the school. The interest of all the nation, therefore, was directed toward Tuskegee. For weeks people interested in the Founder, the Institute itself, the Principal-elect, and the eventful occasion had been sending letters indicating their intention to be present. Several days before the inauguration friends of the Institute had been arriving. Special trains and special cars came from the North and from the South. Practically all of the important educational institutions for Negroes and many others of the white race were significantly represented; likewise the churches and almost every other phase of important activity in the life of the colored people. There was a large representation of the Alumni. It was for them, as well as for former students, teachers and undergraduates, a day of nerve-racking tension and anxiety.

Immediately after the passing of Dr. Washington a great deal of sentiment had been created in favor of different persons who were thought to be qualified to succeed him. Some men busied themselves in creating favorable impressions of their particular friends; some, more zealous than wise, yielded to the temptation to advance their favorites by initiating adverse criticism against other persons whose names had been mentioned for the principalship of Tuskegee. In the case of Major Moton some went so far as to express their unqualified disapproval of him on such untenable grounds that, according to their declaration, he had never made a public address nor shown any particular adaptability for that kind of activity. One can well imagine, then, the very uncomfortable anxiety with which the sincere well-wishers of Dr. Washington and of the Principal-elect approached the day of inauguration.

The hour for the exercises arrived. The spacious Institute Chapel was crowded, even beyond its capacity. Here were people who had journeyed from afar, as well as from places more nearly located, because of their interest in the future of this great Negro institution. People literally stood on tiptoe, leaning forward with hands to ears, mouths agape, eyes straining, to hear and see this new Principal who had been selected by the Trustees, but not wholly accepted by members of his own race; anxious to hear this man tell in his own words what Tuskegee's future was to be under his direction, eager to hear and see this new leader of the race—this man who was to succeed the greatest Negro perhaps the world had ever known.

Introduced by Mr. William G. Willcox, of New York, a member of the Board of Trustees, the Principal-elect began his inaugural address with calm confidence and easy self-possession. In a very little while the audience relaxed and there seemed to run through the whole assembly a sense of satisfaction and relief, aware of the fact that they were in the presence of a sane, patient, big-hearted soul of superior ability and rare common sense.

The address was more than a success—it was a triumph for the Principal and his friends, an inspiration to all. A part of the closing statement is given here:

"No greater or more serious responsibility was ever placed upon the Negro than is left us here at Tuskegee. The importance of the work and the gravity of the duty that has been assigned the Principal and teachers in the forwarding of this work cannot be over-estimated. Along with the responsibility we have a rare opportunity —one almost to be envied—an opportunity to help in the solution of a great problem, the Human Race Problem, not merely changing the modes of life and the ideals of a race, but the ideas of other races regarding that race.... Not by arrogant self-seeking, not by bluff, sham, or bombast, not by flippant fault-finding, not by shrinking at difficulty, or shirking of duty, not by the cherishing of prejudice against white people or black people, can the work of Tuskegee Institute live and prosper.... If we are to be true to the great and sacred trust, if we are to carry out the aims and purposes of Booker T. Washington, the Founder of this institution, we must cherish and maintain the spirit which has always permeated the life and work of this school—the spirit of self-forgetfulness—the spirit of service and sacrifice—the Tuskegee spirit—the spirit of cooperation and consecration. It is only in this spirit that the Tuskegee Normal and Industrial Institute can continue to render service to the Negro, to this State and to the Nation."

The exercises concluded, the audience dismissed, the vast assemblage dissolved into small groups of happy friends gathered with a few converted and disappointed doubters, all scattered about the campus, admiring the wonderful plant that had been created by Booker T. Washington, and joyously echoing the optimistic note that had been sounded a few minutes before by the new Principal in his strong and convincing address. The day passed; friends departed for their homes with benediction on their lips, and joy, satisfaction and hope in their hearts because of what they had seen and heard.

Campus activities gradually returned to normal. A few hours thereafter we were in our working clothes and at our individual duties again. Principal Moton directing? No! Principal Moton observing and studying. The new Principal spent a great part of his time in very careful observation and study of each department and division of the Institute, not even presiding at the meetings of the Executive Council of the Faculty.

Nor did Principal Moton assume full charge at once. He left the school for a time to fill engagements North and South that had been arranged by the Trustees in an effort to raise a Memorial Fund of two million dollars with which to carry forward the work of the Founder. Friends in the North were anxious to hear and see the new Principal. People in the South were just as eager to hear him and get further evidence and assurance of his attitude, not only toward the future of Tuskegee Institute, but also on the question of the relation between the two races. Large audiences greeted him wherever he appeared. He made a favorable and more than satisfactory impression. He grew rapidly in demand as a speaker, and proved himself at once a sound adviser on racial, educational and other questions of national importance. So clear and sane were his interpretations, and so practical and full of common sense and charity were his counsels in the solution of these problems that the leading educational institutions of the land recognized his able and distinguished services to his race and country.

Dr. Moton had come to Tuskegee just at the beginning of the first World War, a time when the strongest minds of the world were taxed to the utmost, and when leaders of thought and action in all races found it difficult to "keep their feet upon the ground." He worked so tactfully and effectively with the different elements of his own race and with the leaders of the nation that he was responsible in no small degree for the fact that the twelve million Negroes in America were practically a unit in their support of the National Government, and in their efforts and sacrifices to win the war. Dr. Moton had a very great influence in getting the Officers' Training Camp at Des Moines for Negroes; and in getting a special representative in the War Department in the person of Mr. Emmett J. Scott, then Secretary of Tuskegee Institute, to handle such matters as particularly affected the welfare of Negro soldiers. Dr. Moton himself was given a commission by the President of the United States to go to France for the special purpose of investigating the welfare and condition of the men of our race overseas and of making such recommendations as, in his judgment, would promote their welfare and efficiency in the American fighting forces.

On the campus Dr. Moton quietly but busily pursued his many duties as Principal of the Institute. He followed with persistence every aspect of the school's work in order to help insure its maximum efficiency. When off the campus he was usually engaged in one or the other of two activities: first, in raising large sums of money that had to be secured annually to keep the Institute in operation; second, and not less important, in interpreting to the nation, both North and South, the needs and aspirations of his struggling but advancing people, and in helping to keep alive the faith, the industry, and the cheerful determination of his own race.

During the earlier years of Dr. Moton's administration it was natural that there should be widespread and inquiring interest in the success of the Institute. Whenever the workers came in contact with outsiders they were instantly besieged with the eager question, "How is the new Principal getting on?" It was only right and fair, therefore, both to Dr. Moton and to the general public who had loyally and faithfully supported the work of Tuskegee Institute and who were doing as much after the passing of the Founder as before to have this question answered fairly and impartially. Since the writer is an alumnus of the Institute and, for a considerable period of time one of its officers, he has two sets of experiences on which to base his judgments. In the former capacity he has seen the administration of the school with the eyes of a student for which class the school was founded; he would, therefore, tend to be prejudiced rather in favor of the Institute itself than in favor of its new Principal. It is easy to look back to "the good old days." As an officer of the Institute, however, the writer has had opportunity to know at least something of the details of administrative activities from a position that admits close observation and evaluation. The resultant analysis, therefore, pleads whatever merit there may be in first hand knowledge and in the candor of an interested graduate.

Some indication of the manner in which Dr. Moton met his responsibilities lies in the improvement and progress made subsequent to his incumbency. One of the first steps taken toward keeping the Institute up to the high standards of efficiency maintained by his predecessor was the appointment of a special committee to make a careful survey of all the courses of study offered by the school, designating as chairman Mr. W. T. B. Williams, Field Agent of the Jeanes and Slater Fund Board, whom he had invited and persuaded to make his headquarters at Tuskegee. School people of both races are familiar with the name of W. T. B. Williams in connection with school methods and school matters generally. No extensive reference to him is necessary, therefore, to indicate the purpose of the Principal to be thorough in his approach to Tuskegee's problems. Along with Mr. Williams were associated the heads of the main departments of instruction at the Institute. At the same time Dr. Paul Henry Hanus, Senior Professor of Education at Harvard University, was invited to make an independent study of the school's method of instruction and courses of study. In this way the Principal placed himself in a position to secure the double advantage of criticism from without and from within the Institute. In due course reports were received from both sources.

After a careful review of the methods and needs of the Institute as indicated by these reports in consultation with the Executive Council, Dr. Moton set out to accomplish the things agreed upon for the continued progress of the institution. Immediate steps were taken to strengthen and to enrich the courses of study in the academic department. Special emphasis was to be laid upon the Teacher Training Course. Students in the senior class were given a regular schedule of observation and practice in the Children's House and in the public schools of the county. To meet the increasing demand for bookkeepers, stenographers and office assistants for Negro business enterprises, a two year business course was organized within the academic department. In addition to these new courses, the regular curriculum was raised to a point representing an advance of practically one year in the requirements for graduation.

In like manner the courses in the industrial and agricultural departments were enlarged. To the mechanical department was added a course in photography. Men, even with college degrees, were soon coming to the Institute for training in this course. Exhibits placed by this division in the various National and International Photographic Expositions were before long receiving honors for the Institute.

Teacher training courses, made possible by the Smith-Hughes Act, were introduced in the girls' industrial division and in the agricultural department. Under the energetic and progressive new director, Benjamin F. Hubert, the agricultural department added a course of graduate study in agriculture, covering a period of three years and requiring twelve months of study each year.

Much, during these early years of Dr. Moton's administration, was done to bring about increased efficiency and economy in the school's internal trading activities by uniting sales for all departments in the general stores of the campus. An unfortunate fire in the old Commissary made necessary space for placing all of the school's stores under the supervision of a single department. Soon the volume of business under this new arrangement totaled $300,000.00 annually.

The military department of the Institute, during this period, was greatly strengthened by the opportunity which came to the school to train some eighteen hundred "fighting mechanics" for service overseas. The Student Army Training Corps was also established. The effectiveness of this work led later to the establishment at Tuskegee of a Reserve Officers' Training Corps under the instruction of a commissioned officer from the United States Army. Along with the several enlargements in the military department of the Institute, an effective piece of work was being carried on in the rehabilitation of disabled ex-service men under the supervision of the Veterans' Bureau. Over a three year period more than three hundred men were enrolled in the courses carried on for this purpose.

Perhaps in no way did Dr. Moton's effectiveness in directing the affairs of the Institute show to better advantage than in the physical improvements made on the campus during his first six years as Principal. The following buildings were erected: a model dairy barn, a modern horse barn, James Hall—a new dormitory for girls—

and five new trades buildings. The old Commissary, partially destroyed by fire, was remodeled.

The new trades buildings are worthy of special mention. If ever the mettle of a school administrator was tested, that of Principal Moton was subjected to the acid test by the situation which necessitated the erection of the new trades buildings. During the fall of 1918, when we were training "fighting mechanics" for the United States Army, the old Boys' Trades Building, which housed the mechanical industries of the school, was destroyed by fire. Although the trades divisions were forced into temporary quarters in various buildings, the work was resumed the next day. Dr. Moton then launched a campaign for replacing what was destroyed. Within little more than two years' time he had raised the money with which to build five substantial, spacious, and attractive buildings to take the place of the old Trades Building. The new buildings were soon equipped with modern machinery to provide for instruction in more than 20 trades.

The second task that the new Principal faced was that of promoting the progress of the race. Here he entered a wider field of activity with many different factors to deal with. Under his supervision the various extension activities of the Institute—the Annual Negro Farmers and Workers Conference at Tuskegee Institute, the National Negro Business League of which he was president, the National Negro Health Week, and the Annual Clinic at the John A. Andrew Memorial Hospital on the campus of the Institute—were prosecuted with undiminished energy and continuing success. While the Farmers' Conference lost some of its picturesqueness with the passing of the gaudy head-gear and dress of some of the farmers' wives which were once much in evidence, together with certain ancient types of vehicles, still this was accepted with satisfaction as a sign of the very progress which the Conference was designed to effect. The meeting that the National Negro Business League gradually developed from the "experience meeting" type to a kind embodying discussions of details of business methods, kept pace with the rise of numerous highly organized business corporations among Negroes. National Negro Health Week was becoming literally a "National Movement," receiving the support and cooperation of the United States Public Health Service, the State and

Municipal Health Departments, the National Medical Association, and other welfare and social agencies. Governors of several Southern states had begun to issue proclamations urging public officials and the people generally to observe and cooperate with this movement.

In addition to maintaining these activities, inaugurated during the lifetime of the Founder of the Institute, Dr. Moton went forward to the promotion of new enterprises in line with Tuskegee's policy of unselfish service. Within the school the John A. Andrew Clinical Society established a postgraduate course for physicians and surgeons in connection with the Annual Clinic. Early in Moton's administration a postgraduate course for nurses was added. In the Agricultural Department the summer work was featured by a course for vocational agricultural teachers, bringing to the Institute teachers of agriculture from all parts of the South; also a summer course for farm demonstration extension agents engaged under the States Relations Service of the United States Department of Agriculture, and a ten day course for farmers. All of these came to be conducted simultaneously with a registration of several hundred persons. In this connection should be mentioned the Annual Clinic established by the Veterinary Hospital of the Institute for the benefit of local farmers needing simple instruction in the care of their farm animals.

The third, and in some respects the most important accomplishment of all, was that of continuing the difficult and delicate work of cultivating good will between the two races in the South. For this service Dr. Moton brought to the Institute an unusual equipment and training. Those who knew him best discerned in him a subtle, intangible power to fathom and appreciate psychic processes and tendencies of various types of men, a gift that was made more effective by his experience at Hampton as Commandant of Cadets where, for twenty-five years, he daily faced the problem of adjusting the relations of white, black and red men in the normal activities of life. The insight and poise thus acquired he brought to bear at once in the wider circles of race relations in the South and throughout the nation.

A striking phase of his activity in this difficult field was, from the first as well as long before he came to Tuskegee, that of making tours in the Southern states, including especially the states of the Southeastern section. In his speeches he attempted to interpret the races to each other. In his addresses to Negroes he advised them to be thrifty, to cooperate with each other and with other races, and to be proud of their own race. In addressing whites he contended for the rights of the colored race in no uncertain terms, always evidencing frankness and sincerity in what he said. Concerning his address in Wilmington, North Carolina, the Wilmington Star said:

"The address delivered by Dr. Robert R. Moton last night could produce no other than a salutary effect. Endeavoring to interpret some of the things which white and colored people respectively keep 'in the back of their heads,' the Tuskegee Principal spoke with refreshing frankness. His directness, his simplicity, his honesty and earnestness are at once disarming and strongly persuasive. He is immediately revealed as a man who loves mankind, whose outlook is that of a clear-eyed Christian. The widespread adoption of the Moton methods would soon clarify the atmosphere of racial relations. His method is that of unreserved frankness and unlimited charity. Nothing is to be gained by a policy of concealment; no adjustment of the race problem will ever be made while there is a lack of understanding, or while a spirit of sympathy is excluded from our councils on race relations."

Scarcely less delicate was the task confronting the new Principal of holding together the highly organized and efficient corps of workers which Dr. Washington had assembled on the faculty of the Institute. Naturally under the new administration as under the preceding one there were some changes in the personnel from year to year. Dr. Moton spent a great deal of time away from the Institute, but students and teachers alike continued to follow their duties with undiminished diligence. Visitors to the Institute continued to find here a highly trained, efficient, and well-organized faculty composed of men and women from the leading schools and colleges of all sections of the country. In their respective spheres the members of the faculty cooperated with the Principal in his efforts to train Negro youth to be useful, self-reliant citizens in whatever community they would eventually live. The outstanding fact in this connection was that Tuskegee was able to supply only a fraction of the demand for graduates as teachers, nurses, mechanics, and workers in other positions of trust and usefulness.

We have mentioned only a few of the services which Dr. Moton consistently rendered the Institute, the race and the nation during the years of his principalship. Through his sincerity, his practicality and his intimate knowledge of what was then called "The Negro Problem," he gained the confidence of the people of both races who came to know him at first hand. Many other institutions—schools and welfare agencies—placed him on their boards of trustees and on various executive committees in order to have the advantage of his counsel and his patient, sympathetic insight.

It is not possible to review all of the work which Dr. Moton accomplished during the first years of his principalship at Tuskegee Institute. Enough has been given, however, of his more important activities to enable the impartial reader to judge for himself the wisdom of the Board of Trustees in selecting Major Robert R. Moton of Hampton Institute to succeed Booker T. Washington at Tuskegee. At the Institute itself he soon won the entire confidence and the loyal support of both teachers and students. Outside the Institute he soon established the confidence of the general public in the methods and spirit of Tuskegee in such a way as to settle forever all questions about their soundness or their permanency. Tuskegee Institute, with a larger plant and a larger enrollment than ever before, has an increasing hold upon the good will and affection of both races throughout the country.

Through all of his accomplishments Dr. Moton remained as simple, as unassuming and as unselfish as anyone could desire. Called to be Principal, he approached his task as modestly as the humblest worker on the staff. Without the least self-assertion he was accorded, from the first, the utmost respect from all about him, so evident were the earnestness and seriousness of his dedication to the Institute's great requirements. And then insensibly, imperceptibly there passed into his hands the fullest authority. He rarely exercised it. He trusted his heads of departments without reserve. However when conflict or confusion arose, or when decision waited upon ultimate responsibility, it was immediately apparent that Robert Russa Moton was the Principal of Tuskegee Institute.

CHAPTER 8

❦ *A Man of Courage* ❦

BY ALBON L. HOLSEY

In his autobiography, *Finding a Way Out*, Dr. Moton has delightfully told his early experiences during the Reconstruction Period of the South. Many of these experiences were character-revealing as well as preparatory for subsequent responsibilities. One such incident, showing his sense of humor and temperamental balance under difficulties, was told concerning his first day's experience at Hampton Institute in 1885. Coming down by boat from his home in Prince Edward County, Virginia, he arrived at Old Point Comfort and took a hack to the school. "Looking upon the well-kept grounds of the Institute," he said, "the water front, the neat and imposing buildings and farms, I felt almost as if I were in another world. A few mischievous boys took occasion to have some fun at my expense. They were already calling out 'fresh fish,' and two or three of them yanked my small trunk out of the carriage and balanced it on their fingers as waiters balance their trays in hotels. Some suggested that it weighed ten pounds, others said five. I must confess that the small trunk was entirely out of proportion to the size of its 175 pound, eighteen-year-old, and somewhat awkward owner. But I went through the ordeal good naturedly, when finally one of the older boys was kind enough to show me to the office where I presented myself to the commandant."

"I went through the ordeal good naturedly." These seven words, better than any I can bring together, are descriptive of Dr. Moton's basic character. This characteristic was his greatest asset when he faced the many ordeals at Tuskegee Institute. Those envious critics who wishfully predicted the end of Tuskegee's prestige, at the passing of the Founder, did not reckon with those intrinsic and latent qualities of leadership with which Dr. Moton was fortunately endowed. These values were enriched by a judicial and elastic temperament, a becoming modesty, a mature judgment, a native refinement, and a delightful personality. As if further to confound those who would challenge Tuskegee's leadership, now that the Founder had passed, fate stepped in with its first real test of Dr. Moton and he met it.

When our country was preparing for action in the first World War, Tuskegee's well-known program for service was immediately in demand by the President and by other Governmental officials at Washington. The selection of Tuskegee Institute as a training center for Negro soldiers; Dr. Moton's quiet and effective influence in the establishment of the training camp for Negro officers at Des Moines; the invitation from Secretary of War, Newton D. Baker, to Dr. Moton to serve as his advisor on problems of Negro enlisted men; Dr. Moton's subsequent selection of Dr. Emmett J. Scott, Secretary of Tuskegee Institute, to fill the post; and Dr. Moton's later cooperation with the Government in the postwar recovery programs—all of these and many more were Tuskegee's contributions to the national cause.

During the late summer and early fall of 1918, there were many rumors afloat, both in and outside official circles in this country, to the effect that the American Negro soldier was a failure on the battlefields of Europe. He was not only cowardly and inefficient as a soldier but, morally, he was a disgrace to his country. So malignant and damaging was "the whispering gallery" in France, that the President and Secretary of War selected and appointed Dr. Moton to go to the battlefronts in Europe with full authority to go anywhere and to get information from any source, as far as the American Expeditionary Force was concerned.

Dr. Moton was fully aware of the difficulties of such a mission and that questions which he might ask and things which he might say would probably be misunderstood or misinterpreted. His purpose, however, was to get at the facts and to allay untruthful rumors. In order to ascertain the facts, he made extended inquiries of those with whom he came in contact, from the highest officers down.

When Dr. Moton reached the General Headquarters of the American Forces, he found that two days before his arrival a young white soldier was sentenced to be hanged for the "unmentionable crime," rape. However, because of his good record as a soldier, the sentence was commuted to life imprisonment. The opinion expressed at Headquarters was that rape was no more prevalent among Negro soldiers than among white soldiers, or any other soldiers, for that matter.

From Chaumont, Dr. Moton went immediately to Marbache, the Headquarters of the 92nd Division. When he asked the Commanding General of the 92nd about the prevalence of the crime in question, he received the reply that it was very prevalent. Dr. Moton was not satisfied with mere opinion. He courteously called for the records, inasmuch as the reputation of a race was at stake.

When the records were brought in and examined, only seven cases actually charged could be found. Of these only two had been found guilty and convicted. Furthermore, one of the two convictions had been "turned down" by General Headquarters. Afterwards, Dr. Moton interviewed the Judge Advocate of the 92nd Division, who informed him that there had been eleven cases charged in that whole division. Out of these eleven, two really belonged to another organization and only three of the remaining nine had been finally approved as guilty, and one sentence out of the three had been reduced from life imprisonment to taking of half the man's pay for twelve months.

In other fighting units, where many of the Service of Supply Troops were located, Dr. Moton made similar investigations. He interviewed American and French commanding officers as well as scores of American and French officers of the lower ranks. Whenever the records were consulted it was found that the number of cases charged was very small. He likewise spent considerable time with members of the Peace Conference, and with Americans engaged in various branches of war activities, in an effort to disprove and set at rest the widespread slander against the Negro race. He spared no pains in carrying out his mission which, no doubt, was effective in reducing to some degree the harmful rumors both in America and abroad.

The following statements are from Dr. Moton's report:

"There was apparently no doubt in the mind of anybody in France, so far as I was able to find out, among the French or the Americans, as to the excellent qualities of the American Negro as a soldier, when led by white officers. There was also little question, if any, about the fighting record of the four regiments—the 369th, 370th, 371st, and 372nd—which had been brigaded with French Divisions; but when it came to the 92nd Division, there was a subtle and persistent rumor in Paris and in other places of Europe, as far as my travels, observations, and investigations, substantiating the rumor which was also prevalent in America—only in France it was much more generally accepted as true; namely, that the Negro officers had been 'practically a failure,' and that it was a mistake to have ever attempted to have a division with Negroes as officers.

"I took a great deal of pains and care, as did also the gentlemen with me, to run down every rumor. We spent much time in and out of Paris ferreting out every statement that came from the 'whispering gallery.' We finally found that, so far as the 92nd Division was concerned, only a very small portion of a single battalion, of a single regiment, had failed. . . . Later in a conversation with the highest American military official in France, regarding this story of the failure of Negro officers, he said that the possibilities were that any officer, white or black, under the same adverse circumstances that these men faced, would have failed, as the very few did. About a dozen officers of the battalion were sent before a board for trial for having shown cowardice. They were not, however, all found guilty; and to offset this, some of the other colored officers of this regiment, for conspicuous bravery in the same engagement, were promoted and decorated with the Distinguished Service Cross!

"It would appear that this small part of a battalion whose failure was so widely reported, had never before been under fire, and had been taken from a quiet sector and brought forward with the expectation that they would not be put into the firing for several weeks; but it so happened that the Germans were much stronger than the French behind whom this unit was placed. When the French troops were badly cut to pieces, the Negro unit in question had to go into the firing within twenty-four hours after reaching the front, which was much earlier than expected. In connection with this alleged failure, there are also some other very important considerations to be brought out officially.

"It was gratifying to find that the Commanding General, who knew all phases of the affair, did not take this failure anything like as seriously as the rumor about it seemed to warrant. The facts in the case in no sense justified the common report. In talking with the Commanding General at Le Mans, I referred to the fact that something like fifteen Negro officers had been sent back as 'inefficient.' He said to me, 'If it is any comfort to you, I will tell you this: we sent back through Blois to America, in six months, an average of one thousand white officers a month, who failed in one way or another in this awful struggle. I hope, Dr. Moton,' he added, 'that you won't lose your faith in my race because of that, and certainly I am not going to lose my faith in your race because of the record of a few colored officers who failed.' "

Just what did Dr. Moton say to the Negro troops in his parting address to them? He said, in part: "The record you have made in this war—of faithfulness, bravery, and loyalty—has deepened my faith in you as men and as soldiers, as well as in my race and my country. You have been tremendously tested. You have suffered hardships and privations. You have been called upon to make many sacrifices. Your record has sent a thrill of joy and satisfaction to the hearts of millions of white and black Americans, rich and poor, high and low. Black mothers and wives, sweethearts, fathers, and friends have rejoiced with you and with our country in your record. You will go back to America," he said, "as heroes, as you really are. You will go back as you have carried yourselves over here—in a straightforward, manly, and modest way. If I were you, I would find a job as soon as possible, and get to work. To those who have not already done so, I would suggest that you get hold of a piece of land and a home as soon as possible, and marry and settle down.

Save your money and put it into something tangible. I hope no one will do anything in peace to spoil the magnificent record your troops have made in war."

What Dr. Moton said in addresses to white officers and soldiers in France was even more significant. The following was the final paragraph in one of his speeches:

"These black soldiers—officers and men—have, along with you, placed their lives willingly and gladly at the disposal of their country, not only to make the world safe for democracy, but, what is equally important, to make democracy safe for mankind, black and white. You and they go back to America as heroes, brave and modest, of course, but there is a difference; you go back without let or hindrance, with every opportunity our beloved country offers open to you. You are the heirs of all the ages. God has never given any race more than He has given you. The men of my race who return will have many unnecessary hardships and limitations, along many lines. What a wonderful opportunity you have, therefore, and what a great responsibility, if you go back to America resolved that as far as in your power lies, you are going to see that these black men and the twelve millions of people whom they represent in our country, who have stood so loyally by you and America in peace and in war, shall have a fair and absolutely equal chance with every other American citizen, along every line—this is your duty and sacred obligation. They ask only fair play and, as loyal American citizens, they should have it."

One feature of the nation's postwar effort brought with it a new and unanticipated angle of the race problem, especially in the South. Along with a number of Veterans' Hospitals to be established in various parts of the country, there was to be a hospital for Negroes disabled in the recent war. Very conclusively, a Government survey had shown the inadequate provisions hitherto made for Negro veterans, many of whom were being "farmed out" to private hospitals of inferior rank or, too frequently, not hospitalized at all even though seriously disabled. Under these conditions, the excessive death rate of disabled Negro veterans, as compared with white veterans of like age and service, was understandable. For these reasons, it seemed desirable that a first class hospital for Negro veterans should be established somewhere in the South.

In spite of the fact that the greatest number of Negro veterans were in the South, many communities were ready to oppose the location of such a hospital in their midst. A contributor to the Montgomery *Advertiser*, in the spring of 1923, declared:

"When the Government agents were trying to find a place suitable for the Negro veterans' hospital, they came to Montgomery. Our people did not want it. . . . The Northern Negro wouldn't have good health in the Southern climate; nothing here would make him happy; and certainly he doesn't suit our people. . . . If the Government wanted Northern Negroes to manage this hospital, they should have located it in the North; and if they now want Northern Negroes to manage it, for God's sake let them move it quickly. . . . Every institution in the South should be managed by white men; for as long as the blood of Southerners courses our veins, white men will control the South. It is necessary that we do so. No Negro officer can do well here. Our people will not stand for it."

The story of how the Negro Veterans' Hospital came to be located near Tuskegee, Alabama, on a beautiful hilltop of 464 acres, three hundred of which were donated by Tuskegee Institute, is interesting but complicated. On February 12, 1923, this modern hospital unit of six hundred beds, erected and equipped by the Government at a cost of $2,500,000, was ready to be dedicated. Representing the Government at the dedicatory exercises held in the chapel of Tuskegee Institute, Calvin Coolidge, then Vice President of the United States, was the chief speaker.

At one point in the program there was a spiritual sung by the Tuskegee Institute Choir. The audience applauded and the choir responded with "We Are Climbing Jacob's Ladder." Again the audience insisted on another. As the choir leader tapped her baton for a third encore and began singing "Let Us Cheer The Weary Traveler," Colonel Clifford, observing that Mr. Coolidge was apparently unmoved and fearing that he was growing weary of the singing, leaned over and whispered to him, "If you are tired of the singing, I will stop them and go ahead with the program." Without turning his head and almost without a perceptible movement of the lips, Mr. Coolidge in his well-known, laconic expression whispered back, "I like it."

Not only did Mr. Coolidge enjoy the singing of the melodies but he was impressed by the whole panorama of the day's events. The inspection of the new buildings and grounds at the hospital and the visit to Tuskegee Institute, with its various activities, awakened in him a new appreciation of the possibilities of Negro leadership. He came to Tuskegee to deliver the address, probably feeling that it was merely one of the duties of his office; but he went away with a broader sympathy for the Negro race and a deeper insight into interracial achievements. It was, in short, a day of mutual understanding and good will.

In words of praise which will outlive even the hospital buildings, Mr. Coolidge said in his address: "For the service of the Negroes at home and abroad during the war, they have the everlasting gratitude of the American people. They have justified the faith of Abraham Lincoln. The dedication of this hospital ... shows the appreciation in which they are held by our Government."

Responding to the words of Mr. Coolidge, Dr. Moton declared: "The colored people throughout the nation appreciate this magnificent effort on the part of our Government to see that these Negro soldiers have a fair chance, under as perfect conditions as modern science affords, for as speedy and complete a recovery as is possible. I am glad to see that this hospital has no earmarks of inferiority. It is as good as the very best and marks the greatest physical achievement of our Government for the Negro race in America since emancipation."

Soon after the dedication of the Veterans' Hospital at Tuskegee, colored people throughout the country were beginning to ask, "Will Negro physicians and nurses be permitted to serve there?" Dr. Moton, in a letter to President Harding, wrote as follows: "If Negro physicians and nurses are not permitted to serve Negro patients in a hospital erected by the Government for them on land donated by and adjacent to an institution which is controlled and managed by Negroes, it will create an embarrassing situation and one which I cannot defend."

There were those in the Veterans' Bureau at Washington who

honestly believed that a Negro personnel, competent to run a large hospital, was not available. In conversation with Dr. Moton, one of these said, "Are there any institutions offering professional courses for Negro doctors and nurses?" Dr. Moton quickly replied, "There certainly are and right here in Washington. There is the Medical School of Howard University for training Negro physicians, and the Freedmen's Hospital and Nurses Training School, both supported by the Government."

The official expressed great surprise and interest. He had never before heard of Howard University or the Freedmen's Hospital nor had he heard of the National Medical Association—an organization composed of between three and four thousand Negro physicians. The task of convincing the Government officials that Negroes are capable of managing the Veterans' Hospital was not easy and required the combined efforts of Dr. Moton, the National Medical Association, and other leaders of both races.

Early in 1923, General Frank T. Hines, the newly appointed Director of the Veteran's Bureau, approached the problem with an open mind and with the sympathy of a master executive. My own impression of the General, during the months of discussion and confusion, was that he considered of prime importance the welfare of the Negro veteran. There was neither sentiment nor prejudice on his part; the whole matter to him was a question of efficiency.

It should be remembered, however, that the negotiations for a Veteran's hospital at Tuskegee were initiated during a Republican administration and that some Negroes of the Republican Party were inclined to consider the prospective hospital as a patronage-dispensing opportunity. The two conflicting ambitions over the control of the hospital were Dr. Moton's dilemma. Once he realized the nature and magnitude of his task, he unhesitatingly went into action. Prior to this, however, he had been in more or less continuous contact with the authorities at Washington, who in this situation as in many others, were receptive to any suggestions or recommendations he might care to offer.

In the meantime, on February 23, 1923, President Harding's secretary wrote the Director of the Veterans' Bureau as follows: "I have brought the text of your letter of February 20th to the attention of the President. He has directed me to say that it is his wish that there be no designation of doctors and nurses for the care of the colored soldiers at the United States Veterans' Hospital at Tuskegee until there has been a thorough and determined effort to secure a civil service list of eligible Negro citizens. Dr. Moton, Principal of Tuskegee Institute, has assured the President of his willingness to be helpful, and the President asks that you seek his cooperation."

As soon as General Hines had made a careful survey of the situation and had become convinced that a competent Negro personnel was available, he proceeded on his program of selection and replacement. With the assistance of Dr. M. O. Dumas of Washington, D.C., a well-known official of the National Association, competent men and women were gradually selected from different parts of the country for the various posts at Tuskegee. Following a careful canvass begun several months before, General Hines selected Dr. Joseph H. Ward of Indianapolis, Indiana, as a possible head for the hospital. Aside from being a successful physician and surgeon, Dr. Ward had served overseas during the war and had been promoted from the rank of second lieutenant to major for conspicuous and well done service in the Medical Corps. Subsequently, he received the rank of lieutenant-colonel. Before going to Tuskegee, he was sent by the Veterans' Bureau to study administrative policies operative in other Government hospitals. Three of Dr. Ward's prospective assistants in the neuro-psychiatric section received special training at the Boston Psychopathic Hospital. Others awaiting specific assignments were graduates of Harvard University, The University of Pennsylvania, Columbia University, the University of Chicago and other institutions of higher learning.

Before the replacement of personnel at the hospital began, several events of a disturbing nature took place. When the white people of Alabama learned of the President's decision, a storm of protest arose in certain sections of the state. The Governor of the State and a State senator, the latter a resident of Tuskegee, were among the leaders of the dissension. The senator, a candidate for the governorship at the coming election, declared, "We do not want any Governmental institution in Alabama with niggers in charge. White supremacy in this state must be maintained at any cost, and we are not going to have any niggers in the state whom we cannot control."

It was then that the Ku Klux Klan entered the scene and became loud in its insistence that a Negro personnel in the Veterans' Hospital would be opposed by them in every way possible. Rumors of threatened harm to Tuskegee Institute were persistent. The buildings would be bombed or burned to the ground. Dr. John A. Kenney, who for twenty years had been Director of the Institute Hospital, a surgeon of national reputation, was "advised" to leave the community because of his open statement favoring a Negro personnel in the Veterans' Hospital.

Under the circumstances, it was expected that Dr. Moton would receive something of the aroused wrath of the Klan. His influence with the Veterans' Bureau at Washington; his part in bringing the Veterans' Hospital to Tuskegee; and his follow-up contacts with the President of the United States while the personnel problem at the hospital was being solved, were not unknown to those who were causing the disturbance. At one stage of the unhappy events, a committee of fifteen malcontents of the county—a committee self-styled "the leading citizens of the community"—came to Dr. Moton's office with a petition and the demand that he sign it. Some time afterward, Dr. Moton gave the following account of what happened in the conference:

"Booker Washington," said one of the white group, "gave thirty-five years of his life to build up this school. You, unless you are too stubborn to sign a little paper here, are going to have it all blown up in twenty-four hours." Another added, "You understand that we have the legislature, we make the laws, we have the judges, the sheriffs, the jails. We have the hardware stores and the arms." Still another "representative of the community" declared, "A thousand men—their spokesman called me up this morning—we will be over on an hour's notice and wipe out the whole —— institution if things are not going the way you want them to go." In conclusion, the speaker addressing Dr. Moton, threatened, "Your life is in our hands."

The committeeman who delivered this threat, accustomed as he was to cowering reactions on the part of frightened victims, had not anticipated the deliberate reply of Dr. Moton. "Gentlemen,"

Dr. Moton said, "I would be sorry to have any harm come to Tuskegee Institute.... You say my life is in your hands. I do not doubt it. You have in your hands all the things you have mentioned—the laws, the judges, the jails, and even the guns.... I haven't a gun in my pocket or anywhere else.... You can wipe me out; you can take my life, gentlemen; but you can't take my character."

Continuing, Dr. Moton declared: "If Negroes who are thoroughly educated and trained for such service can't serve their own people, can't serve in that hospital, on land given by a Negro school, for Negro veterans, provided by the Federal Government; if they can't practice in that hospital, then you may as well wipe out Tuskegee Institute and every other Negro institution in the world. The sooner you do it the better . . . so far as I am concerned, gentlemen, I have only one life to give; but I would gladly give a dozen for this cause.... If I were to sign that paper, I would be deceiving my people and my country.... It's a Negro hospital, built for Negroes; and, gentlemen, if Negroes trained for the job can't run it, you can wipe out the hospital and the school and Moton."

Throughout all the heat and uncertainty of the hospital controversy there had been occasional but persistent rumors of a Klan parade. Such a demonstration was to remind any doubting persons of the "powerful and eternal supremacy of the white race" and to show the determination of the white people of Tuskegee to prevent Negroes from being installed as officers in the Negro Veterans' Hospital.

On July 1, 1923, there was circulated a final and decisive word that the parade would take place on the eve of Independence Day. The officials of Tuskegee Institute, however, were notified that the demonstration would not come upon the grounds nor pass through any of the school thoroughfares; that no one at the Institute need fear of being molested; but that the event should be looked upon just as if it were a Masonic or Pythian parade.

The cleverly devised stage-setting for the day was nearly upset by a young man of the colored race. John H. Calhoun, a graduate of Hampton Institute, was among those who had recently taken the Civil Service examination for the position of disbursing official at the hospital. Among others taking the examination, was a white woman who was already holding the position temporarily. When the examinations were over, it was found that Mr. Calhoun had made the highest average grade, while the white woman had actually failed. Mr. Calhoun, then in Virginia, received his orders to report to the Veterans' Hospital at Tuskegee and to begin his work immediately.

On the morning of July 3, the day on which the Klan parade was to take place, Calhoun reported to the commanding officer in charge of the hospital, where he was given a desk but no immediate assignment. It had been assumed that he would be only too glad to make a "hasty retreat" upon receiving the final threats from those who would "kill him on sight" should he attempt to remain there. Such threats, no doubt, were contained in a sealed message handed to Calhoun on this occasion by the commanding officer with the casual remark, "I was requested to deliver this." But Calhoun did not hasten away. It was the commanding officer who became frightened when he observed the unexpected calmness of the intended victim. The report had it that the commanding officer left the hospital and telephoned back giving orders for Calhoun to be put off the premises. Three armed guards of the hospital were instructed to see that the orders were carried out. Calm and unruffled by the threats of those who would do him bodily harm and unaffected by the entreaties of his friends, Calhoun, without any effort at concealment, remained in the community until after the Klan parade when he departed for Washington.

Scarcely had the Tuskegee Klan demonstration ended when Director Hines of the Veterans' Bureau was on his way for a conference with white representatives of Tuskegee. There in the Court House, on July 5, a very frank discussion of the interracial problem took place. In his introductory remarks, General Hines stated very clearly that it had been the intention of President Harding from the beginning to place colored physicians in charge of this hospital—provided, of course, that competent physicians of that race could be found. "I say to you," declared General Hines, "such a staff has been found, but it has not yet been appointed."

The state senator, spokesman for the local group, then reviewed at some length the story of the establishment of the Veterans' Hospital at Tuskegee, pointing out that Montgomery and other Alabama communities had refused to allow the hospital to be located in their midst. "We in Tuskegee did not want this hospital located here," he said, "and when Major Kenzie first came here, he said his purpose was to sound out the local sentiment to see whether Tuskegee would be a proper place for such an institution. I told him, as frankly as I purpose to talk with you, sir, that in my judgment he was misstating his mission and that he had probably come here to convince Tuskegee citizens that they should permit its location here."

Continuing, the senator said: "Now, sir, I say to you that Alabama is not a suitable place for the location of this hospital, especially if it is to be officered and manned by colored physicians. The place for such a hospital is in the North. We, here in Tuskegee, have fostered Tuskegee Institute from the beginning. We have given Booker T. Washington and his successor, Dr. Moton, every possible protection. The Institute, as Washington said many times, is founded on the goodwill and friendship of the Tuskegee white man. If Dr. Moton and his associates on the faculty have told you what they have told us about the proposed Negro personnel at the hospital, they have told you that it will be a menace to the great school. ... If they have told you and the President anything different, they have deceived us. In such case the protection and friendship of the Tuskegee whites will be withdrawn from the institution and it cannot, in the future, prosper."

"Colored physicians," continued the senator, "cannot manage that hospital staff and its patients. We of the South, we who have lived here for generations, know the Negro far better than the Northerner does. We know that the Negro cannot control even himself.... The white race is the controlling race. Wherever the white man has set foot, even in the ratio of one to fifty, he has controlled; he has always conquered and controlled the colored.... Here in Tuskegee, our ratio is about one to four and a half. Here the white man has controlled and will continue to control.... The white man controls that great institution for the education of the Negro.... The teaching there is done by Negroes; but the hand of the Tuskegee white man is on the pulse at all times and the white man controls."

During the Klan parade, it should be mentioned, the people of the campus of Tuskegee Institute went about their usual activities. To most of the summer school students and teachers, Klan parades were no novelty. They did not look on the demonstration with "awe and silence" as one of the newspapers reported. They were curious and somewhat depressed but not especially fearful. One member of the faculty made the following comment: "For forty years, we have had as we thought, the full confidence of the white people of the community and of the South; we have supported their business enterprises; we have, many times, at the sacrifice of the confidence of others, made every reasonable overture to secure the goodwill of our white neighbors; in a word, we have tried to prove that the Tuskegee experiment in interracial cooperation is good."

However embarrassing the hospital affair was at the time, it brought out many encouraging facts concerning interracial progress in the South. With very few exceptions, the metropolitan newspapers of the South took a stand in opposition to that of the Ku Klux Klan. Southern editorials on the subject would fill a large volume of hopeful opinion. In the *Asheville* (N.C.) *Citizen* of July 8, 1923, we read:

"The Tuskegee protests in this matter do not represent Southern opinion on the race question. It is an established Southern tradition that Negroes should have their own preachers, teachers, and physicians. Such a mode of living represents the sanest kind of common sense with regard to the social contacts of whites and blacks. This policy increases the efficiency and self-respect of the colored man; it opens to the race avenues of work other than common labor.... But the truth is that in Alabama, and to some degree in other Southern states, a minority of whites still hold that the Negro should hew wood and draw water and only that; that he should be virtually a serf."

In the *Louisville Courier-Journal*, July 9, 1923, the Klan's activities were condemned in no uncertain terms:

"That demonstration in Alabama the other day was typical of the Ku Klux Klan. Seven hundred members marched through the streets of Tuskegee as a protest against placing Negro officials in charge of the Government hospital for disabled Negro veterans....

Such a display of race animosity would damn the Ku Klux Klan were it not already damned. They might as well have paraded against Tuskegee Institute having at its head a Negro and having been founded by a Negro.... Ordinarily the clowning of the Ku Klux Klan is laughable. When they set in motion the doctrine of race hatred they are a menace. When they try to take into their own hands the law they are outlaws."

The *Greensboro* (N.C.) *Daily News*, July 5, 1923, was no less caustic in its criticism of what happened at Tuskegee. It asked:

"Is this a true reflection of the spirit of the South? Are we determined to bar the Negro out of the learned professions, even when he has no idea of attempting to practice his profession except within his own race? Are we going to deny to a man on account of the color of his skin opportunity to make the best of the talents God has given him? ... The *Daily News* cannot believe that. But if it is not true, then this benighted attempt to drive Negroes out of the Government hospital at Tuskegee should be repudiated vigorously by Southern opinion. Doubtless the attempt of the Klan will be fruitless. The Government cannot conceivably yield to it. But for the protection of its own good name, the attempt should be hotly denied by the South. The attempt in itself will do no harm, for the world understands perfectly that the South, like every other section, has its due proportion of morons and toughs whose actions cannot always be controlled by the decent and intelligent element of the population. The danger is that the country may believe that this outrage is supported by the better element, at least tacitly. It is to correct any such impression that the South should condemn the outbreak unsparingly."

In many editorials of the Southern press, the inconsistency of opposing a Negro personnel in a strictly Negro veterans' hospital was pointed out. Surely Southern people, at all loyal to the traditions of the South, were not clamoring for an opportunity to wait on sick Negroes! The Ku Klux Klansmen, even if they wanted to humble themselves to the extent of becoming servants of Negroes, could not qualify. In all probability, there were no white physicians in the Klan demonstration. The Ku Kluxers—if they cared to be consistent in their alleged beliefs about racial separation—could well parade in protest against white nurses and white doctors serving the Negro sick and wounded.

Significant was an editorial which appeared in the *Daily Times*, Chattanooga, Tennessee, July 25, 1923, as follows:

"Just a reminder of how it happened that so many persons do not respect laws, the incident at Tuskegee, Alabama, where there has been an open if not violent demonstration against putting Negro doctors and Negro officials in charge of the Negro hospital for disabled Negro veterans located in that city, it might be well to suggest that the 'protest' is in defiance of the Fourteenth and Fifteenth amendments to the Constitution of the United States. The clamor is not against the men who are being put in charge of the institution, but against the color of their skins and character of their antecedents.... The attempt is being made at Tuskegee to so terrify men of black skins, and to agitate the emotional whites against the blacks, that the administration at Washington may feel it best for the peace and tranquility of the community and the proper functioning of the hospital to withdraw its order putting Negro surgeons and officials in charge. That, of course, would be government by 'mob suasion,' and not government according to the Constitution.... The people of Tuskegee are attempting to nullify the Fourteenth Amendment, —the state authorities have not interfered to stop it—by threatening the Government with a 'reign of terror' unless it shall retreat from its position and withdraw its action, for the reason that it is repugnant to certain elements of Tuskegee society.... We cannot have a sound and just government when part of the Constitution is to be enforced and another part of it is to be repudiated. Expediency and opportunism have been having their day in this great country of ours, and that may in some measure explain, although it does not justify, the wide-spread disrespect for law we are now experiencing. We cannot fairly hold the violators of one law to strict accountability when we openly and notoriously justify ourselves in violating another law just as binding upon our good citizenship and conscience."

Some editorials, however, were more concerned about the probable ineffectiveness of the tactics used than about the principles involved in the controversy. The *Macon* (Ga.) *Daily Telegraph*, July 7, 1923, declared:

"The recent demonstration on the part of the Klan tended to play the whole situation into the hands of the radicals among the Northern Negroes.... The result of the parade held in the vicinity of Tuskegee was that rumors began to float to the effect that President Moton's life was in danger. The rumors could have been manufactured by the Northern radicals or they could have easily been created in Tuskegee in one of the excited quarters.... Alabama wants no such sorry spectacle as Federal troops coming down to camp on her soil to 'protect' somebody. The very suggestion was an insult to Alabama's Governor and Militia; but as long as we play into the hands of radicals, such suggestions can be made and sometimes listened to."

A week later, in the same daily, the following appeared:

"Really, there should be a Negro staff in charge. There should also be Negro nurses. . . . In simple justice to the Negro, he should be given opportunities for his own development. . . . As we understand it, the Negro's Republican friends of the North are robbing him of his opportunity at Tuskegee. As is generally known, the Republicans of the North have very little sense about the Negro in the South—they play politics with him caring little about what eventually becomes of him. . . . But if the Negro hospital at Tuskegee, since it is a Federal institution, is put in charge of a Negro staff, what guarantee has the South that white nurses from the North will not come down and work under a Negro staff? None at all! And if this should occur, trouble will result as surely as the sun rises in the east and sets in the west. . . . The real Southern Negro has about as much respect for white people who dwell in the Negro realm as a real Southern white man has. Of course, this makes matters all the worse."

At times during the hospital controversy, as to whether the personnel should be black, white or mixed, the situation became embarrassing to Dr. Moton. The vexing triangle of groups consisted of Northern Negroes who were opposed to any kind of separate hospital; Southern Negroes who favored a colored personnel; and Southern whites who contended that all the professional staff should be white. No one in Dr. Moton's position could have pleased all of these disputants. Even the Negro papers, especially in the North, presented Dr. Moton as an "Uncle Tom" in the South and a bold advocate for the rights of race in the North. Cartoons setting forth the assumed double personality of Dr. Moton were sometimes seen in these papers.

While Dr. Moton did not choose to answer these rebukes publicly—it was never his policy, when attacked, to use the public method in answering charges—he did work quietly and effectively with those who were in a position to bring about, eventually, a hospital for Negroes, manned and directed by Negroes.

Finally, in a speech before the National Negro Business League, in convention at Hot Springs, Arkansas, in August 1923, Dr. Moton made the following statement concerning the hospital controversy:

"In all of this affair," he asserted, "two great motives have been actuating those of us at Tuskegee who have had directly to deal with the situation. The first was the conviction that Negroes have a right above all other people to serve their own; and second, the necessity of preserving intact those relations of goodwill and mutual helpfulness between white people and black people at Tuskegee, in the South and all over the country—which latter was the outstanding achievement of the career of Booker Washington.

"So far as the first motive goes," continued Dr. Moton, "we have abundant evidence that our physicians and nurses are capable of rendering the services demanded. This is not only my own opinion, but it is the testimony of those in authority outside of the Negro race. I have steadfastly and unswervingly taken that position from the beginning and have said that by every right of sentiment and justice our physicians and nurses should have the opportunity to serve in that hospital, and I have made this assertion where it would mean most; namely, before the Superintendent of the Veterans' Hospital at Tuskegee, the Director of the Veterans Bureau in Washington, and before the late lamented President W. G. Harding, himself. I stand on that position today and there is no man living who can make me change it, and there is no force on earth that can make me surrender it.

"On the other hand, there is the question of goodwill between the races to be considered. For 35 years, Washington so conducted the work at Tuskegee that the school and the town were constantly moving forward in hearty cooperation, and there were those among our white friends in the town of Tuskegee who were equally as steadfast in their determination that these harmonious relations should not be disturbed. Therefore, to avoid any possible rupture of these harmonious relations, I have avoided as far as possible any public statement on the situation; I have preferred to make my recommendations to those in authority who were in position to adjust the matter on a satisfactory basis. And in every instance I have reinforced my recommendations with the statement that if Negro physicians were debarred from serving in this hospital it would be the occasion of great embarrassment to all concerned."

President Harding assured Dr. Moton that his wishes would be followed. The procedure agreed upon called for the temporary assignment of key white personnel. These were promptly replaced as rapidly as suitable Negro professional personnel could be recruited and installed.

During the intervening years since 1923, the continuous development of the Veterans' Hospital at Tuskegee under Negro management has proved beyond doubt the wisdom of Dr. Moton. As we have already noted, his sponsorship, in spite of a troublous beginning of the institution, has been most fruitful. A hospital, once considered by the critics beyond the abilities of a Negro personnel to manage, has grown steadily in services rendered and in modern buildings and other equipment. While originally the institution was of considerable size—six hundred beds and a dozen doctors and dentists—it is now, twenty-five years later, a hospital of 2200 beds, 55 doctors and dentists, 150 nurses, and a total of 1400 full-time employees. Its nearness to Tuskegee Institute, especially its proximity to the John A. Andrew Memorial Hospital of that institution, has proved advantageous in many ways. Cooperative relationships between the two hospitals have been effectively established.

Although located in a small community, effective planning and leadership on the part of the management of the Veterans' Hospital have resulted in a variety of cooperative relationships not only with the John A. Andrew Memorial Hospital but with a number of hospitals and medical schools within a range of 150 miles. Two of the cooperating medical schools—the Emory University School of Medicine and the Medical College of Alabama, both white—cooperate continuously. Each week now, three physician teachers travel the 140 miles to Tuskegee from Emory University, in Atlanta, Georgia, on Mondays and from the Medical College of Alabama, in Birmingham, on Thursdays to lecture and teach and to make ward rounds. This program, it is agreed, has unlimited possibilities. Also of vital importance in the teaching program is the full-time and consultant staff of the hospital.

No longer is there doubt concerning the ability of Negro personnel to manage such an institution. The surrounding community, including the city of Tuskegee itself, have long been convinced of the wise sponsorship of Dr. Moton from the beginning. His foresight, once questioned even by the members of his own race, has been fully realized in the extraordinary development of an institution which now ranks high among all of the Veterans' Hospitals of the country. Frequently during two decades, its rank has been placed, as measured by objective standards, among the best 10 per cent of all Federal hospitals in the United States.

The story of the origin and rise and development of the Veterans' Negro Hospital at Tuskegee would be incomplete without reference to the sincere resolutions of the white City Council of Tuskegee upon hearing that Dr. Moton, because of poor health, was contemplating the resignation of his official position at the Institute. This was in September, 1934. The resolution, approved unanimously, was as follows:

"It is the sincere hope of the citizens of Tuskegee that the rumor regarding the physical condition of Dr. Robert R. Moton is unfounded and that the statement implying his considered resignation is without basis of fact; that it is the sincere wish of the citizens of this community that Dr. Moton be restored, during the summer, to good and normal health so that he may carry on his work at the Institute for the ensuing year, and for many years to come, in the same excellent manner in which he has served as President during the years that have passed; and that it is the general belief of our people that Dr. Robert R. Moton has filled the position left vacant by Booker T. Washington in such a manner as to win the approval, not only of the Board of Trustees of the Institute but of the intelligent, honest, and patriotic citizens of the State of Alabama as well as of the country as a whole. His administration of the affairs of the Institute, from an executive standpoint, has been marked with success; the equipment and facilities for educational purposes have been greatly enlarged and increased in number; costly and magnificent buildings have been erected, and extensive improvements have been made in the buildings and grounds of the Institute. The accomplishments in the form of increased valuation in the physical properties of the Institute, the growth of the endowment fund established and perpetuated for the present and future development and expansion, and the greatly increased opportunities for educational advantages to the people of his race have all demonstrated, in the highest degree, his executive ability, and the lofty ideals and patriotic impulses that always prompted Dr. Moton in the administration of this great institution."

At the end of this hospital story, Dr. Moton could have well used the seven words, already quoted from his early biography, "I went through the ordeal good naturedly." This is the way he went through innumerable ordeals of life—always with optimistic determination to do, in accordance with his best judgment, whatever seemed right to do. And the passing of the years have, almost invariably, stamped the goodness of his major judgments.

CHAPTER 9

❧ *The New Negro* ❧

BY JESSIE DANIEL AMES

With the death of Booker T. Washington, there ended one period in the development of the Negro American and the beginning of another. The war in Europe was opening the door of opportunity to advance with renewed determination into areas of life which had been closed to the race since the overthrow of Reconstruction days. The minds as well as the emotions of the dominant Southern class were diverted from its almost constant attention to domestic affairs, except as these related to political and economic activities. In both of these latter, the aggressiveness of the Negro race indicated that the old order of racial adjustment was on the way out. The approaching Presidential election and the rising price of cotton were of overwhelming importance, the one to the Northern Negroes, the other to the Southern ruling class. It was through the changing relation of the Southern Negro to white society that the first signs of a new age for the Negro race were appearing. The white man was no longer the boss whom the Negro must obey. Increasing migration from the cotton fields to Northern industries, though ruthlessly opposed in many places by planters, gained such volume that the economy of the cotton belt was being endangered. The South as a whole was not greatly disturbed by this defiance of the white man's law nor, at first, did the planters grasp its full significance.

There was, in general, little importance attached to this migration. The South, presumably, had solved the race problem. It was considered natural, though inconvenient, that for a time ignorant Negroes should be lured away by stories of prosperity and freedom which seemed within their grasp if they could only get away. But after they had been up North a little while many came streaming back. They were not quite comfortable in a cold climate where Northern white people seemed not to understand them as Southern white people did. When hard times came, as they did rather soon, they found few friends who would give them handouts and discarded clothing. Amusing stories circulated then, as now, contrasting the misery of poor old Uncle Rastus among the heartless white men of the North and his happiness and well-being among the warmhearted and sympathetic white people of the South. Southern white men thought they knew what the Negro wanted as well as how to treat him. Just be patient, many Southerners thought, and the migrant Negro would soon be back. This attitude, however, foreshadowed the course of future race relations and the tragic conflicts which later developed as the Old South, deeply buried in its traditions, was confronted with a new Negro living in a different time.

Fundamental changes in an accepted pattern of social adjustment are usually of slow development, each generation making some adaptation of the old ways to a new situation. Gradually, through several generations, the changeover becomes more nearly complete. But the South was facing a revolutionary condition in its pattern of life as the new Negro refused to accept it as his own. He had not been a part in the fixing of the pattern. He had been, unfortunately, its victim. In this pattern, the Negro had been forced into a social, economic, and cultural status similar to that of slavery. He had to live in his relations with the dominant society according to the traditions of that society. Within his own race, he could grow and expand in any manner of which he was capable provided that he did not appear to question the dogma of inherent racial inferiority.

In this manner, the white South had solved the race problem as they thought, for the good of both races and for all time to come. The Negro knew his place and kept within it; the white man knew the Negro's place and saw to it that he was kept there. It was so strong a conviction that Southern Negroes accepted and liked this solution of the race problem that white Southerners were blind to the real meaning of migration, namely, that it was a kind of defiance of the law of subservience to the white man's command. Since it was God's plan, as widely declared and supported by selected texts from the Bible with warped interpretations, that the white man should rule over the black man, then the former could develop the latter and train him in ways which would be a benefit to himself and to the support of the white civilization without endangering the laws of God for either white or black peoples. This, in effect, was a part of the religious creed to the South. After the carpetbaggers had been driven from the region and the Old South was again in power, the freed but ignorant ex-slaves became a drain on the resources of an impoverished land. They must be re-educated for their new role of service—for their own good and for that of the white man. Thus it was that Tuskegee Institute was created and the seed sowed for a future harvest of incalculable disaster to the white man's traditional solution of the race problem.

A few years after the days of Reconstruction, Booker T. Washington, a Virginian-born slave, was invited to establish a manual training school in the Black Belt of Alabama to teach and train the poverty stricken and illiterate ex-slaves and their children to earn a living for themselves and to help rebuild the fortunes of the white South. Having deprived them of all rights of citizenship and reduced them to the status of wards of the white man, some white Southerners felt a responsibility for the Negroes' welfare. Booker T. Washington was an ideal man for the work he was chosen to undertake. He possessed amazing flexibility and was richly endowed with skill in dealing with people. His faith in himself and his sense of mission gave him the power to stand firm in the face of discouragement. He had to convince the white South that his people could be developed along economic lines without disturbing unduly the pattern that the white man had set for them; he had to persuade philanthropists of the North that money given to the school would not in the end be thrown away by his failure to secure the goodwill of his white neighbors; he had to instill in

Negroes respect for themselves, belief in their integrity and renewed hope for the future. At the same time, he had to persuade them to work with their hands at all kinds of labor in order to attain their goals. This latter was one of the most difficult parts of his work, for work done with hands instead of minds was the badge of slavery. As success came to him in his work, he became the target of attack from the small segment of his own race who held firmly to the conviction that the upper class Negroes should be developed first, forming an elite social stratum which would lead the great masses of their people out of darkness. Dr. Washington became the first leader of the Southern Negro, accepted as such by the white people, and recognized as the supreme leader of the whole race by Northern men of wealth. His stamp of approval on requests for financial aid to Negro projects became almost a requirement. In time, opposition to his work at Tuskegee Institute grew so intemperate that he was accused of being a willing tool in the hands of the white South in perpetuating the slave psychology of former times.

Tuskegee Institute grew and expanded in its physical plant and in its student body, and especially, in its influence throughout the white South. Its students could find work more easily than those from other schools. They became independent farmers, home owners and teachers, machinists, carpenters, and masons. As the Southern States built schools for Negroes, school boards turned to Tuskegee Institute for teachers to take charge of them. During the times in which Dr. Washington served his people, the accusation that he was serving the white South was only half true. He was building, whether or not he completely foresaw it, toward a generation which would be free of slave psychology.

In November, 1915, Dr. Washington died. As the leader of his people, he had established his name at home and abroad as a man who could be trusted to hold to a conservative course. He had founded an institution for his people which was proving an asset to the South. His name would be honored and revered as the man who had brought his people out of darkness into the light of a new day. He had served his times well. With the dawn of this new day, he passed on his cause and his office to Robert Russa Moton, a man whose abilities as a leader were unknown. Yet the leadership was an inseparable part of the office of President of Tuskegee Institute.

As an intimate friend of Dr. Washington and a co-worker with him in many field activities of two institutions, Major Moton had become familiar with the affairs of Tuskegee Institute. In addition, he knew that he must keep open the sources of financial support which Dr. Washington had found, and that he must uncover others if the school was to continue to grow as the needs of the people increased. No small responsibility were these duties. The chart, which Dr. Washington had drawn out of his experience, and which had raised him to eminence as leader of a cause and a people, was in harmony with the temper of the times in which he served. But the times were changing. The chart was safe for Dr. Washington to follow. By it he had reached the peak of his success. An uncharted road, in fact, lay ahead of Major Moton whose status of leadership was ex officio. He had to establish himself in his own right. If he was to succeed in guiding his people, he would have to adapt old ways to hold the confidence of a people irresistibly moved by a new spirit of daring and adventure, no longer a flock of sheep blindly following a shepherd. But it was the old spirit of the white South, its reaction to the new Negro, which Major Moton had to face at the beginning. Threatening signs to the pattern of racial adjustment had appeared before Major Moton became President of Tuskegee. The signs had now become fact.

The white South was at last seriously alarmed by what it considered the increasing contumacy of Negroes. The trickle of migration had become a fast flowing stream. The price of cotton, so low in the first year of the World War as to bring disaster to the planters, was rising to unbelievably high levels. Without an adequate supply of Negro labor, recovery of the South's economy, based on cotton, would not be complete. Agents from the North recruiting workers for war industry were set upon and even driven out of the region. The Southern press was in full cry with propaganda designed, if not intended, to increase suspicion and fear among white people and, by implication, to justify acts of violence against Negroes which might halt their migration from the cotton belt states. Editors were lifting sentences and single words from the pages of Negro newspapers from the North to sustain their charge that Negroes were openly demanding social equality and intermarriage. Some of these white editors were saying that it was the duty of every white citizen to keep an eye on every Negro for none was to be trusted. Some of the most indignant and outraged white men were those who claimed to be the best friends that Negroes had. Every Negro who was lynched, mutilated, or beaten to a pulp was, in the eyes of disturbed Southerners, a bad Negro and got only what was coming to him. White men, taking the law into their hands were upholders of racial supremacy and declared protectors of Southern womanhood. Negro preachers and teachers, educated Negroes and Negroes who dressed above their stations were classed as especially dangerous to the white man's law. Fear and hatred spread throughout the cotton belt while migration to the North continued.

At the head of Tuskegee Institute in the heart of the cotton belt of the South was Major Moton.

In these days of tragedy a vainglorious man might have sought to establish himself as a bold leader by calling for resistance and retaliation; a timid man might have fled danger, and from a safe haven, preached the justice of the Negro's cause and the infamy of the white man: Major Moton did neither. He stayed where he was. He had held his office too short a time to have built up a partisan group of followers. He dared not, for obvious reasons, inject his office into the conflict. The fate of Tuskegee Institute, symbol of the Negro's faith, was not to be rashly endangered. Even though in later years it might be rebuilt, if destroyed, the spirit of the institution would not return. If he kept silent to save the school from the wrath of white people, he might save the physical plant as evidence that Negroes had something that even white men in their madness would not dare to destroy. "There was a time to speak and a time to keep silent." This, to him, was the time to keep silent.

As future events were to prove, Major Moton's decision enhanced his own value and increased the opportunity of Tuskegee Institute to serve the race. The Presidential election was approaching. The Republican campaign to unseat President Wilson was growing increasingly tense and emotional. The Democrats were resisting every attack by the Republicans with strong counter attacks. Since Southern Negroes could not vote, politics did not enter into the conflict between the races in the South. Northern Negroes, traditionally Republican, were rallying their forces to support the Party's candidate without attracting the attention of the white South. This was not because they were working under cover. Far from it. Because they were Negroes, they were considered unimportant; because they were in the North, they were no danger to the Solid South; because they were few in number, they wielded no influence in the Republican Party even if the Democrats should lose. Nothing was more illustrative of the failure of the South to keep abreast of the times than this attitude in regard to Northern Negroes as voters. Migration over the years had finally endangered cotton profits. It had also increased the number of Republican votes. Most Negroes lived in the rural sections, scattered throughout the South, with neither ability nor opportunity to organize their people. When migrating to Northern urban centers, they were generally packed together in large numbers and under the influence of shrewd politicians of their own race. Furthermore, most of the cities to which they went were located in politically doubtful states. Even had the South known these facts, there would have been no attention given to them, for the stereotype of the Negro in the white mind would still have remained unchanged.

The slight margin of victory for the Democratic Party may have given pause to Southern Congressmen but it did not disturb the Solid South. But Northern Democrats, the Party leaders, believed that votes were votes regardless of the color of the hands that marked the ballots. If Negroes continued to concentrate in doubtful states, if they all lined up with the Party of Freedom, doubtful states might soon cease to be doubtful. Some such reasoning must have been carried on among Democratic State and National Committeemen and Congressmen outside the South. For the month after President Wilson was inaugurated for the second time, war was declared on Germany by the Congress, a law providing for compulsory military service was enacted; draft machinery was set up, and Negroes along with white men were called before draft boards. Northern Negro leaders immediately became active. The best way to prevent a course of action from crystallizing into a set procedure is to forestall its inception. These Negroes believed that if nothing was done to prevent it, all Negro soldiers would be assigned to labor battalions and other service companies which would not give them an opportunity to distinguish themselves to the honor and glory of the race. There was ample reason for their fears.

Pressure was brought on the Federal Administration to authorize an officers' training school for Negroes. The boldness of Negroes who had worked for the defeated Republican candidate in demanding recognition of the Democratic administration as their right, and not as a favor, was a shocking departure from political etiquette. If the recent election was still fresh in the minds of the Negroes, it was also fresh in the minds of the Democrats. There would be another election in four years; Negroes were still coming up from the South; they were still concentrating in the cities of doubtful states. Both Democratic and Republican members of Congress from these doubtful states would be seeking re-election in less than two years. In less than four years, there would be another presidential election. But President Wilson had other and greater issues to handle than those of Party politics. The country was at war. He had to have the utmost cooperation of the Congress in order to carry on. The slogan, "he kept us out of war," had done more than little to gain the votes of women in the North—Southern women like Southern Negroes could not vote. He could count on the patriotism and party loyalty of Southern Congressmen to give his war program support up to a point. Beyond that point, they might feel that the preservation of white supremacy and support of racial superiority were their patriotic duty. The President, a Virginian by birth, reared and educated in the South, could understand their motives and emotions, but the long years he had spent in the North and the offices he had held had erased sectionalism from his mind. He had become both national and international in his thinking. Too, now the slogan which stirred the country, his own words, was to "make the world safe for Democracy." Democracy meant certain unalienable rights to all citizens, and the Negroes were demanding these rights—to fight as equals with all other citizens; to preserve the rights of life, liberty and the pursuit of happiness which in their own lives they were denied. In his dilemma he turned to the South for counsel. Not to the white South, but to the black South. The President of Tuskegee Institute, Robert Russa Moton, was summoned to the White House.

When a white man speaks of the race problem, he is thinking of the problem that the Negro race is to him. He leaves no one in doubt as to his meaning. When a Negro refers to the race problem in the presence of a white person, he knows that it will be taken for granted that he means the Negro race. He resorts to double-talk, for to him and all Negroes the race problem is the problem of the white race. Major Moton and President Wilson together were facing the problem of the white race. These two men, one white, the other Negro, both Southern, knew the race problem they faced. It was not whether to train Negroes for commissioned officers but how to go about it so as to keep the white South in line. President Wilson was thinking of Congressmen; Major Moton was thinking of Southern people—both white and Negro. He held to the belief, later explained but not in reference to this incident, that Negroes should be willing to take a half loaf and use it to build up strength to go back for the rest of the loaf. As white people became accustomed to seeing a few Negroes filling positions to which only white men had access, more Negroes could break out of the ring to which they were confined, and more Negroes and still more Negroes, until their strength would be great enough to obtain the rest of the loaf. The opportunity to prove themselves as able to be commissioned officers opened a new field for the race. However, the white South must not be exposed to the sight of them in the process of being trained. For this they would not stand. The friction and tension in race relations had lessened with the declaration of war, but Negroes in training as candidates for commissions would arouse the dormant fear and hatred to greater excesses than migration had caused.

The Negro race was proud of their military record in all the wars of their country, from the Revolutionary through the Spanish American War. They had acquitted themselves well but without public recognition of their contribution to victory—except to a limited degree by the Northern army in the Civil War. Here was the war to end all wars. It would be the last chance Negroes would have to receive the same training and pay, wear the same uniforms and discharge the duties of the same rank as white officers. It was not a question of how many but of some to whom the race could point with pride as symbols of racial achievement. To be able to do this would increase the power of all Negroes to reject the white man's assumption of inherent racial inferiority. It would also sustain their morale in the dark years ahead so that they would have the determination to hold every inch gained and the courage to press forward to greater heights. What the white South might do to all Negroes because a few had got out of their place could not take away the glory of having had Negro officers in this war.

In June 1917, by authority of the President of the United States, an officer candidate training school for Negroes was opened for applications at Fort Des Moines, Iowa, with a waiting list of twelve hundred educated Negroes from all parts of the country. Subsequently, 639 Negro officers were commissioned.

Racial conflict broke out after the Armistice both above and below the Mason-Dixon line. During the war, hatred of the German was stimulated as an efficient weapon to spur soldiers to fiercer and more merciless combat and civilians to greater efforts to do their "bit" to support the boys overseas in the war bond drive, food conservation, hospitality to soldiers both in camp and troop trains as they were passing through towns and villages on their way overseas. All social functions were patriotic in purpose, flags were waved, speeches made, terroristic methods adopted to force citizens to buy savings stamps and bonds in the amount that local men decided they should have. Dizzy excitement prevailed. Hatred was a patriotic virtue and a Christian obligation. At the height of this hysteria the shooting stopped. One last patriotic binge in celebration of the Armistice and the people were left with a high fever of emotional hate in their hearts and no way to allay it. Flags were furled, bands were gone, troop trains were of the past, hostess houses at Army camps were closed, windshield stickers inviting soldiers to have free rides were washed off, war bonds were being liquidated, restlessness and discontent had seized the citizenry. The war, it would seem, was too short. The vacuum, which Nature abhors and which must be filled, was soon occupied in the South by an organization of hallowed memory which would supply the needs of unsatisfied men, and later, more unsatisfied women, by giving them objects to hate and a uniform to wear. Religious bigotry or racial hatred or both provided the incentive to bring volunteers to the Ku Klux Klan to serve as patriotic protectors of the church, the home, the state, the nation and Southern white womanhood. The enemy without had been vanquished, the enemy within called for all native-born, one hundred per cent American men of red blood, Protestant faith and a Caucasian ancestry. The number who could qualify was far greater than the number who could not. Those who could qualify but did not answer the call felt it was expedient to imitate the Tar Baby and say nothing. With objects to hate, and in the case of Negroes all around them and right at hand and not overseas, action followed as soon as they had their uniforms. Civilians who were not in the war, as well as those who were, in the uniform of a bed sheet and a pillow case, following a Fiery Cross, marched forth at night to destroy the enemy to the music of their theme song, "Onward Christian Soldiers." At first attacks were limited to Catholics, Jews, and Negroes. The first two were hard to find in the South, for they were few in numbers and lived mostly in urban centers. Negroes were many and could be hunted out of hiding in every locality. The Klan patriots found it more advantageous to direct major assaults against those of the Negro race living in rural areas where their local membership was almost one hundred per cent of the inhabitants and their victims legitimate prey. Gradually they extended their attentions to white men and even women whose lives were not Christian, according to the interpretation of a Christian life as outlined by the wholesale membership of Protestant preachers. White men who were said not to stay at home nights with their wives were taken out and disciplined with the lash and then treated with a coat of tar and feathers; women, who were not attentive to their homes, husband, and children were warned, which was all that was needed to return them to the paths of virtue. A few women were dealt with more severely. Alcoholic beverages, sale or possession, had been declared illegal by the Congress and a sin by the Southern

Baptist and Methodist churches. An overwhelming majority of Southern white people throughout the Southern states were Baptists and Methodists. Without these the Ku Klux Klan could not have existed. Treatments given to white men suspected of possessing, selling or drinking liquor, were sanctioned on the grounds that they were breaking the law of the land and sinning against Christianity. The Ku Klux Klan was an American version of Hitler's Gestapo which was still more than a decade in the future.

What this terrorism meant to Negroes in small towns and rural communities and on plantations, only Negroes could know. What spiritual degradation, physical cowardice and disintegrity it brought to white Southerners only one who lived through those years can know.

One faint ray of light flickered in the darkness. It came from a small group of white churchmen and educators, determined to hold out a hand to Negroes and help them through the trials and tribulations inflicted upon them by other members of their own race. Their discussion of the course of action to be taken, the problems that should be solved, disclosed the fact that there were almost as many opinions as there were men present. In this confusion, they decided that the first move should be to invite an equal number of Negro leaders to sit with them and tell them what they wanted. They were aware that this was a diversionist decision, for by it they admitted that they, Southern white men, did not know the Negro and, therefore, could not decide what he ought to want. They were asking Negro men to come and sit down with them as equals and fellow human beings. This was an intelligent procedure that marked a radical deviation from approved conduct. They were surprised, and gratified, that their guests told them that all they wanted were security for their person, property, and family; better homes in improved surroundings, if they were able to buy them; better schools for their children; the opportunity to work in any occupation for which they were fitted; and protection of their women from advances of white men. That day the idea of a Commission on Interracial Cooperation took root—an idea expressed much earlier by Dr. Robert R. Moton and a resulting organization to which he gave his best thought and service. Since this meeting with Negro leaders had given them a new opinion of the race problem, they believed that if white and Negro leaders in the Southern states could be induced to have similar meetings, the race problem would be started on its way to solution. Before the Klan had grown so monstrously powerful that it intimidated many men of good will, all the states had held initial meetings of the Interracial Commission and many counties had thought well enough of the idea to put it into practice.

When later the Commission decided to take a "calculated risk" and enlist women of both races in the movement, they assigned to them the work of studying conditions in the Negro home, school, and church and to pass resolutions condemning lynching for any cause whatever. Being one of the women invited to participate, I was puzzled by the inclusion of lynching in the women's work since white men did the lynchings and Negro men were the victims. It was in the first joint meeting of men and women that I saw Major Moton in action.

It was at this first meeting that I was told of an attempted invasion of the campus of Tuskegee Institute by the Ku Klux Klan the year before. The story lost nothing in the telling, every detail was included, the size of the mob, the bed sheets, the pillow cases, the Fiery Crosses, the flight of the shadowy figures when they were met at the gates by a student officer and an armed cadet corps. The local Klan had become enraged over the Government's policy of staffing the hospital for Disabled Negro War Veterans with Negro professional men and women. Administrator, Purchasing Agent, surgeons, nurses, specialists for the treatment and care of mentally sick veterans, all these must be replaced by white men and women. The hospital grounds were adjacent to Tuskegee Institute which was held responsible for this insulting infraction of white supremacy. Even worse was the implication that the head of the Institute and its officials had encroached on the dogma of racial superiority by presuming to think these Negroes were as well trained as white men and women and equal to them in professional ability. Shocked and frightened, I asked anxiously what Major Moton and faculty members had done afterwards. This the white women did not know, but they were sure that nothing was done. Although I was new in this work and was not sure that I knew as much about Negroes as I should, I was sure that I knew white people well enough to believe that something had happened of a curious nature if there was not an aftermath of violence initiated by white citizens in retaliation for the humiliation they had suffered. They were a different breed of white people from any I knew. I did not doubt that there had been no violence, for that would have been carried widely by the press and the white women would have read about it. They did know that the all-Negro staff remained, which by itself was a blow to white pride that should have been avenged from ambush at least.

Several years later, the Commission on Interracial Cooperation held its annual meeting at Tuskegee Institute. It was my first visit there, and so it was the first time I had had a chance to do a bit of research among the faculty to find an explanation of the mystery surrounding the attempted invasion of the Ku Klux Klan. I was expecting to learn a great deal, but even a little would help. At first I found a great reluctance to discuss the issue. I was sure from their manner that some were suppressing deep feeling and fighting an urge to talk. Several did finally tell what happened. Their stories differed in details but from all of them I gathered enough of facts, with interpretations, to put together the story of what did happen. These were culled from the talks which Major Moton had made at Faculty meetings, at Vesper Services to the student body, and from personal interviews as they were remembered then.

A white citizen of Tuskegee believed that the ex-slaves around the town and in the county should be given some training in manual arts. A school should be provided for this purpose, open to all Negroes. With the approval of other citizens and an appropriation from the Legislature, an invitation was sent to Booker T. Washington, who was recommended by the President of Hampton Institute, to come down and open a school. The school had firm friends among the local white citizens from the beginning; they had taken pride in its development and its success; their wisdom had been justified; their doubts had been dissolved. This relation between the town and the school had passed from father to son for forty years. Dr. Moton knew that these friends were deeply humiliated by the attack on the Institute and that they were tense with fear that the student body might commit some act in retaliation which would lead the Klan to believe that their attempted invasion was justified and that further action should be taken against individual students.

If the students and the faculty evinced no disposition to retaliate, if nothing was said or done that would afford the slightest justification of the lawless act of the Klan, then their white friends would show their disapproval and gradually return to their former friendly relation to the school. Every white person everywhere, in their home towns, on the campus, on the trains, must be shown the greatest courtesy and respect. They must remember that they represented Tuskegee Institute and the school would gain or lose according to the way in which its representatives, the students, conducted themselves. He wanted no talking about what had happened among themselves. Talk would develop anger, anger would cause them to boast of what they would like to do to get even. Before they were aware of it, they would begin to plan how they would do what they would like to do. Then, some one of them, would try out the plan to see whether or not it would work. Fear was the root of hate. If anyone of them hated another, then he was afraid of the one he hated. Students of Tuskegee were not afraid of any man or woman, white or colored, so they could not hate. The future of Tuskegee Institute was in their hands. He knew that not one of them would do anything unworthy of himself or as a representative of the school. His theme was love as the only force to bring peace and friendship among all people.

He had evidently controlled the student body, at least, as far as public demonstration was concerned. He had evidently controlled the teachers, but he had something more than the philosophy of love to use with them. Their position on the faculty was precious. They would hesitate to jeopardize it. But not all of them approved of the course of conduct laid down by Major Moton. Some of them said that failure of Tuskegee Institute to show their anger and contempt openly was even more humiliating for them than the indignities they suffered at the hands of Klansmen. White people had reason to believe that they could do anything to Negroes and not have to pay for it.

I never thought to consider how rigidly maintained was segregation of the white visitors to Tuskegee Institute. There was no intermingling of the races in dining halls or dormitories. Dorothy Hall was the guest house reserved for white guests. On Sunday, white people were taken into the Chapel through a side entrance and seated in pews at the side of the rostrum and choir loft with no Negroes in occupancy with them. This was the normal way to treat members of the ruling class. It was some time before it occurred to me that possibly Negroes had no greater urge to mix with white people than whites had to mix with Negroes. I had heard Negroes speak with bitterness on segregation of their race by the white race. Some Negro colleges refused to entertain white guests who expected to have quarters outside the dormitories and their meals served in private. I learned to what extent many upper class Negroes held Tuskegee Institute responsible for strengthening the barriers of segregation and prolonging this custom when several Negro women refused to attend an interracial conference to be held there. Their reason for doing so was explicit, and their manner of refusal indicated that extending the invitation was an assumption that they would demean themselves by submitting to any form of segregation for any reason. To balance this attitude were several white women who refused for the equally explicit reason that they would be subjected to the indignity of intermingling with the Negro women on the basis of equality extended to the limit of having to eat with them. However, after the conference had adjourned, some of the white women who did attend confessed that it required all their courage to agree to be present. As Christians they could not refuse. They were glad that they had come on. Nothing that they had feared might happen had happened.

On another occasion, some twelve years after the attempted raid by the Klan, a recognized leader from the North with a large and powerful following, was the guest speaker at Sunday night Vespers. He happened to be on the campus over the weekend, and, as was his custom with all visitors, Major Moton invited him to address the student body. At the close of his talk, he lashed out at the young people in his audience and, with withering contempt charged them with having a "slave psychology" that kept them

submissive to the will of the white man. It was no general indictment of all Negro youth but a specific indictment of the young
people sitting before him in words and voice that could shrivel
their souls.

Regardless of how many attacks were launched against him,
Dr. Moton remained firm in his determination to follow any
honorable course that would preserve the usefulness of Tuskegee
Institute for future generations. That he was wise in his time was
proven in the days of the depression when banks were failing
throughout the nation. For a time the only bank open for business
in Tuskegee was that of Tuskegee Institute. Businessmen of the
town did not hesitate to open accounts with it. A white man could
show no more convincing evidence of confidence in the integrity
of the Administration and the sound business methods of Negro
bankers than to trust his dollars to their keeping.

In the late twenties, a new type of hysteria swept the country
and the Ku Klux Klan out of power. Everybody was getting rich
in the stock market. Buying stock on margin and selling at a
profit, reinvesting the profits in more margin stock, over and over,
creating millionaires, or near millionaires, on paper, out of men
and women who never dreamed that so much wealth could be
theirs. As usual, when white people are prosperous, or think they
are, an atmosphere of racial peace and goodwill settles over the
South. White people in growing numbers gave their blessings on
interracial meetings and not infrequently joined them. Material
abundance is a powerful force in all good works. Respectable
white citizens were a bit embarrassed by unfavorable publicity
the South had achieved in the one area of human relations in
which the white Southerners claimed to be liberal and just. Tuskegee Institute grew; the physical plant was enlarged; the steady
consistent policy of courtesy to all white people was winning the
goodwill of the whole South as well as the local community.
Courses in race relations were put in high schools and colleges.
The Commission on Interracial Cooperation inaugurated a series
of essay contests, preparing a special number of pamphlets to be
used as basic material. There were several lynchings which merited
national coverage, but minor ones—those in isolated rural districts—

got scant publicity even within the local communities in which they occurred. Everyone was excited and happy. It was more satisfactory to get rich and wear silk shirts than it was to march at night in a bedsheet. After nearly fifteen years of continuous crisis, Dr. Moton was given a reprieve.

CHAPTER 10

❧ *A Pragmatic Educator* ❧

BY JOSEPH L. WHITING

In a Founder's Day Address at Tuskegee Institute, Dr. John R. Finley declared: "No program for Negro advancement which does not include the fundamental principles laid down by Booker T. Washington and carried on by Dr. Robert R. Moton, present head of the Institute, is complete." His judgment was not unlike that expressed by many leaders of educational thought in America.

Shortly after Dr. Moton became Principal of Tuskegee Institute the United States Government passed legislation which enabled the Federal Government to assist the several states in their desire to give vocational training to high school youth.

It is well known that the framers of the Federal Vocational Education Act, popularly known as the Smith-Hughes Act, which became effective in 1917, were favorable to the Tuskegee type of industrial education. On one occasion, during a visit by a Federal Commission to the Institute, the chairman announced that what was most urgently needed of Tuskegee was a continuation of its role in vocational instruction, in its traditional manner, so that when requests came to Washington for advice and direction, the Federal Board could say: "Make a visit to Tuskegee. Inspect, observe, and imitate its methods in vocational instruction."

With Robert R. Moton, working with the hands was an experience of great worth. He wholly approved the Tuskegee method of providing manual work both in the shops, as vocational training and in the self-help jobs which were an integral part of the Tuskegee Program.

Early in his administration at Tuskegee, Dr. Moton became perceptibly disturbed by an excerpt from the auditor's report. "It will be seen," stated this report, "that there has been an increase, within a ten year period, of 191 per cent in the annual cash payment per student, while the amount paid in labor has actually decreased. The average student, in 1912-13, paid $21.58 in cash, and $70.70 in labor; while, in 1921-22, the figures stood at $54.58 in cash and $61.12 in labor. One possible interpretation of these comparative amounts," the report continued, "is that the figures represent a change in students' attitudes toward work—that now, in many cases, they are willing and able to pay cash for their education and do not wish to spend any more time on particular industrial tasks than is sufficient for learning its principles. They seem unwilling to do practical work for the sake of earning money with which to defray expenses." Continuing, the author of this report declared: "If this tendency continues to manifest itself, it will, I am sure, have a profound effect upon the character of the Institute. The result may be that the Institute will become a mechanical training school in which principles will be taught and paid for, rather than an industrial school in which boys and girls learn trades and earn their way by actual work."

Dr. Moton was determined to correct these trends and implications. With this in mind, he sought and directed such remedial modifications in instructional technique and in interdepartmental organization as would bring about greater efficiency in educational procedures. In the words of Dr. Moton: "The Tuskegee plan enlarges considerably the usual program of education by taking the traditional program of the public school and adding to it a vocational objective in such a way as to give deeper meaning and larger interest to both features in the combined program."

Following Dr. Moton's pronouncement that the Tuskegee plan "considerably enlarges the usual program," he gave his approval and support to a general reorganization of courses of instruction in the industrial fields. He felt that the courses should be more specifically analyzed and that the units of instruction should each be centered about some appropriate objective. Furthermore, he thought that the objective in each case should be typical of a definite productive activity, marking a worthwhile step in a logical and progressive course of instruction. The productive effort, essential to such a program, must draw upon related technical information peculiar to other courses of learning, the aim and purpose of which should be clear, and the objective definite and both immediate and ultimate. Thus, with the project as a center, attracting to it all the desirable information at the time of its instrumental usefulness, there is in this plan an effective binding together into a pattern of complete learning. Such a plan, as may easily be seen, calls for intelligent and purposeful cooperation of trades teachers and academic teachers in the various fields.

The reorganization of the courses of instruction in the mechanical industries entailed further simplification in procedure, and Dr. Moton readily assented to the following suggestions presented for this purpose:

1. The allocation of beginning students to their respective assignments of vocational training, based upon a study and examination of their fitness and experience

2. The compilation of students' shop and class progress records with the authority to effect adjustments according to individual cases

3. The clarification of the distinction between production and non-production jobs, i.e., such work as may come under the head of scientific and organized industrial training, and routine school work

4. The listing of all production jobs in the form of an analysis of operation and difficulty, and the time required to perform it on an economic basis

5. A student placement bureau with contact of prospective graduate employees with industry.

The above points would involve the following modifications:

1. That the cost of acquiring a trade be ascertained, for instance, a fee of twenty dollars ($20.00), minimum, per year, to the student (exclusive of the regular tuition fee)

Dr. Moton and Dr. Mordecai W. Johnson, President of Howard University, May 30, 1929

Fiftieth Anniversary Celebration at Tuskegee, 1931. *L. to r.*, Dr. Harry A. Garfield, President of Williams College; Dr. Anson Phelps Stokes, Canon, Washington Cathedral; Dr. George H. Denny, President, University of Alabama; Dr. Moton; Dr. William Jay Schieffelin, Chairman of Board of Trustees

William G. Wilcox Trades
Building, Tuskegee Insti-
tute, 1920 (P. H. Polk,
Tuskegee Inst., Ala.)

Interior of Logan Hall, Tuskegee's auditorium-gymnasium

2. That a scale of shop wages be determined for each shop, after commercial standards, reaching a maximum as wages obtained under economic conditions in industry

3. That all student earnings, beyond the charged fee, be paid over to the student in cash

4. That all routine shop and classroom work be done at the end of the day, or at night by students under supervision and paid for as is done for outside labor

5. That all routine and necessary school work (non-productive), such as sweeping, cleaning windows, office work, hauling, driving, messenger boys, etc., be evaluated, listed, and paid for as ordinary, unskilled labor

6. That there should be established an exchange, or job-routing center for the purpose of getting the job through the shop; that orders for all jobs should begin and end in this center, all specifications and other desirable information having been ascertained

7. That the shop instructor be relieved of all financial transactions, such duties being placed in the job-routing office

8. That the student load be definitely established, both academically and industrially, based upon such facts as may be ascertained under vocational guidance

9. That as students progress in their respective vocations, as determined by objective shop records, they become, automatically, shop assistants, foremen, and assistant instructors with requisite credit and compensation, accordingly

10. That the distinction should be allowed between those students desiring to work towards a degree and those who desire to become technically trained to enter industry; that the latter be permitted to select a curriculum most suitable to their needs in industry—such students above high school to be designated as non-degree college students

11. That the school shops be operated upon modern and scientific methods; for instance, upon modern methods of commercial practice a shoeshop is no longer equipped with settees, but standing machines

12. That for the purpose of effective instruction and training there should be not more than fifteen to twenty students under one instructor at one time

13. That students may be rotated among allied shops before definitely selecting their major shop

14. That the importance of the vocational shop should be determined according to economic needs and probable placement

15. That the trade instructor should be an expert craftsman, not of necessity a degree-man

16. That there should be a sufficient number of degree-men from standard technical colleges to offer supplementary courses in fundamental technical principles underlying the applied trades

17. That there should be designated related subjects teachers attached to the academic faculty and considered as such.

In August, 1920, Dr. Moton suggested that I should attend a Work Shop seminar in trade-student instructor training, conducted by Mr. Charles R. Allen, Special Agent, Federal Vocation Division, in process at Hampton Institute, Virginia. I spent one week with Mr. Allen and his assistant.

Permission was granted to inaugurate such changes at Tuskegee in the organization of the courses in the trade classes so as to distinguish more clearly the functional technique, job analysis, safety-first notions, learning difficulties, etc., for the purpose of establishing an impressive student-instructor consciousness, and to create a pattern of the instruction job in brighter perspective. The time-consuming method of absorption is an easy and tempting rubric of the laissez-faire trade instructor, and he will not readily respond to any innovating stimulus, or recognize a revolutionary process of imparting his familiar trade experience.

A persistent weakness in trade shop training is a failure to recognize and formulate as an objective the fact that certain students are going to be blacksmiths, others tailors, tinsmiths, auto mechanics, house carpenters, plumbers, or power plant operators. The idea that a general education will function in any vocation rather than a particular vocation and should draw from a general education course whatever is essential to make it most effective is rarely of immediate concern.

An alert group of young men from the trades—machine shop practice, carpentry, auto mechanics, plumbing, auto painting, electric wiring, tailoring, printing, cabinet-making, and brick masonry

—having already spent the required time in the shops to entitle them to trade certificates, were formed into a "Student-Instructor Class in Lesson Planning" for group instruction on the job. This was an experimental, and something of a pioneer undertaking to interpret and carry out the suggestions emphasized by Mr. Allen in his Work Shop at Hampton.

In the Principal's Annual Report, 1925-26, the following statement was carried:

"In the Department of Mechanical Industries, a college course in Technical Arts is being developed to prepare young men for supervision of the vocational phases of high school work. Students registering for this course numbered thirty including ten graduates from our own vocational courses. This two year course contains the studies fundamental to any well-grounded Junior College course in education together with a carefully selected series of courses in industrial arts, shop work and professional subjects. Students act as assistants to the instructors in the shops and as student-teachers of shop operations in the vocational classes."

This enrichment of the preparation of the prospective manual arts teacher was intended to meet the increasing and urgent demands for manual arts teachers with a wider professional experience. Therefore, Dr. Moton enthusiastically welcomed the suggestions presented, later, in the following communication:

Julius Rosenwald Fund
925 South Homan Avenue
Chicago

Dear Dr. Moton:

In making some observations in the field of education . . . the thought occurred to me that a certain phase of the experiment that Cincinnati and Antioch are doing could be applicable to schools like Tuskegee Institute . . . especially in the industrial lines . . . since Tuskegee is so near Montgomery and other large steel districts in Alabama, I was wondering if some plan could not be worked out whereby students at Tuskegee in the field of general iron work could not spend some of their time in the plants in the steel mill district and there acquire the practical knowledge that would make them so valuable after graduation.

... the question of the Negro economic status in the South, as well as in the North, has become of such grave importance, I believe that every means ought to be tried whereby the Negro can keep his hold, at least, in the basic industries of the country. . . .

Yours truly,
George R. Arthur

Dr. Moton immediately appointed a committee to explore the possibility of placing cooperative students from Tuskegee with the Tennessee Coal, Iron & Railroad Company at Birmingham, Alabama.

Tennessee Coal, Iron & Railroad Company
General Offices: Brown-Marx Building
Birmingham, Ala.

Dr. Moton, President
Tuskegee Institute, Ala.
Dear Sir:

I desire to acknowledge receipt of your favor of the 27 ult., in which you advise that your committee has made a report of its conference with Mr. Crawford and myself, and further advising that you expect to appoint a coordinator in the early Autumn to confer with the writer on the question of placing cooperative students of the Tuskegee Institute with this Company.

The writer wishes to assure you he will be very glad indeed to cooperate with this coordinator, and would suggest that the work be undertaken somewhere between September 15th and October 1st.

Yours very truly,
J. F. Vance
Manager Labor Department

The cooperative venture was henceforth undertaken by Tuskegee Institute, under very happy auspices. Five students were selected, one from each of five shops—electrical, forge, brickmasonry, foundry, and machine—and taken to Birmingham. Once in Birmingham, the group was directed to attend a conference with the manager in one of the well equipped executive offices. The manager invited the students to be seated around a glossy mahogany table, and passed cigars. Not a single student was tempted to accept the delightful hospitality, and the manager immediately began the conference with a frankness of speech that might be regarded as a prelude and forecast, twenty years in advance of the "Jackie Robinson Story":

"This Company," said the Company Manager, "has gone to some considerable expense in making arrangement in five of our shops so that you boys may get experience and training under our expert mechanics. Much depends upon your success in this undertaking. If the experiment is successful, it will mean other students in greater number from Tuskegee will follow you into these shops.

"You are not going to get any favors; you may be the object of a few unpleasant contacts. But the Company is behind you, and you are assured of a square deal. I have carefully selected the shops and foremen where you are to be assigned. These foremen are sympathetic and interested in you. Remember that your main purpose is to acquire skill and competence in your trade. The Company is primarily concerned in developing competent mechanics to be eventually taken over by the Company permanently."

The students were immediately transferred to their respective shops, or camps, given a preliminary examination, and assigned to work. The shops first selected were: Electrical Department, Fairfield Steel Works; Machine Shop, Transportation Department; Forge Shop, Ensley Works; Foundry, Fairfield Steel Works; Brickmasonry, Ensley Works.

After eight months' contact and cooperation by ten students with the Tennessee Coal, Iron & Railway Company, the following points were regarded as significant:

1. Ten students, composing two groups of five, each, have been placed in training in five Company Shops, viz., two in the machine shop, two in the electrical shop, two in the steel foundry, two in the forge shop, and two in the brickmasonry shop, for periods of three months.

2. The progress reports have been uniformly satisfactory, and indicate the degree of attention and supervision on the part of each shop foreman to act justly toward these cooperative students, and to accord them every opportunity to advance in manipulative skill while acquiring a varied shop experience.

3. The cooperative students, young men of prudence and common sense, realizing that such contact was in the form of an experiment involving new relationships, have displayed a keen appreciation of their opportunity, met every expectation of the Company management, and have cultivated a wholesome morale among themselves.

4. The cooperative student reports that he has been unable to observe any appreciable distinction between the white cooperative student from Georgia Tech and the University of Alabama and himself.

5. That while the wages paid the cooperative student does not dominate their main purpose, it is, however, a desirable incentive to effective training, stimulates effort, and instills in the trainee the proper attitude and appreciation both with respect to the elements of time and quality of work on production under normal standards.

In order to allay any misunderstanding on the part of the parents of the cooperative student, during his period of non-residence training, the following letter of information was dispatched to each parent:

My dear Madam:

The Institute is now in a position, for the first time, to directly cooperate with the large industrial organizations in the South for the purpose of affording its technical college students the advantage of contact with the highly trained expert mechanics to supplement their training and instruction under practical and ideal conditions. Such advantages have a most important prospect for the future placement of such trained students in highly acceptable positions. Therefore, the school has entered into a policy of having these students in the technical college to pursue their regular school courses three months, and then pursue their technical instruction and training three months. This schedule is to be continuous, at three months' intervals, until the students have reached the point of successful skilled mechanics and to graduation from the college.

Your son has elected to be one of the group to accept this advantageous arrangement. There were several more, also, qualified and willing to go. Your son was chosen because the Institute wanted to have in this group the very finest type of representative students. Much depends upon this experiment. It means the opening of an important field for the future employment of Negro mechanics, technically and skillfully trained. In fact, these boys were told by an official of the organization that the Company was primarily interested in developing successful skilled mechanics for permanent employment in their organization.

Thus, you will appreciate, at once, that your son is not only carrying on his college work, but at the same time building a record with an important industrial organization, where the chances are he will be immediately taken over permanently at the end of his training period.

Of course, these young men are still under the supervision of the Institute, whose representative makes frequent visits of inspection to see after their welfare, their progress, and other conveniences necessary to their complete comfort and success.

Very cordially yours,
R. R. Moton,
Principal.

Dr. Moton, whether on the campus, or on one of his frequent road trips, was constantly on the alert to the improvement of the Institute's educational program.

Institutions more recently assuming an industrial or vocational character, were beginning to have faith in their programs. There were some disadvantages at first, due to the conventional curriculum with a long line of traditions and indefinite evaluations. Concessions to any attempt at interfering with the usual schedules and courses of study were sparing and reluctant. However, the inevitable justification of an educational procedure that combines practical utility and cultural appreciation has become so impressive and popular that the traditional curriculum is now more elastic and susceptible to diversification and enrichment of subject matter.

CHAPTER 11

～ *Cooperative Action* ～

BY SPRIGHT DOWELL *

My personal interest in Tuskegee began with my first visit to the institution soon after I became a member of the Alabama State Department of Education in 1913. Superintendent Feagin, who had appointed me as his assistant and whom I later succeeded in office, believed firmly in the Institute and was a great admirer of Booker T. Washington, who visited the Department of Education in the capitol, now and then, for conferences on some educational project or problem. Invariably and with a deferential modesty that was characteristic of him, he sent a runner to inquire whether it would be convenient to have him call. This was not because of any disinclination on the part of the Department to confer with him, but out of respect for custom and the prudence that he always displayed in seeking to avoid the slightest cause for any misunderstanding of his motives and the sincerity of his purpose.

I soon learned to think of Tuskegee Institute as the lengthened shadow of Dr. Washington, an orator, patriot, statesman, and educator of the first rank. The story of his life, of his long and eminently successful administration as President of Tuskegee Institute, of his matchless oratory, and of the monumental service he ren-

* Moton Memorial speaker in Tuskegee Institute Chapel, December 4, 1949. This chapter consists of excerpts from his address.

dered, entitled him to a place of high honor among the notables in our American history.

Quite naturally, the relations between the Alabama State Department of Education and the Institute were harmonious, friendly, and intentionally helpful. Mr. James L. Sibley of the Department of Education, who served as State Supervisor of Negro rural schools by courtesy of the General Education Board, worked in close relationship with Tuskegee and rendered practical and praiseworthy service in improving the work of the Negro schools, in building schoolhouses with a limited amount of State aid and the help of the Julius Rosenwald Fund, and in helping develop their use as community centers. He was deeply interested in his work, loved it with a passionate devotion, maintained a keen sense of values and of the proprieties, and worked with and depended upon Tuskegee very largely as a base of operation in planning and performing the type of service expected of him and so greatly needed to better conditions in rural districts and in rural homes.

Mr. Sibley was a man of fine cultural and family background, and he did his work so well that he attracted the favorable attention of the General Education Board and was requisitioned for larger service in the South and later in Africa where his accomplishments in Liberia brought him deserved distinction, recognition, and lasting gratitude. Unfortunately, during his stay in Africa in which he did such a signal pioneer work, he contracted a disease that proved fatal, and Alabama, and more particularly, the Negro people, who loved him perhaps as they did no other white man of his day, lost a most faithful and devoted friend.

It is unnecessary to say that the Negro of the South and the whole nation suffered an inestimable loss at the death of Dr. Washington. Hundreds of thoughtful people were deeply concerned; many were apprehensive about the future of Tuskegee and were inquiring who would take up the mantle of Elijah. He had done a unique, pioneer, and monumental work in such a difficult and exacting field that any hope of finding a worthy successor seemed to be vain. I must confess that the magnitude of the work to be done and the problem of finding a competent leader to carry it forward were of such serious concern that I shared in the deep feeling of doubt and depression.

Again Hampton Institute led the way in the person of Dr. Frissell, who arranged for a conference of the trustees with Major Moton. The invitation to succeed Dr. Washington resulted. Fortunately for all concerned, his acceptance followed after serious deliberation. In this connection, Colonel Theodore Roosevelt expressed his impressions in the following excerpt from a letter to a fellow trustee who was not present for the conference:

"We all of us ardently wish you had been with us on the train when we saw Major Moton. . . . It is the greatest relief to me to say that I believe if he is appointed we insure for ourselves every reasonable probability of success in carrying on the great work of Booker T. Washington. I believe that he can run the institution. I believe that he can get on with the Southern people as well as any Negro now living. . . . I believe that he will get on with Northern white men and be able to help us in getting the necessary funds. He has a very powerful, and at the same time, an engaging and attractive personality. I cannot speak too strongly about the favorable impressions he has made on me. Finally I believe that he will be able to wisely interpret the feelings and desires of his people to the white people of both the North and the South."

The Alabama State Department of Education was a great admirer of Dr. Moton, as it had been of Dr. Washington, and shared the popular feeling that he was the man of destiny to build on the foundation laid by his illustrious predecessor. The State supervisor of Negro rural schools, Mr. James L. Sibley, enjoyed the special privilege of access to Dr. Moton's office and, as official representative of the State Department of Education, conferred with him regularly about the program and problems in Negro education in Alabama. After his resignation for a larger work in Africa, Mr. J. S. Lambert succeeded to the position from which Mr. Sibley had resigned. With like zeal and ability Mr. Lambert magnified the office and strengthened the ties between the State Department of Education and Tuskegee Institute.

Furthermore, the spirit of progress and the fine working relations made possible thereby owed greatly to the breadth of vision, and the untiring labor of Dr. Moton, under whose wise leadership Tuskegee was dedicated not only to the uplift of the Negro race, but to the general welfare of mankind.

As State Superintendent of Education, I had the opportunity to visit Tuskegee in a semiofficial capacity, to attend an occasional formal meeting, to accompany this or that distinguished visitor, to meet trustees and distinguished guests, among them Dr. Wallace Buttrick, Dr. James H. Dillard, Dr. Thomas Jesse Jones, Dr. Jackson Davis, Dr. William G. Willcox, and many others, and to learn firsthand of their impressions, their interests, and their loyalties, to sense their activities, the atmosphere and the seriousness of purpose that pervaded the institution, and to get a glimpse of the celestial fire that glowed in the heart of Dr. Moton. I can never forget the occasional visits I had with him in the privacy of his office—his absolute candor, his profound common sense, and his unmistakable devotion to the work entrusted to him as the leader of his people and as an ambassador of humanitarianism and interracial good will.

As I look back on these associations, I well recall that I shared very much the feelings of his predecessor, Dr. Washington, "He is a man who makes you believe in him the very first time you meet him and at the same time makes you love him. I have learned from him that one does not need to belong to a 'superior race' to be a gentleman." My contacts with him and the impressions that grew out of them commanded my hearty allegiance and dedication to the services of society, church and state.

Of the legislation for education enacted during my term of office as State Superintendent of Education, chief of which was the preparation of the first Alabama School Code, one of the things in which I experienced great pride was an increase in the annual State appropriation to Tuskegee, a private institution, to $10,000. This increase, although small, revealed a growing appreciation and wholesome example that were both positive and propitious. I am happy to report that during the administration of Governor Chauncey Sparks, who is an alumnus of both the College of Liberal Arts and the Law School of Mercer University, the annual appropriation was raised to $100,000, a source of pride to all friends of education and good citizenship.

The opportunity for better acquaintance and cooperation afforded me was considerably increased after I resigned as State

Superintendent of Education and entered upon my duties as President of the Alabama Polytechnic Institute at Auburn. The proximity of Tuskegee to Auburn—only twenty miles apart—their similar interests, their semiofficial relations in the field of agricultural research and agricultural extension, and the growing feeling of neighborliness so well begun during the administration of Dr. Washington and so fittingly carried forward by Dr. Moton made it not only the natural but also the desirable policy to be as mutually helpful as practicable.

Soon after the beginning of my presidency at Auburn, Mr. S. J. T. Price, our business manager and other members of our institutional family, expressed the desire to visit Tuskegee some Sunday as a matter of interest and information. This wish on our part was expressed to District Agent T. M. Campbell at Tuskegee. Immediately we received a most cordial invitation from Dr. Moton. "We will provide for as many as will come," he wrote, "and will prepare supper because we would like to have you remain for the evening Chapel service."

"We have with us over Saturday night and part of Sunday, Dr. Wallace Buttrick, Chairman of the General Education Board, Dr. Abraham Flexner, Secretary, and Dr. James H. Dillard of the Jeanes and Slater Boards, with some other friends.

"You will be interested to know that the school has opened with the largest attendance in the history of the Institute—1721.

"District Agent Campbell will go over with you the details that you may wish regarding the trip."

The invitation was gladly accepted, and a party of nearly one hundred, composed of faculty members and relatives, spent a very delightful and revealing day as guests of the Institute. They attended an inspiring worship in the Chapel, witnessed the cadets numbering nearly two thousand as they assembled and enjoyed the noon-day meal, visited a number of places of interest on the campus, were entertained for dinner in Dorothy Hall, and were guests at the vesper service in the Chapel featured by music by the incomparable Tuskegee Choir. Dean Judd of the School of Education at Auburn voiced the appreciation and gratitude of the party in a very fitting and effective address.

Among the celebrities included in the interchange of courtesies between Auburn and Tuskegee were Will Rogers, the inimitable philosopher-humorist, and Dr. Stockton Axson, a noted English scholar and professor at Princeton, brother-in-law of President Wilson, and leader of the American Red Cross.

The cordial relationship between the two institutions was continuous and owed much to Dr. Moton, who exhibited a wholesome pride in race and country and the quality of courage that enabled him to go forward with enthusiasm and without friction or loss of friendship.

Among the avenues of contact, the agricultural work was the most intimate and active. The directing heads and staff members at Auburn and Tuskegee, the various county farm and home demonstration agents, and the community of interests that began to grow out of their leadership provided contacts, incentives, and ideals that made for mutual understanding, good citizenship, and fair play. The far-reaching effects of these cordial relations are indicated in a letter from Dr. Moton to Mr. J. A. Evans, Chief of Extension Work in the South of the United States Department of Agriculture, from which I quote:

"You will, I hope, forgive me for this letter, but I just wanted to send this word of congratulation and tell you how glad I am that you have taken up the work so successfully handled by Dr. Bradford Knapp and his father before him. I want also to assure you that Tuskegee and its Principal stand ready to be of any possible aid in the furtherance of your work, especially as it affects the Negro people.

"Through Dr. Duggar of Auburn and District Agent Campbell with headquarters here, we have been able to do what seemed to me most excellent work in many of the Southern states, not only in increasing the agricultural output from the standpoint of the Negro, but what seems, I think, sometimes of even greater importance, in cementing cordial, sympathetic, and helpful racial relations in our part of the country."

Another example of this friendly spirit of cooperation is shown in a letter from District Field Agent T. M. Campbell to Dr. Moton, from which I quote:

"I am informed by Mr. L. N. Duncan, Director of Extension Service at Auburn, that Dr. C. B. Smith, now chief of Extension Work for the United States, headquarters at Washington, will spend Sunday at Tuskegee Institute.

"We had hoped to have Dr. Smith visit Tuskegee during the week, but we find that Sunday will be the only day he can spare. I am asking Mr. Duncan to invite Dr. Smith to remain throughout the day to witness the Sunday activities. In addition, he wishes to meet a few of the agricultural extension workers."

Various other conditions and developments growing out of the relationships between the two institutions and their representatives tended to bind them together in praiseworthy fashion with an attendant unconscious influence and a usually wholesome rivalry that grew out of the more notable achievements of this or that scientist or specialist at Auburn and this or that scientist or specialist at Tuskegee. In this mutually helpful relationship, the marvelous achievements of Dr. George W. Carver deserve special and honorable mention. One of the most interesting and most frequently visited buildings on the Tuskegee campus is the Carver Memorial in which are hundreds of products from the peanut, sweet potato, and other evidences of his unique and wonderful genius.

The practical effects of the institutional relationships which have been already referred to, and which are typical, are shown pretty clearly and convincingly in the two letters to Dr. Moton and in the resolutions that follow in order:

"I am sure you have noticed in the press that the second day of the next meeting of the Alabama Press Association will be spent at Auburn with a return trip of the editors via Tuskegee in the afternoon. The first day of this meeting will be May 10 and the second, May 11, which is the day the editors will spend in Auburn and Tuskegee.

"For more than a year we have been working on this proposition, and we at Auburn are greatly pleased over the coming of the editors, and feel sure that you people at Tuskegee Institute share this pleasure with us.

"You, no doubt, noticed the program for the day in the press, and it is not necessary that I relate it here. However, we shall keep you advised of any developments in connection with this visit of the Alabama editors."

This was written by Editor P. O. Davis.

The following resolution is typical of expressions of approval and official recognition of the increasing effectiveness of Negro extension work in the South. This resolution, adopted unanimously by the Court of County Commissioners of Talladega County, Alabama, on the 8th day of October, 1934, is similar to many other official expressions in several states of the South.

RESOLUTION:

WHEREAS, On or about October, 1930, the Extension Department of Auburn and Tuskegee put on a Negro Demonstration Agent to work among the Negro farmers of this County, without cost to this County, and

WHEREAS, The Farm Demonstrator, Demus Frazier, has done good and efficient work among the Negro farmers and much good has resulted therefrom, and

WHEREAS, It is now proposed to put on a Negro Home Demonstration Agent to work with the Negro women and girls of the County, the expense to be paid by the Federal Government, therefore be it,

Resolved, By the Court of County Commissioners of Talladega County that we do hereby endorse this work and believe that the same will be of great value in raising the standard of the home and result in a general improvement in the life of the Negro farmers of this County.

Dr. Moton became one of the leading spirits in the Committee on Interracial Cooperation, which was organized in Atlanta in 1918, and spoke frequently in various gatherings in Alabama and throughout the South. He spoke frankly and effectively about delicate points and phases of race relations. So human and happy were his presentations and so searching and striking were the stories he told that the minds and hearts of many were touched and his words were liberally applauded. He disarmed many who were disposed to be

[179]

critical or even unjust, and he greatly stimulated and strengthened those who were working to improve conditions. He always revealed his sincerity of purpose and his soundness of judgment convincingly even to some of his own people who objected to his public utterances and who otherwise might have been disposed to obstruct rather than promote understanding and friendship.

Like Dr. Washington, Dr. Moton exerted tremendous influence over present day pedagogical methods, particularly in the field of vocational education, and followed rather consistently the Tuskegee policy for Negro schools which was in harmony with the State Department of Education: (1) to improve facilities; (2) to exercise more helpful and effective supervision; (3) to have the teaching vitally connected with activities in which the people were engaged; (4) and to have the school, in addition to its regular teaching work, actually to assist in the general improvement of the community.

In *What the Negro Thinks*, Dr. Moton says:

"As things are happening in the world today, America has in the Negro an asset of indispensable value. Bound together by ties of common suffering and sacrifice in times of national distress it is unthinkable that these two elements should be anything else than allies in whatever undertaking they may face in the future. Meanwhile, nothing can contribute more toward the establishment of our national welfare than the continued effort to realize for the humblest in our national life, whether black or white, that full measure of justice and equal opportunity for which America stands as a symbol before the world. To this task thousands of the noblest spirits in our country are dedicated. It is such as these that make all, regardless of race, proud to be an American."

In his report to the Board of Trustees on April 1, 1930, Dr. Moton further defined the policies of Dr. Washington and his own objectives. Tuskegee, first was to be a demonstration of Negro capacity in maintaining "a community in which Negroes are responsible for all the activities incident to the maintenance of community life; second, a social laboratory for the advancement of the Negro race as a whole and for national welfare; third, a research

Above, Hollis Burke Frissell Library, Tuskegee Institute.

Below, Samuel Chapman Armstrong Science Building, Tuskegee Institute (P. H. Polk, Tuskegee Inst., Ala.)

Moton Residence, Holly Knoll, Capahosic, Virginia

center for investigation and study of the problems and the processes of racial development and interracial contact." Furthermore, it was to be a point of interracial contact between two races in America in their efforts toward understanding and cooperation and in the promotion of good will, without which one of the major instruments for justice and equality before the law and for the promotion of self-respect and mutual good will between the races would be sadly lacking. "I have faith to believe that succeeding generations will supply the institution with resources necessary for its successful functioning."

He closed the report with this highly significant paragraph:

"Because of its past, as well as its prospects for the future, I am anxious that whatever we do at Tuskegee shall be done as well as it can possibly be done by anybody under the circumstances. I am anxious that our equipment shall be of the best, consistent with rational economy and intelligent efficiency, I am anxious, too, that our teachers and workers shall be representative of the best in character, culture, training, and spirit that are found anywhere. In our methods of service, changes are unavoidable to meet the changing times and conditions; but always the institution must be faithful to the heritage of unselfishness, service, and good will left us by the Founder. It is a proud privilege to work at Tuskegee Institute.... My own conviction is that nowhere else in the world is a larger opportunity presented to be of direct, helpful, and lasting service, not only to the Negro race, but to all mankind. It is our constant desire to measure up to this opportunity and its responsibilities."

In this connection I quote from a very significant address of Dr. Moton over Radio Broadcasting Station WMAV, the Alabama Polytechnic Institute (now WAPI), Auburn, Alabama.

"The South is primarily an agricultural section. Its wealth is wrapped up in its rich soil and warm climate, which makes farming possible the year round. No agency in the South has contributed more to its development than the Extension Service of the United States Department of Agriculture working in cooperation with the State A. & M. Colleges and through demonstration agents.

"Here in Alabama we have seen the most interesting development of this service, in which both white and colored have shared and have been mutually benefited. One cannot think of the extension service in Alabama without thinking of Dr. Thatch of Auburn and Dr. Washington of Tuskegee. No finer example of interracial co-operation has been exhibited than is true of the two schools, Auburn and Tuskegee—the one for whites and the other for blacks. The same traditional cooperation has been handed down and developed through Dr. Dowell and the present administration at Tuskegee. As a result, Negro agents are scattered throughout the State of Alabama, who are preaching the doctrine of better farming, and in all this work Auburn has led the way and, through Tuskegee Institute, has extended its helping hand to the Negro farmers.

"I have been asked to say something on the subject of Negro migration. The large numbers of Negroes who have left the South left primarily for economic reasons. There has been greater demand in the North for laborers with much higher wages, and in many instances, I am sure that other factors have entered in to induce the Negro to leave the South, which deep down in his heart, the Negro sincerely loves. Whatever may be said to the contrary, the white man of the South loves the Negro. Many who have gone North have not found conditions as they expected, but in most instances they have gained certain other advantages, such as greater opportunities for the education of their children and greater civic advantages. There is, however, less reason now for Negroes to leave the South than ever before, because the best sentiment in the South today, official and otherwise, is determined that the fundamental desires of the black man shall be assured him, and this can be done without violating any of the best traditions of the South and greatly to the advantage of black and white alike."

Among the careful plans and effective agencies that had been established in accordance with the idea that whites and Negroes should work together without suspicion and prejudice was the Conference for Education in the South, initiated by a few Northern and Southern men for the purpose of developing sentiment and securing the facilities for educating all the children of the South. Among those attending the Conference were Robert R. Moton, Robert C.

Ogden, business executive and statesman; William H. Baldwin, Jr., first chairman of the General Education Board, which had its inception in the Conference; Walter Page, Albert Shaw, George Foster Peabody, John D. Rockefeller, Jr., Edgar Gardner Murphey, Edwin A. Alderman, Charles D. McIver, Wallace Buttrick, H. B. Frissell, and other men of like vision and dedication. It is noteworthy that these men included both Southerners and Northerners who, first of all, were Americans. No movement in America has been quite so influential in creating and spreading sentiment and support for the improvement of educational service. The General Education Board and the Rosenwald Fund which grew out of it, have all made their respective outstanding contributions to the advancement of the Negro race and of the public welfare.

Among the great friends and admirers of Dr. Moton and of Tuskegee Institute was Dr. James H. Dillard, a cultivated Virginia gentleman and scholar, a man of nobility of character and sublimity of spirit, a great Southerner, and a great friend of man. He fully realized that there would be no substantial and permanent improvement in the condition of the Negro in the South without serious and sympathetic effort to create among Southern white people an intelligent interest in the conditions and needs of the colored people by whom they were surrounded and who formed so important and indispensable a part of the life of the South. As executive secretary of the Anna T. Jeanes Foundation and of the John F. Slater Fund, he gave this estimate of Dr. Moton, "It would be hard to find a man anywhere in America who has developed more tact, thoughtfulness, patience, and courage in dealing with the intimate and delicate problems that we must meet in striving to adjust race relations in the South."

During the administrations of Dr. Washington and his successor, Dr. Moton, Tuskegee Institute was and still is the center of many conferences by representatives of the two races for understanding and good will. The most important of these has been those sponsored by the Commission on Interracial Cooperation. According to Dr. Will W. Alexander, foremost among the leaders of the South, it was begun in France soon after the signing of the Armistice that marked the close of World War I, and the idea was originally conceived in the mind of Dr. Moton. In this connection Dr. Anson

[183]

Phelps Stokes, a great patriot and philanthropist, gave this appraisal of Dr. Moton's influence in this movement, "When the history of the South is dispassionately written, Dr. Moton will be inscribed permanently as one of the half dozen most useful and distinguished Southerners of his generation."

The more recent activities of our National Government in defining the rights guaranteed by the Constitution, of those public spirited organizations and agencies that are playing worthy parts in cultivating and in advancing the principle and practice of friendly relations and fair play, and of the churches of every denomination in working for a genuine Christian attitude in all our relations, owe much to the life, the labors, the spirit, and the ideals of Robert Russa Moton, who merits our everlasting gratitude for the purity and grandeur of his motives and the greatness of his mission.

Recognizing the implications and importance of the race problem in America, the Carnegie Corporation decided to attack the problem practically, scientifically, and thoroughly. Dr. Gunnar Myrdal, a distinguished social economist of the University of Stockholm and economic adviser to the Swedish government, and now executive secretary of the UN's Executive Committee for Europe, was secured to do this work. His searching and scholarly study and findings were given in his two volume report, *An American Dilemma*, and in four other volumes by members of his staff of noted scholars. Dr. Myrdal declares that the problem is not based on any separate factor such as economic exploitation, color prejudice, or Southern malice and conservatism, but that it is a combination of many factors, intricate and subtle, which basically have to do with a moral issue. This very important book, in which Dr. Moton is quoted many times, has attracted the attention of the whole country, and in connection with this appraisal of the monumental service to society of Dr. Moton, I am attempting a brief summary, which, incidentally, it not unlike the principles of human relations set forth by Dr. Moton.

The moral issue, the author insists, is the lag between the American profession and practice of its democratic creed and its many ramifications. *Politically*, that creed defines democracy as government by the majority through duly elected representatives where the voice and right of the minority are always heard and respected.

Economically, that creed defines democracy as looking after the welfare of the people so that no group shall fall below the minimum standard of living, arbitrarily set in terms of the nation's growing sense of values and its increasing economic production. *Socially*, that creed defines democracy as a good society in which there is free intermingling of peoples according to their abilities to contribute their self-realization to the total welfare.

If this creed is admitted to be a moral issue, we must accept it as a religious issue, for democracy as formulated in the Declaration of Independence and in the Constitution itself is based on the fundamental principles of Christianity. Our sense of values of personality and of individual worth are similar to those expressed in the Christian tradition. Our sense of the unity of the great human family, in which each is given according to his needs and to which each contributes according to his ability, stems from the Christian concept of the fatherhood of God and the brotherhood of man.

And so the thing that concerns us politically is not so much the civil rights program *per se* as the extralegal interpretations by which most of the discriminations against a minority group have been justified in the past. To be sure we stand for the guarantee of civil rights, but by the same token we need to be constantly reminded that, so long as the fourteenth and fifteenth amendments are so frequently misconstrued to selfish ends, we have not won the fight by legislation. The thing that concerns us economically is not only substandard housing, clothing, or diet, but the drag, the hindrance to the over-all economic progress of our commonwealth that persists so stubbornly among our citizenry. As Christians we cannot help being indignant that many are deliberately kept from employment, or from employment that is wholesome and profitable, that they, therefore, are denied their share of the goods of life. The thing that concerns us socially is not only the ghetto-like existence imposed upon so many of our fellowmen but the moral callousness, the all too prevalent insensitivity to human feelings and the psychological frustration of those who think themselves superior and who would keep others inferior—a spirit that not only damages, but destroys. In this connection, I do not forget the many exhibitions of discourtesy, discrimination, and injury, usually given without real cause or provocation, that have come under my observation

[185]

and that hurt my feelings and aroused my sense of justice and fair play.

In the light of the conditions that prevail today and the part that Doctors Washington, Moton, Patterson, and others who share their faith and courage have played, and are playing, in the life of the country, what should we as citizens of America do about it? What are the difficulties to be overcome? Is it not true that the problem is complicated by the fact that Negroes remember slavery and emancipation and, with the liberating rights of education and progress, are claiming full freedom; and that the whites remember war and reconstruction and hold on tenaciously to the traditional role of master, still regarding the Negro as a servant race? Is it not also pertinent to say that as long as two self-conscious races live together in the same territory, there will be continuing problems of adjustment that must be solved rationally and in the spirit of good will? Are we not already convinced that the solution does not lie merely in some law or theoretical device, but in the spirit of mutual respect and regard? Have we not learned from experience that men of good will in both races may come to understand each other through conferences and collaborations participated in by members of both groups, in which ways of cooperating are discussed and developed and to which each contributes according to his ability? Dr. Moton was an apostle of good will.

CHAPTER 12

❧ *A Southern Statesman* ❧

BY CLAUDE A. BARNETT

When Robert R. Moton became principal of Tuskegee Institute, he stepped into the shoes of Booker T. Washington, a many-sided individual, who had risen from the very bottom to the heights of leadership in all matters pertaining to the welfare of his people. Few men of any race had accomplished so much in a lifetime. In education, in politics, in almost every area in which Negro life touched that of the white population, Washington's counsel was sought by both white and Negro. Tuskegee and Booker Washington had become synonymous in the minds of the public, white and black, so that it was to be expected, after his passing, that his mantle should fall, at least temporarily, on the shoulders of whomever succeeded him.

Thus the Washington role of educator and pioneer in the field of race relations—head administrator of a great educational institution, president of the National Negro Business League, member and confidant of numerous philanthropic boards and foundations, as well as political sage and adviser to many leaders of the nation—all were assumed, almost automatically, by his successor.

Dr. Moton, who had the rare ability of intuitively sensing the fitness of things, recognized that one of the outstanding values in the Washington leadership had been his ability to work with other people and to discover in them the ability and qualifications necessary for leadership. The Tuskegee seer thus developed a large following of men who, while far overshadowed by Dr. Washington, still were persons of quality and competence.

During the lifetime of Dr. Washington, these men, in most instances, stood loyally behind him. There was little or no grumbling even when he became almost the sole arbiter on important Federal appointments which were parcelled out to Negro applicants. Each year, when he called the National Negro Business League together for its annual session, there would be found assembled most of the leaders of the race, men of all professions and shades of opinion. From these gatherings emerged more unanimity of feeling and opinion on problems affecting the race than from almost any other single assembly.

Inevitably, therefore, when Booker Washington passed from the scene, men who had been content to serve as subalterns and lieutenants began to surge forward in the varied fields where he had occupied the role of commander-in-chief and to assert what they regarded as their rights to succession.

Perhaps no more reliable measure of the man who stepped into Dr. Washington's shoes could be given, aside from the growth and expansion which Tuskegee itself experienced, than the manner in which Dr. Moton sought to cooperate, and even yield in one field and then in another, to capable men who, like himself, had grown up in association with Dr. Washington. Often, however, his retirement was more apparent than real. White leaders had come to know Dr. Moton, through his close association with Dr. Washington, so that it was only natural for them to turn to Tuskegee and Moton for counsel and guidance when problems of an interracial character faced them. To these he gave the benefits of his experience and thought, often while remaining modestly in the background himself.

Dr. Moton, in describing the Washington role, has written: "In politics, Booker Washington was the recognized leader of the Negro people. He was a Republican, although he himself rarely took part in open political combat. During the period when his influence had been established, there were very few important appointments made to Negroes which Booker T. Washington did not pass upon, and it would have amazed the white South of that day had they known how many important political posts went to white men in the South simply because Dr. Washington had pointed them out as capable, high class men with a sense of fairness as to race."

Robert R. Moton followed much the same pattern. Astute, a student of human nature, with a great fund of common sense to temper his idealism, he was sought by men in high places who had quickly learned to trust his judgment. Dr. Moton's association with leaders high in public life—indeed, with presidents of the nation—extended over a long period of time. He knew William Howard Taft well because of Mr. Taft's association with Hampton Institute as a trustee. Through the administrations of five other presidents—Woodrow Wilson, Warren Harding, Calvin Coolidge, Herbert Hoover and F. D. Roosevelt—Moton's counsel was sought and his influence deeply felt at the White House, although he went there in person infrequently.

An examination of his correspondence with these men is illuminating. It was February 21, 1918, when a letter from Dr. Moton went to President Wilson, requesting him to see a small committee of colored leaders. They were interested in discovering some method through which the United States could help the struggling little Republic of Liberia, which, at that time, was being sorely pressed by Great Britain, France, and other European countries who were not in favor of an independent African country on the West Coast of Africa.

Dr. Moton wrote: "The Negroes of this country are deeply stirred by Liberia's plight. As President Roosevelt and President Taft exhibited an interest in the little Black Republic ten years ago, I am thinking, Sir, you may not object to such a conference as is herein suggested."

Although the conference of colored representatives was held, matters lagged until June 18, 1918, when President Wilson wrote Dr. Moton as follows: "Thank you for your letter of June 15. I have been seeking an opportunity to do what you suggest, and if I do not find it soon, I will do it without an opportunity."

On September 11, 1918, Dr. Moton had occasion to write a grateful letter to President Wilson in the following words: "I notice in today's paper that Liberia has been granted a loan of five millions of dollars, as requested by the committee which waited upon you last

April. This act will serve not only to help a struggling people, but it will tremendously strenghthen the morale of the American Negroes. I am taking this opportunity now to thank you for your efforts in our behalf. . . . I speak the sentiments of the colored people of this country and of Liberia when I tell you we are grateful for what you have done in this instance."

Immediately, President Wilson replied: "Thank you sincerely, Major Moton, for your letter of September 11. It gives me real gratification. You rightly interpret my desire, which is to help in every way that is possible and legitimate, and I am always glad when thoughtful men agree that I am doing the right thing."

Soon after this, in the fall of 1918, Dr. Moton, at the invitation of Secretary of War Baker, made a trip to Europe and the war front with instructions and full authority to inspect conditions under which Negro troops were living in France, to hear their complaints, and to counsel with them.

On January 1, 1919, President Wilson, writing from Paris, France, expressed to Dr. Moton his appreciation: "I wish to express my appreciation, Principal Moton, for the service you have rendered during the past several weeks with our colored soldiers in France. I have heard not only of the wholesome advice you have given regarding their conduct during the time they will remain in France, but also of your advice as to how they should conduct themselves when they return to our own shores. I very much hope, as you have advised, that no one of them may do anything to spoil the splendid record that they, with the rest of our American forces, have made."

In a letter written by Secretary Baker to Dr. Moton on February 25, 1919, appreciation was again expressed: "I have received your letter of February 20," he wrote, "and the interesting summary of your experience abroad, which you have been good enough to prepare for me. . . . All in all, I find myself cheered by the observations you make. It is always difficult, of course, to extract comfort out of a situation which has so many elements of more or less permanent disquiet; but I am persuaded that the service rendered by the colored men in France, the sacrifices they have endured, and their gallantry in action are real assets, and an approach hereafter to the problem must always be with a keener realization of what these services to America meant at a critical period in her history.... Your whole trip abroad was most helpful, and both the President and I appreciate the sacrifice you made to undertake it."

Again, on November 1, 1919, Secretary Baker wrote Dr. Moton as follows: "I have your letter of October 29 and am happy to inform you that upon my recommendation, the President has directed the disapproval of the proceedings involving the four officers convicted by Court Martial abroad in connection with the retirement of a portion of the 368th Infantry. This disposes of the cases of all the officers involved. My own statement on the subject, which I submitted to you sometime ago, will appear in the newspapers shortly."

Feeling that a statement from the White House concerning lynching, mob action, and various forms of interracial injustice and unfairness would have a salutary effect on the country, Dr. Moton, on August 8, 1919, wrote a letter of considerable length to President Wilson:

"I know you are besieged from many and various angles touching many phases of life in this country. I have some slight appreciation of the burdens you have been carrying, and the fine courage and wisdom with which you have faced the situation. I am very glad you are again back on American soil. We somehow feel happier and safer with you at home.

"I want especially to call your attention to the intense feeling on the part of the colored people throughout the country towards white people, and the apparent revolutionary attitude of many Negroes which shows itself in a desire to have justice at any cost. The riots in Washington and Chicago and near-riots in many other cities have not surprised me in the least. I predicted in an address several months ago at the fiftieth anniversary of Hampton Institute on the 2nd of May—ex-President Taft and Mr. George Foster Peabody were present at the time—that this would happen if the matter was not taken hold of vigorously by the thoughtful elements of both races.

"I think the time is at hand, and I think nothing would have a more salutary effect on the whole situation now than if you should in your own wise way, make a statement regarding mob law, laying special stress on lynching and every form of injustice and unfairness. You would lose nothing by specifically referring to the lynching record in the past six months, many of which have been attended with unusual horrors, and it would be easy to do it now because of the two most recent riots in the North, notably Washington and Chicago. The South was never more ready to listen than at present to that kind of advice, and it would have a tremendously stabilizing effect, as I have said, on the members of my race.

"Of course, you must have seen the account of the lynching, in Georgia, of an old colored man seventy years of age, who shot one of two white men in his attempt to protect two colored girls who had been demanded to come out of their homes in the night to meet the two white men. The colored man killed the white man after being shot by one of the disturbers. The colored man's offense was merely that of protesting. I have not the lynching record for the past six months, but will have it sent on from Tuskegee to you. I am enclosing the *Atlanta Constitution* editorial which strongly denounced mob violence.

"With all good wishes, and assuring you of no desire to add to your burdens, but simply to call attention to what seems to me vital, not only for the interest of the twelve millions of black people but, equally as important, for the welfare of the millions of whites whom they touch...."

The immediate reply from President Wilson, as of August 12, 1919, was sincerely appreciative of Dr. Moton's "public-spirited cooperation." The President wrote: "Thank you sincerely for your letter of August 8. It conveys information and the suggestions you make are under very serious consideration, because I realize how critical the situation has become and how important it is to steady affairs in every possible way."

Soon after the election of President Warren G. Harding, Dr. Moton wrote a significant letter of congratulation in which he set forth some suggestions related to interracial conditions. This letter, dated February 14, 1921, was as follows:

"As an American citizen residing in the South, who is interested in the fullest development of our country, I am venturing to offer some suggestions which, in my opinion, would help in harmonizing and bringing about the heartiest sympathy and understanding between the two races, who must live together here in the South.

"First of all, I wish to express to you my personal appreciation of the liberal attitude you have manifested in all of your speeches during the campaign and since the election. A demand for justice for all humanity has been evident in your public utterances and actions, and this reassures us that under your administration the country will take forward strides in making more real the rights and privileges which our constitution guarantees.

"In making these suggestions I desire only to be of service to you and your administration in the furtherance of the best interests of our country. The suggestions which I respectfully offer are as follows:

"First. I do not desire any office nor have I anyone to suggest for office; but in the matter of appointments in the South, whether white or colored, I hope the men selected may be those who will insure the promotion of interracial understanding and cooperation.

"Second. During the past fifty years, the majority of Negroes in the South have been loyal to the spirit and principles of the Republican Party. It is earnestly hoped that in any plans for the reorganization and rehabilitation of the Republican Party in the South the Negro may be included.

"Third. During the administration of your predecessor in office, he issued a strong statement against lynching. This open letter had some effect in strengthening the hands of those who are endeavoring to encourage law and order; but lynching has continued unabated, and most of the victims have been members of the Negro race. In this connection, it is earnestly hoped that you may take some steps looking toward the further strengthening of the hands of those who are endeavoring to promote law and order, and also that will appeal to the nobler sentiments of the American people, and cause them to take steps to crush this continued evil. A brief reference to lynching in your inaugural address would have a very reassuring effect and would, in my opinion, meet the hearty approval of the American people both North and South.

"Fourth. As far as I have been able to ascertain, there has grown up in the countries south of us a feeling of distrust of the motives of our country with respect to them. I also understand there has grown up in Haiti and San Domingo, not only a distrust, but a bitterness against this country. I hope that you may find it possible to use, if necessary, an utmost of your authority to re-establish confidence in the minds of these sister countries. With respect to Haiti, San Domingo, and also Liberia, I hope you may in your own wise and sympathetic way take a firm hand in the economic, educational, and sanitary rehabilitation of these countries and, especially, in the development of their wonderful natural resources. It is further hoped that whatever America does for these three Negro republics it will be done in the spirit of cooperation and not of domination, and that there may be no encroachment on their rights and prerogatives as individual nations. I strongly urge and respectfully suggest that, as soon as you can take the matter up after your inauguration, a joint commission composed of American white and colored people be appointed to make a careful survey of each one of these countries and to make a definite report and recommendation to the President with respect to their immediate and pressing needs."

Not least of Dr. Moton's influence on the White House was that related to appointments made, from time to time, by the President. Many times the opinion of Dr. Moton was sought in such matters. At other times, he took the initiative in making suggestions and recommendations. The following communication, dated December 12, 1921, was addressed to President Warren G. Harding:

"I sent you a telegram on yesterday as follows: 'I wish to urge appointment of Louis Edelman of Montgomery, Alabama, for the position of Minister to Jugoslavia. For many years he has stood for the highest and best for black and white in the South without regard to race or color and has the confidence of both races. His education, which was largely in Europe, as well as his experience and temperament amply fit him for such a post. Letter follows.'
"Dr. Edelman told me that he had a conference with you while you were at Birmingham, and that he filed with you on October 28, application for the appointment of Minister to Jugoslavia. You, of course, understand that he is familiar with European questions, especially as they affect the Slavs, as well as the Jews. From my

acquaintance with Dr. Edelman, and judging from the excellent service which he has rendered both races in Alabama, I feel that he would make a very acceptable diplomatic representative of our Government. His views and sympathies are broad. His loyalty and patriotism, and his very great respect for you and your administration, all lead me to say this strong word in his behalf. Any consideration you may give him, I will appreciate as a personal favor, and at the same time, I am sure you would make no mistake in such recognition of him."

On May 31, 1922, President Harding wrote the following letter to Dr. Moton in regard to the unveiling of the monument to Booker T. Washington: "I want to contribute my little part to the satisfaction I know you and your associates of the Institute feel on the occasion of the unveiling of the monument to Booker T. Washington. I think there will be little divergence from the opinion that he was one of the most useful Americans of his time, and that the work which he inaugurated, and so long directed, is already demonstrating the wisdom of his attitude toward one of the great public questions of the nation. My own views on this subject, which have been expressed heretofore with all the earnestness I could command, were in no small part the result of my observation of Mr. Washington's work and its results."

A letter from President Harding to Dr. Moton, about this time, in regard to federal appointments, was significant. "Since it is impossible," he wrote, "to have Negroes appointed to federal offices in the South, the next best thing is to secure nominations of high class white Southerners." Dr. Moton gladly responded to this and to other suggestions from the White House. The following letter, in this connection, to President Harding is typical: "In presenting Hon. N. L. Steele to you, I feel that I am putting you in touch with the best that Alabama produces. Mr. Steele is a Republican of long faith and high standing. He is an excellent lawyer and enjoys the confidence of the best elements of both races in the State. I understand that he is an applicant for the position of District Attorney for the State of Alabama and I am very glad to say as strong a word as I can in his behalf. In my opinion, his appointment would help to strengthen the party in this State. He and Hon. T. H. Aldrich are really two friends of ours who are absolutely dependable and who are worthy of any recognition they may secure from your administration."

On April 16, 1921, Dr. Moton wrote a similar letter to the President in regard to the application of Mr. Aldrich for the position of Collector of Internal Revenue: "Hon. T. H. Aldrich, bearer of this communication, is one of the strongest men in Alabama. He stands well with all classes throughout the State and is a man of high character evidenced by a life long record of fair dealing with those with whom he has come in contact. Mr. Aldrich is an ardent believer in fair play for every one. He has the confidence equally of the best white people of the State as well as the best Negroes. I understand that he is an applicant for the position of Collector of Internal Revenue of this District and I am very heartily recommending him for it."

A letter written to President Harding on February 14, 1923, relates to the personnel of the Veterans' Hospital at Tuskegee. Dr. Moton wrote:

"You know, of course, about the Hospital which Vice President Coolidge so graciously dedicated here at Tuskegee on Monday the 12th–Lincoln's birthday–and I want to thank you, the Vice President and many others of your administration, for the large share which you had in bringing the Hospital here. I was in the Veterans' Bureau in Washington on the 3rd of this month. Matters there seemed somewhat confused. . . . I went in to see the Director because I had been informed that this hospital here for Negro soldiers is to be manned entirely by a white staff, no colored persons holding positions above the rank of laborers. These instructions, I understand, have come from the U.S. Veterans' Bureau to the officer in charge of the hospital here.

"I think it entirely proper that the Commanding Officer of the Hospital should be someone already experienced in Government service of this kind, and that his expert assistants should also be people of experience; but I am writing you to say that if Negro physicians and nurses are debarred from service in this Hospital, without at least being given the chance to qualify under the civil service, where that requirement is necessary, it will bring down on my head, and on Tuskegee Institute, an avalanche of criticism which, I think, would be entirely justified, especially since I have been very active in bringing the Hospital here and in doing everything I could to facilitate matters for the Treasury Department, under whose charge it was constructed. What is more, it will bring down upon your administration throughout the country a storm of protest on the part of the Negro press and from Negroes, North and South, which would be most unfortunate. I am therefore writing you thus frankly, because I think that, whatever happens, you ought to know at first hand from me, as you have been so kind and considerate of me personally in many ways, as is also true of many others in your administration."

A short time later, President Harding wrote Governor "Wild Bill" Brandon of Alabama. His letter dated May 1, 1923, read:

"I have your telegram of April 28. It is quite correct that we are working upon a plan of organizing the Tuskegee Hospital with colored officers and staff. It is an institution for Negro Service Men and located adjacent to the great Negro University. These people have a right to prove their ability to be of service among themselves. The decision is not final, but certainly such a program will be followed out if we find available an abundance of experienced professional people to inaugurate such a program. I would not, for anything in the world, do that which suggests the making of racial trouble. I am at a very great loss to understand what your telegram means to convey to me relating to that phase of the situation. Meanwhile, the survey is going on with very great care and no small degree of hopefulness of being a fine and helpful undertaking. If there are urgent and specific reasons why our plans should not be carried through, I shall be more than glad to consider them."

Negroes, who were hoping great things of Massachusetts-born Coolidge, became alarmed when they learned that Basom Slemp, Virginian and reputedly "lily white" in leanings, had been appointed Secretary to the President and would be his political advisor. In a letter from Dr. Moton to President Coolidge, dated September 14, 1923, some suggestions in relation to this disappointment were stated as follows:

"I know your hands are more than full with matters of the gravest importance to our country as well as to the rest of the civilized world; but permit me to make, in your own interest and that of our nation, one or two suggestions: As you probably know, Negroes, rather generally, were disappointed, not to use a stronger word, at the appointment of the Honorable Basom Slemp as your private Secretary.... With no ax to grind, and with no one to be rewarded or punished, and with wholly unselfish motives, my suggestions are these:

"I hope Mr. Slemp will send for a few people and discuss with them the political situation as it pertains to the colored people, without, of course committing himself or you in any way. Second, I wish to suggest that Mr. Slemp, in his own way, call in Mr. Robert R. Church of Memphis, Tennessee, one of the most substantial and reliable men of the Negro race, and one who has been most unselfish in his efforts to be of service to the Republican party. Mr. Church is a man of culture and wealth, a man who has no selfish motives, so far as holding office is concerned; but a man who believes thoroughly in the Republican party. His advice would be most helpful, I am sure, in lining up the colored people. His suggestions with reference to other people to be dealt with would also be worth considering."

Dr. Moton was alert, too, when it came to action intended to place Negroes in strategic posts. Fred R. Moore in his letter to Secretary of War Newton D. Baker, written April 21, 1919, is related to a significant appointment resulting from Dr. Moton's influence. The letter follows:

"I am writing to congratulate you for acting on the advice of Dr. Moton, in appointing Mr. Emmett J. Scott as Special Assistant to advise you on matters relating to the Negro. You could not have made a wiser selection. We are proud of the record made by Mr. Scott. He has reflected credit to his race, and I am sure he has justified the confidence reposed in him by you. The race has been helped forward by your desire to see that the Negro receives a square deal in so far as you have the power to give it. You were always willing to listen to complaints of discrimination and unfairness, and quick to do what you could. Your heart was in the right place. While no man should be thanked for doing his duty, I think my race owes you appreciation for standing for the right."

There were times when civil service or military examinations seemed not intended for colored youth. Secretary of War, John W. Weeks, in writing Coolidge's Secretary, December 21, 1923, indicates something of Dr. Moton's interest and influence in relation to this situation:

"I am returning the letter from President R. R. Moton of Tuskegee Normal and Industrial Institute, with respect to the question of holding a special examination of a number of colored young men for appointment as commissioned officers in the Army, which you referred to the Department on December 17, asking for information in the premises.

"The Department does not consider it necessary to hold such a special examination of colored applicants for appointment in the Army, at this time, since a general examination of applicants for appointment as second lieutenants in the Regular Army is scheduled for the week of April 14, 1924. This examination is open to colored as well as white candidates who meet the requirements of eligibility. ... The April examination has been duly announced by the War Department and all corps area and Department commanders have been instructed to give such examination wide publicity within the limits of their jurisdiction. To insure the students at Tuskegee Institute, Wilberforce University, Howard University, and Hampton Institute, an opportunity to compete in the coming examination, the Adjutant General of the Army has this date addressed letters to the corps area commanders in which such institutions are located, directing that necessary measures be taken to furnish the students at these institutions full information concerning this examination so that they may apply if they so desire."

On December 27, 1924, Dr. Moton wrote the following letter to President Coolidge relative to the Agricultural Commission recently appointed by the White House:

"In connection with the Agricultural Commission which you have appointed to study agricultural problems of the country, I wish respectfully to suggest for your consideration the appointment of an additional member from the South to the commission to represent the interests of this particular section. This, I think, can be done without a disproportionate emphasis upon the relative place of the South in the agriculture of the country, as indicated in the accompanying map.

"With this in mind, I wish to commend to your consideration Professor L. N. Duncan, Director of Agricultural Extension Work for the State of Alabama, with headquarters at the Alabama Polytechnic Institute, Auburn, Alabama. Aside from his qualifications as an agriculturist, which are detailed in the accompanying memorandum, I wish especially to commend Professor Duncan to your notice because of his success, in dealing with both races, in the discharge of his duties in this connection. He has, in a very notable way, dealt with the interests of the Negro farmers of the State in fairness and justice, thereby winning their complete confidence, and, at the same time, losing nothing whatever of prestige in his relations with white farmers and officials of the South. Because of the large part which the Negro plays in the agricultural interests of the South, this addition to the Commission would be of incalculable benefit to my people and to the entire South."

Dr. Moton was on more intimate terms with Herbert Hoover than was any other colored citizen—more intimate, in fact, than many outstanding whites. Even before Mr. Hoover became Chief Executive, while Secretary of Commerce, the two had important contacts. In 1927, for example, during a devastating Mississippi flood, Dr. Moton was appointed by Hoover to organize a committee of outstanding colored people in the South to work with the Red Cross.

The colored committee investigated needs and reported any inequalities of treatment in the flood area. Headed by Dr. Moton, the committee rendered signal service and was backed to the limit by Secretary Hoover, no matter what problems arose, even to discharging offending civilian supervisors. In a letter written by Dr. Moton to a Mr. Sidney B. Thompson, March 26, 1928, we have a sincere statement concerning the fine qualities of Mr. Hoover: "Suffice it to say," wrote Dr. Moton, "that the Secretary of Commerce did everything that the Advisory Commission, of which I was the chairman, asked, and at least one woman in Louisiana was dismissed by telegram when it was found that she was notoriously unjust in her dealings with Negroes.

"In my judgment," he continued, "Secretary Hoover is a man who disregards differences in race, color, creed, and condition. He sees and serves humanity in terms of equality, justice, and absolute fairness. I have known him for many years and, rather intimately, during the past eight months in connection with the Mississippi flood. And, furthermore, this is the impression he has universally made on all who have come in intimate contact with him."

To a Mrs. C. C. Goines in West Virginia, Dr. Moton wrote the following letter, October 1, 1928:

"I am sorry that I have not had an opportunity to reply to your letter before this, and I fear now it will not reach you in time for your meeting. I want to say, however, that the statements circulated about Mr. Hoover to the effect that he was unfair to colored people are a gross misrepresentation of the facts. Indeed, Mr. Hoover took definite steps to prevent that very thing by appointing a Colored Advisory Committee as a part of The Red Cross organization, in the distribution of relief in the flood area, whose special duty it was to see that the Negro people of that section should receive the same consideration as was accorded any others.

"It was true that before this Committee was appointed, there were discriminations in various places, but this was not the fault of Mr. Hoover or of the Red Cross itself. It was the result of location conditions of the sort with which all of us are familiar. When complaints reached Mr. Hoover on this score, he proceeded to appoint the Colored Advisory Committee with power to take whatever steps were necessary to correct any such abuses and to supply any needs of the people they might discover.

"As a further step, and in response to the recommendations of the Committee, he appointed Red Cross supervisors for the colored people corresponding to similar supervisors among the white people in the same area, who gave their attention directly to meeting the needs of colored people. When this was done, the colored people received the same attention as was given to the whites. Mr. Hoover has, furthermore, recommended that this Committee remain a permanent organization to assist the Red Cross in its relief work among colored people at any point where there may be need of such service.

"As Chairman of the Advisory Committee meeting frequently in conference with Mr. Hoover himself, I am in position to testify to his unfailing and impartial interest in people of all classes who have need of relief and assistance."

The following letter, written by Dr. Moton to President Hoover, April 1, 1929, has to do with Federal patronage in the Southern states:

"I wish to indicate my hearty endorsement of your proposal to handle Federal patronage in the Southern states through committees for this purpose in each state. From information in my possession, I am sure that this method is equally appropriate to the state of Alabama as to other Southern states. The plan would not work an injustice to anyone in these states and it would be the means of correcting abuses of various kinds. In my opinion, these committees should be representative of all groups who voted the Republican ticket in the recent campaign, including the Hoover-Democrats, and particularly the Negro Republicans.

"In this connection, you will be interested to know that both Hoover-Democrats and Smith-Democrats in the South have expressed to me their approval of such a course regarding the Negro: that in the recent campaign, the South knew perfectly well what your attitude was on this question, and that they naturally expected you to do nothing less than what was fair and just. Any failure, they thought, to give representation to this element of the Republican constituency would fall short of the expectations even of Democrats—to say nothing of Republicans. This, you will agree, represents decided progress in popular thinking, and is a great gain."

Herbert Hoover planned, as is well known, to use his vast engineering experience in developing a model, large farming settlement operated by Southern Negroes. He was sure that he could prove the ability of Negroes to conduct a big scale operation of this kind with profit to all concerned. The writer was present when he invited Dr. Moton to lunch at the White House with a group of financiers to discuss the project. Dr. Moton preferred to handle it in another way. The project, in the form first conceived by Herbert Hoover, did not materialize. Later, however, under the planning of Rexford Tugwell, Will Alexander, Charles S. Johnson, and Edwin Embree, the Farm Security Administration embraced the idea on a larger scale.

Robert R. Moton was a far more powerful factor in the life of Negroes, during his administration of Tuskegee Institute, than the ordinary observer could have known. He desired results and was active in every legitimate way to bring them about. Living, as he did, during a period when there was little civic or political freedom for a Negro citizen in Alabama, he still wielded an influence which was the more definite because it was quiet and unobtrusive.

A decade after the passing of this Southern statesman, Herbert Hoover wrote: "I am glad to join in any tribute to Dr. Moton. He was one of the great educators and leaders of his time. My many personal contacts with him were in discussion of the problems with which he was confronted and I did what I could to help him. He was a welcome visitor to the White House. . . . My total reaction to him then and since was that he was a great gentleman and an inspiring soul."

A statesman of the best type, he used his great influence to elevate a disadvantaged people. He was a tactful master in getting things accomplished. The fact that the public scarcely knew the ramifications of his many efforts and seldom gave him acclaim for his substantial though quiet achievements, was only incidental. Many a man in high office, with whom he made important contacts, knew and appreciated his statesmanship. They knew that Robert R. Moton was responsible for much more than was ever published and they knew, also, that he never claimed the recompense of credit.

CHAPTER 13

❧ *Jennie B. Moton* ❧

BY CHARLOTTE HAWKINS BROWN

I would like to pay a tribute of respect and honor to Mrs. Jennie B. Moton. Her calm and understanding attitude in situations involving difficulties and misunderstandings so often encountered in a big school like Tuskegee and its large faculty coming from every part of the country proved a valuable asset to Dr. Moton's administration. She was a woman who loved her husband, her home and her children above everything else, not with a love that hid the faults of her children, faults which I never regarded as outstanding, but nevertheless things that most mothers do not see and notice. She would so often refer to these faults to me in confidence and I remember these words distinctly: "Charlotte, it is a big job to rear children on a big campus like Tuskegee Institute and to have them courteous to the other children and at the same time maintain a sort of dignity that I feel that persons in responsible posts should have their children exhibit."

Jennie Dee Moton was born in Gloucester County, Virginia, in February, 1880. She was one of twelve children and number eleven in the succession. Her parents were a mixture of Negro, Caucasian and Indian. Her paternal grandfather was a full-blooded Indian.

After graduating from the Old Poplar School of Gloucester, Mrs. Moton entered Hampton Institute. Like many students of the time who could not pay the full cost of their education, she took a "work year." She was a good student, liked poetry well enough to memorize many of the poems of Paul Lawrence Dunbar and Henry Wadsworth Longfellow. She had a keen sense of humor which often proved its value during her adult professional life.

Mrs. Moton's mission of service began on a voluntary basis at Hampton where, as the Commandant's wife, she took a great interest in student activities and in community welfare.

At Tuskegee Institute Mrs. Moton succeeded Mrs. Margaret Washington as head of the Department of Women's Industries. The all-encompassing duties of this post, combined with those of wife to the principal and mother of five children, resulted in her participation in a wide range of activities which were without end. In addition, Mrs. Moton found time for many volunteer activities away from the Institute to which she gave creative leadership. These included the Alabama and National Federations of Colored Women's Clubs, an organization of Southern women for the prevention of lynching, the Alabama Reform School at Mount Meigs, and movements for better homes and gardens.

After Dr. Moton's retirement from Tuskegee Institute, Mrs. Moton became a field officer in the U. S. Department of Agriculture. Through this post her concern with women's activities in rural areas resulted in frequent travel over much of the South. She was a hard worker, drove herself constantly, and evinced at all times a vital concern in the welfare of the Negro people. She rivalled Dr. Moton in her dedication to interracial harmony and her belief in American democracy.

As chief hostess for Tuskegee Institute, her abundant good will for all mankind expressed itself in the contacts she had with those from many foreign lands who were frequent guests on the campus of Tuskegee Institute.

Mrs. Moton's warm friendship for the students of Tuskegee Institute manifested itself in many ways and on many occasions. Few students were forced to leave the Institute for any reason if she was able to help them to remain. She seemed never happier or more dedicated to unusual effort than when helping persons in distress.

As frequent as the summertime came the Moton family, with their big dog, would stop over at Canary Cottage, my home on the campus of Palmer Institute, on their way to Hampton. It was a place at which they could stop without any notice because we were never crowded during the summer months, being eight or ten miles from Greensboro, N.C., and it was always a great joy for any member of my family who happened to be there to find room for the Moton family and make them comfortable. I do not know anyone who ever came into the Canary Cottage, the president's home, who made themselves more at home, helping me to move mattresses about, changing beds and maneuvering to make a place for the great big Russian wolf hound who really was never welcome because he kept me frightened all the time.

In our public lives and in our private lives Jennie B. Moton and I were understanding, intimate friends and yet took the liberty to disagree on various matters regarding interracial and club matters without breaking our fine friendship. I do not feel that any woman in public life knew Jennie B. Moton as intimately as I did. I sensed her ambition and noticed her methods and procedures, and never felt that I couldn't disagree with her point of view and maintain her friendship. I held and I still hold a deep devotion for her children whom I came to know, and I was justly proud as President Emerita of Palmer Memorial Institute to see on our roster one of the finest young men here, her grandson, Robert R. Moton, III. The Negro women of the deep South lost valuable, cultured, Christian leadership in the passing of Jennie B. Moton, and I lost a devoted friend whose memory will always be green.

CHAPTER 14

❧ *Administrator and Man* ❧

BY FREDERICK D. PATTERSON

In the relatively brief association of seven years, my opportunities to observe those characteristics which contributed to Dr. Moton's record as an administrator came in two distinct periods of service at Tuskegee, and from two vastly different vantage points.

The first spanned the years between 1928, when I joined the faculty, until 1931, when I took leave for graduate study at Cornell University. During the initial period, my impressions were those of a young teacher filled with awe of the very position of president and by the aura of greatness that already surrounded the man. My contacts with him, as a newly appointed Instructor, were both impersonal and infrequent, yet even those were sufficient to give some insight into those qualities which made Dr. Moton the natural heir to Booker T. Washington's mantle of leadership.

The opportunity to know him more intimately began upon my return to Tuskegee from Cornell in December 1932. During the next two years I was to observe him under the strain of a series of tragic events.

Actually, the first of these had taken place in the summer of 1931, before I left for Cornell. In that year Dr. Moton's sister-in-law, Miss Mary Booth, who was head nurse at Tuskegee's John A. Andrew Hospital, was shot fatally by a maniacal killer. A year later a Mrs. Helen Howard, a restaurant operator, was shot and killed in a similar manner. The circumstances surrounding the two crimes led to the suspicion that the still unapprehended killer of Miss Booth had shot Mrs. Howard also. This suspicion proved to be true, but it was not until after the same person had taken the life of Russell Atkins, Director of the School of Agriculture at Tuskegee, in 1933, that the killer was caught.

One could only surmise the depth of suffering which such senseless killings involving family, close personal friends, and his beloved Tuskegee, caused in such a warm and sensitive person as Robert Russa Moton. For some years he had relied heavily upon Russell Atkins in matters of administration, and he was usually the first person he called to his side when he returned to the campus from one of his many trips for the Institute. Atkins was frequently mentioned as the person most likely to succeed Dr. Moton as president.

During this trying period, Dr. Moton's sorrows were made heavier by the hostile attitude of the Negro press. He accepted this, as he did the tragic happenings themselves, in silence.

It was only a short time later that a series of incendiary fires started. On October 17, 1933, Douglass Hall burned. Six days later, James Hall was seriously damaged by fire. Toward the end of that same month, a young girl was caught setting fire to Chambliss Children's House, a newly built practice school for teachers. Clearly a pyromaniac, she admitted to having set the fires that destroyed Douglass and James Halls. Again, Dr. Moton underwent ordeals that would have broken a lesser man with a fortitude that revealed great inner strength.

In September, 1933, I was asked by Dr. Moton to assume the acting Directorship of the School of Agriculture, a position that carried with it membership on the Executive Council of the Institute. The Council met weekly with Dr. Moton presiding. These sessions provided the greatest opportunity of all to witness his masterly application of administrative techniques and to measure his capacity for leadership.

His method was to encourage full discussion of all items on the agenda. Occasionally, however, when he felt the welfare of the Institute demanded it, he would make clear his opinion of the merit of a proposal before it was voted upon by the Council. Rarely did he insist upon shaping the outcome of the vote, but his logical and persuasive presentation of his point of view usually left few members voting against it. He accomplished this, not through the unwilling acquiescence of the Council members, but rather by gaining their respect for and confidence in the wisdom of his opinion.

One incident at the Council session revealed him to be a truly humble man. There had been much discussion on the campus as to which one of the Institute's first two Principals had done more to build Tuskegee. There were many who felt that Dr. Moton's contributions entitled him to equal recognition with Booker T. Washington. When he learned of this, Dr. Moton spoke out in Council and ended further debate by stating firmly that he knew and rejoiced in the knowledge that the only head of Tuskegee Institute who would be remembered permanently in history would be Dr. Washington. His words made it clear to all that it was because of his devotion to Booker T. Washington, his ideal and his close friend, that he had given the best that was in him to Tuskegee.

Dr. Moton continued Dr. Washington's custom of speaking before Southern interracial audiences, and on such occasions his talent for logical persuasion was at its best. His tact and grace made it possible to deliver what could have been interpreted by white Southerners as a stiff rebuke in a manner that made his pronouncements not only acceptable, but also effective.

His friends of long standing affectionately referred to him as "Major Moton" when they visited at Tuskegee, a title that recalled his long and highly successful tenure as Commandant of Cadets at Hampton Institute, where they had come to know him. He brought their friendship with him when he came to Tuskegee in 1916, not to the exclusion of Hampton but to the great good fortune of both institutions as the results of the Hampton-Tuskegee Endowment Fund Campaign testified. The pressures of that unique fund-raising effort so taxed his strength that he was given a trip around the world to restore his health following it.

Dr. Moton was an avid fisherman, and it was my happy privilege to share several weekends devoted to his favorite sport at his riverside home in Capahosic, Virginia. There, relaxed from the pressures of his work, he revealed quite another side of his personality—the charming raconteur. Many entertaining anecdotes, drawn from his experiences as head of the Hampton-Tuskegee Endowment campaign, helped to explain his success as a fund-raiser. All pointed up his gift for sensing the propitious moment to ask for funds. It was his rule never to do so during the time for filing income tax returns. When his schedule of appointments made it impossible to avoid calling on prospective donors during that period, he deftly turned aside all references to the real purpose of his visit and confined his remarks to the pleasantries of the moment. His wise approach succeeded in making close friends, as well as eventual benefactors, of such philanthropists as Arthur Curtiss James and George Eastman.

Few, if any, persons were more revered over the Virginia countryside in Gloucester county than Robert Russa Moton. He was a kind of patriarch of the community, and people of both races vied with each other to please him. They proudly referred to him as a Chesterfield, and in his dress and manner, as well as in the material comforts with which he surrounded his family, he gave substance to the picture of a man of culture, thoroughly accustomed to gracious living. The impression he created was not without purpose. He believed it fitting to live up to the standards associated with accomplishment and he regarded his physical well-being as a necessary investment in the future growth and progress of Tuskegee.

Certainly it was an investment that paid great dividends, for in the years before poor health caused his great energies to wane, and eventually prompted his voluntary retirement, Dr. Moton increased Tuskegee's physical plant and endowment four fold. When the Trade School was destroyed by fire in 1918, he raised $300,000 in two years to erect five new Trades buildings. Immediately after his inauguration on May 24, 1916, he arranged for an examination to be made of all of the Institute's courses of study. The reports, collaborated in by distinguished experts in education, as well as a completely independent evaluation by Dr. Paul H. Hanus of Harvard, were given careful study by the Executive Council. As a result, teacher training was strengthened, a two year business course was initiated to meet the growing demand for well-trained business personnel and an additional year of general academic study was made a requirement for graduation.

The Forty-fifth Annual Catalogue for the school year of 1925-26 stated that: "Therefore, in addition to those courses of secondary grade in the specialized vocational schools leading to special diplomas, there have been added the following new courses on the college level:

1. The School of Agriculture, offering a four year course leading to the B.S., and a two year course leading to a diploma.
2. The School of Education, offering a four year course leading to the degree of B.S., and a two year course leading to a diploma.
3. The School of Home Economics, offering a two year course leading to a diploma.
4. The Trade Technical School, offering a two year course leading to a diploma.
5. The Summer School for Teachers."

In the Principal's Annual Report, 1929-30, Dr. Moton justified raising the academic program to college and degree levels. Though assurance was given that Tuskegee would continue its emphasis upon vocational education, it was made clear that he felt that failure to advance the level of the Institute's program would be inconsistent with its previous effort to qualify youth for more advanced instruction: "There is no reason why Tuskegee should not keep abreast of the progress which it has so effectually stimulated," he wrote. "Any other course would be suicidal."

Dr. Moton's dedication to the original concept of life-related education and his convictions of the importance of Tuskegee's unique program devoted to the developing stature of the Negro people, were equal to those of his predecessor, Dr. Washington. He also made full use of the Department of Records and Research, initiated by Dr. Washington, relying heavily upon the data compiled in analyzing trends in Negro life in the United States. He encouraged the Department to issue the annual report on lynching which became accepted officially on a national scale. This report, combined with the widespread editorial denouncement of the practice in the Southern press, unquestionably contributed to the steady reduction in lynching to the point of its virtual elimination.

Finally, the fact that Tuskegee passed through the difficult period of readjustment which followed the first world war without the

serious difficulties experienced by many other educational institutions is further proof of his skill as an administrator. Actually, the
closing years of his administration brought many improvements to
Tuskegee's educational program and to the Institute's physical
plant. The Science building, a new library, the Gymnasium, along
with substantial renovations of old structures were testimony to the
confidence so many displayed in Dr. Moton's leadership. Some
measure of that confidence and respect for his abilities is apparent
in the following tributes.

In his "Recollections of Major Moton," Anson Phelps Stokes
wrote, "Whenever I think of Major Moton, I visualize him leading
the processions of trustees, faculty, and students as we marched
across the Institute campus on the morning of commencement. He
was an impressive figure ... tall, well-built, ... and marched forward with his head high and looking very earnest. One could well
see the effects of his early military training at Hampton. He could
be picked out in any group as a probable leader; and the more one
saw of him, the more one realized that his bearing was a true reflection of his character. I remember very well persuading a diplomat
in Washington—one rather prejudiced against the Negro—to make
a trip to Tuskegee that he might see the Institute and its Principal.
After the visit, he returned to Washington enthusiastic about almost
everything he had seen. What impressed him most of all, he said
was the compelling personality of Major Moton. Some time after
that he was proud to have Moton as a guest in his home.

"... It was my pleasure, over a considerable period of time, to sit
with Robert Moton in trustee and committee meetings having to
do with Negro education and progress. We were all impressed by
his keen vision, his balanced judgement and his profound wisdom.
He was never to be rated as an extremist; he was always willing to
reach a constructive, forward-looking decision based on evidence
and reason.

"I remember remarking that if a court of law had to have a lay
member, I could think of no layman who would add more dignity
and good judgement to the proceedings than Major Moton. It was
because of his demonstrated wisdom that we chose him to be a
trustee of the Phelps-Stokes Fund ... the first of many members of
his racial group to be given that position.

"... Although born and reared in the South, and especially interested in its welfare, Major Moton was a true American. He had no sympathy with those who condemned all Southerners just because their views concerning the Negro and his needs were unlike his own. He knew the delicacy of the Southern situation, not yet recovered from the effects of slavery, and he was always tactful, as he could be, in dealing with the issue of race, although he was never willing to subordinate major principles to temporary expediency. He was conscientiously American, intensely loyal to the principles of the Declaration of Independence and to the Constitution of the United States. He was anxious that his own people should share in the rights and duties of full citizenship."

John D. Rockefeller, Jr. expressed his admiration for Dr. Moton in these words: "My first recollection of Dr. Moton is in connection with a visit to Hampton which I made on one of Mr. Robert C. Ogden's Southern Education trips about the turn of the Century. I can see him now, Major Moton he was then, tall, powerful and commanding as he drilled the cadets for the assembled guests, he being the Commandant in charge.

"During the years that followed, my friendship for Dr. Moton grew as well as my admiration for him. Letters passed between us from time to time. In the spring of 1925, in answer to a beautiful letter which he had written me along personal lines, I wrote him on June 5th: 'You, in turn, are a great inspiration as well as an example to me. Your courage, your modesty, your patience, your optimism, your sweetness of spirit, all combine to give you great influence for good. May you be used in the best possible way for the advancement of the interests of the people of this land, both black and white.'

"Six years later, in a letter which Dr. Moton wrote me on February 5, 1931, replying to a note I had written him expressing concern about the operation he had recently undergone at the Strong Memorial Hospital in Rochester, he said: 'My operation was in every way satisfactory and I am improving. I am now relieved of the trouble that has annoyed me for the past ten years, off and on. The people at the hospital at Rochester were as kind as they could be. Dr. Rhees was most kind and gracious, and Dr. Eastman, though not very well these days, was good enough to come in to see me every Sunday. He kept my room filled with flowers from his greenhouse. Of course, I don't deserve such consideration, I know, but I have for forty years done the best I know how—at Hampton and for the past fifteen years at Tuskegee.' Replying to that letter under date of February 19th, I said: 'I am grateful to note that as a result of your recent operation, you are looking forward to enjoying so much better health. The experience, although trying, must have been almost worthwhile because of the kindness of the many friends of whom you write.

"Your long record of useful, unselfish service entitles you to the fullest recognition and appreciation of your friends and fellow countrymen. Few men have used their lives in more worthwhile ways than you have. In a very real sense you have put this country under obligation to you.' At the time of Dr. Moton's death, being unable to attend his funeral, I telegraphed Dr. Patterson on June 3rd, 1940, as follows: 'The passing of Dr. Moton will be mourned by the North and South alike. The Nation owes him a profound debt of gratitude for the far-reaching influence he has had on the improvement of the standards of practical education in this country and for the example of modest, courageous, unselfish, useful living he has given it. Mrs. Rockefeller and I with our family join in expressions of deepest sympathy to Dr. Moton's family.'

"One day at Fifth Avenue and 42nd Street when the late afternoon traffic rush was at its height, a woman, heedless of the signal, started to cross the Avenue. Seeing that her life was in danger, a man standing on the curb, threw himself in front of the traffic and at the risk of his own life, rescued the woman. When asked his name by the police that they might report his act of bravery, the man replied: 'Just say a black man did it.' That story about Dr. Moton, which has been told many times during the past twenty-five years well illustrates the spirit which animated him throughout his entire career. Modesty, courage, love for his fellowman and a burning zeal for the uplift of humanity have been the qualities which, coupled with his splendid powers of head and heart, made him the great force for good in the world which he was throughout all the years of his fruitful life. His example is a challenge to mankind."

It would be difficult to find a man as devoted to his friends as

Robert Russa Moton. In 1932 he wrote these lines which he dedicated to his associate, Julius Rosenwald.

Julius Rosenwald—A Friend to Humanity *

"It seems especially fitting today; it seems very beautiful and touching and inspiring, too, that colored people all over the country, with white cooperating, should give special thanks to God for the life and work and service and sacrifice—and I say sacrifice advisedly—of Julius Rosenwald, the most active Trustee of Tuskegee Institute outside of members of our own staff who are on the Board. There was none more interested than he at any time; none more devoted to all phases and interests of the Institute than Mr. Rosenwald; no Trustee, no member of the staff more devoted to the best interests of the Negro race than was true of Mr. Rosenwald.

"I said 'sacrifice' because he amassed a great fortune running up into the millions of dollars, in all probability; and yet, as some of us remember, once when he was here at the Children's House, he took us a little bit into his confidence—speaking to the children whom he loved; he especially delighted in the Children's House—he told them of his early experiences as a boy, how he pumped an organ in the Presbyterian Church in Springfield, Illinois, for ten cents a Sunday in order to make a little money; how he peddled tinware on the streets of Springfield, sometimes selling almost nothing a day; and yet he rose to the point where he had amassed perhaps one of the largest fortunes of the world and had established one of the largest and most unique business enterprises in the world. This man, simple, unassuming, hardworking, with patient industry was able to accomplish so much in his lifetime.

"We think of Mr. Rosenwald in terms of his beneficence, his financial support and that is well. He gave a great deal of money to a great many causes and to a great many peoples, races and creeds. Indeed he saw no race, and he saw no creed, and saw no land, when there arose a real human need where he thought he could help and that he could help permanently. He liked to help people get on their own feet so that they could help themselves. He gave with the same sagacity that he manifested in establishing his business.

* A Memorial Address in Tuskegee Chapel, February 1932.

[215]

He put the same thought and businesslike effort into giving that he put into establishing his business in Chicago.

"We think of him in connection with the Y.M.C.A. One Sunday afternoon a man strolled into a meeting in Chicago presided over by the late William E. Hunton and Dr. Jesse E. Moreland, a meeting of colored men. He walked in and sat in the gallery and apparently as leisurely strolled out. He met the men at the door, Mr. Hunton and Dr. Moreland, told them who he was and asked them to come to see him. They went and that day Julius Rosenwald said, 'I will give $25,000 to any city in the country that will build a Y.M.C.A. for colored people to cost $100,000, if they will agree to build it and support it.' Thus began the great Y.M.C.A. building program for Negroes. And then he put some money into Dr. Washington's hands for building rural schools for our people. You know the story all too well. He was interested in these little schools among underprivileged people, for children who didn't have a chance to go to school. He believed in attractive, healthful surroundings. He was impressed with the results obtained. He said, 'I will give you as much as you want. Build as many schools as you please for colored people in the South; I will put in my share.' He put in some four or five million dollars and he got some fifteen million more from colored people and white people; got sympathetic co-operation from school officials as well as the populace in general; got white people in sympathy with Negro schools; brought them into sympathy with Negro churches and Negro development.

"It was a great thing for our people; at the same time it was indirectly a great interracial, cooperative movement. The white people saw it and appreciated it. They went further. You will find that wherever there was built an up-to-date school building for Negroes, and the white people did not have one there, they soon built one. In this way he helped to build schools not only for black people but for white people as well. He built model schools—the plans were made by a school architect. A Rosenwald school is a modern school with reference to light, ventilation, and sanitation. Soon the whites tried to get one better. Rosenwald laughed and said, 'If they want to do it, let them go ahead. So much the better.' Today nearly three-quarters of a million Negro children in the

South are in Rosenwald schools, built under the direction and supervision of the Julius Rosenwald Fund.

"But he was interested in all phases of life among Negro people. He sent presents every year to the children of the Children's House; he was the children's Santa Claus, and then he would read the little notes that they sent him. He showed me a batch of them which he had kept. They came from people here and elsewhere—colored people—not always well written, but that made them more beautiful to him. How he cherished those notes as well as the flowers and things they sent him!

"One day we visited a little school here in Macon County, Brown Hill, one of the first Rosenwald schools, with Mr. Rosenwald and a party. Near the close of the meeting one of the teachers working out there, or perhaps a demonstration agent, came and said that one little girl wanted to present flowers to Mr. Rosenwald, but she didn't know what she was going to say because she hadn't had time to prepare. He said, 'Let her say anything she wants to say.' The flowers were brought up. I don't think they were tied with ribbon; it was a calico string as I remember. The flowers were not put together in an artistic way; the child was not well-dressed; there were holes in her stockings; her shoes were not of the best quality. But that was nothing against her; it was all the more impressive. She made her little speech to Mr. Rosenwald in presenting those flowers for her class. It was her own language, her own ideas and her own flowers and her own arrangement. Mr. Rosenwald sat there and looked at this child's feet, looked at her dress, and when he got up to receive the flowers he could scarcely speak. Tears ran down his cheeks. As I rode back with him in the car he said, 'You know, that is one of the most touching experiences I have ever had and one of the most beautiful,' and he held on to those flowers. He brought them home and put them in water in Dorothy Hall. It was the evident poverty of this child and the evident sincerity of one who loved him and expressed appreciation of what he was doing for her people. It went straight to his heart.

"That was the Julius Rosenwald we knew here at Tuskegee; that was the Julius Rosenwald who built nearly 6,000 Negro schools; that was the Julius Rosenwald who built the large apartment house in Chicago which taught philanthropists that they can build good homes for colored people and yet make a reasonable profit.

"As Mr. Rosenwald sat in my office one rainy day he said to me, 'I would like to tie my children up to Tuskegee. The greatest comfort and satisfaction and joy I have ever gotten out of life has been through my contact with Tuskegee Institute and with colored people.' I have a letter he wrote to me afterwards, which I think was written with his own hand, marked personal, in which he said again that he wanted to tie his children up to Tuskegee Institute and the Negro race because he had more satisfaction and got more pleasure and joy out of what he had done for colored people than out of anything else he had ever done. He has helped a great many causes of his own race and creed in this country and in other countries; yet he said that the greatest satisfaction and comfort came from helping the Negro.

"These, friends, are some of the reasons why the colored people, the white people, too, all over the world are thinking and talking and praising and thanking God for the life and the work and service of Julius Rosenwald."

These words represent more than a tribute to a friend. They take you straight to the great heart of the man from whence they came, giving insight into his appreciation of those human qualities and services which contributed so much to the advancement of education for Negroes.

It seems fitting that the concluding and summarizing pages of this volume should be taken from a chapel address given at Tuskegee by Dr. Will Alexander—a man who knew and loved Dr. Moton so well.

"The story of Dr. Moton is typically American. He began his life in the cabin of a farm laborer in a rural county in Virginia, and rose to a position of national leadership. Though his parents had been slaves, they were ambitious that their son should have an education. His mother had acquired a limited education and early began to teach the boy to read and write and use figures. Fortunately, the family of their employer was in sympathy with the ambition of the parents and some members of this family actually helped to teach the child. Finally, public schools of a sort were established in the neighborhood, to which he was sent.

"We know now that the roots of personality are hidden in the obscure and unremembered incidents of childhood. The unusually well integrated emotional life of Dr. Moton no doubt grew out of the sense of dignity and security which he had in his early childhood. The secret of his unusual personality is to a large extent in the unrecorded events of that period.

"... Having exhausted the local opportunities for education this young giant worked for a few years as a laborer in a local lumber mill before going to Hampton Institute when he was eighteen years old.

"In spite of having availed himself of every opportunity offered locally to improve his education, young Moton was unable to pass the examinations for entrance into the lowest regular class at Hampton. The school authorities, however, encouraged him to remain. He accepted work in the school sawmill and attended night school. In less than a year he was able to enter the regular classes.

"The years at Hampton, as student and staff member, were unusual years of preparation for his life work. He received a good education at Hampton, for Hampton was an outgrowth of the best educational tradition in America. I am sure that the education at Hampton at this time was superior to most of the education provided in Virginia. His teachers were honest and thorough. Though the curriculum was restricted, it was thorough, and Dr. Moton left Hampton a well educated man. A few of his teachers there did for him what great teachers do for eager youth—which is the essence of real education—they gave him not only information, but habits and attitudes that were to make him an effective person.

"As a student young Moton continued to demonstrate qualities of leadership. During this period as a student he was elected to almost every position of leadership in the student body. He was the head of most student organizations. There is evidence that his faculty advisors were apprehensive about all this recognition. But there is no evidence that it ever went to his head or caused him to neglect essential work in the class room.

"At that time there were both Indian and Negro students at Hampton, while most of the teachers were white, many of them persons of distinction. The relations of the three groups must have been entirely normal and satisfactory—for this one student, at least, came out of Hampton entirely free from race consciousness or racial bias. In all my intimate association with him in after years there was not once when he made me feel that I was white or that he was colored. I never saw any evidence that any judgment of his was warped by racial bias.

"The founders and supporters of Hampton Institute were among the most distinguished leaders in American life. The public figures, business leaders, educators and literary creators of the time were frequently visitors at Hampton. Young Moton came to know these national leaders and many of them became interested in him. As an officer at Hampton he dealt with people of many types. Out of these varied contacts he developed poise and judgment in dealing with people in all walks of life. Dr. Moton came to know personally as many of the leaders of American thought and life as almost any man of his generation. This wide acquaintance among outstanding American leaders became one of his sources of power.

"While still a student this young man traveled with the representatives of the school as they went about the country telling the story of Hampton. Though a member of the quartette, he was sometimes asked to speak. These trips enlarged young Moton's outlook. He came to know the great cities of the country—outside the South—and important people in these cities—for always it was the important people who were interested in Negro education. He learned to take great pride in the quality of the people who were interested in Negro welfare and development. This gave him confidence and poise—and a great faith in the final outcome of American democracy. He began to see and understand the America that lay beyond his small Virginia rural county. He came to be as much at home in New York and Chicago as he was in Amelia County, Virginia. He became an American in the fullest sense.

"During the school years at Hampton, young Moton went to teach for two years in the rural schools in his own section of Virginia. While there he studied law and passed the examinations which admitted him to the bar. At that time he seriously considered law as a career. He never lost his interest in the law and court procedure.

"The authorities at Hampton, General Armstrong and Dr. Frissell, particularly, had recognized the unusual qualities in this young man and, at his graduation asked him to remain on the staff at Hampton in administrative work. In the office of Commandant, Major Moton, as he came to be known at Hampton, exercised many of the functions of a present day dean of men. His responsibilities increased rapidly and he soon became the right arm of the administration—on the campus—and one of the most efficient representatives of Hampton on many important occasions in all parts of the country. He did well whatever was assigned him and he made friends wherever he went. He soon became second only to the president in the contribution he was making to the development of the institution. Major Moton was the kind of man who could take a secondary position and give it primary importance. In his position at Hampton in ten years he became one of the well known leaders in Negro education. He spoke with authority and was known throughout the country.

"In the early days as a staff member at Hampton, Major Moton went for three months travel in Europe. He toured the British Isles and on the continent—seeing how the people lived, and becoming acquainted with the cities and cultures of Europe. Here, again, the horizons were extending.

"Soon after young Moton had become a student at Hampton—Booker Washington, then in the early days of his work at Tuskegee, was a visitor. It was a memorable occasion for the young man. Soon after becoming a member of the Hampton staff young Moton began to be involved in the larger activities of Dr. Washington in the nation in everything that affected Negroes. Dr. Moton's leadership and influence did not come to him because he succeeded Booker Washington. He was already recognized as a man of importance when he came to Tuskegee. His glory was not the reflected light of Dr. Washington. If he had never come to Tuskegee, he would have been one of the marked men of the generation.

"It was characteristic of the man that when Dr. Washington died everyone familiar with the situation recognized that the successor was ready, except the successor. So modest was this man that I am sure it never occurred to him that the principalship of Tuskegee would be offered to him.

"It is not easy to succeed a genius of Dr. Washington's stature. His methods were unique. If he had lived two generations later he would probably have been an actor. He was, in fact a great actor, dramatist and showman. Never did any man use superb showmanship to a higher purpose. He so dramatized the life of a humble people in the deep South as to arouse the nation to their needs.

"Tuskegee had been founded on faith and had been kept alive and developed by the unusual gifts of its founder. Such men of genius never have successors, and the men who carry on their work are wise to recognize this. Dr. Moton did just that. He never attempted to use Dr. Washington's methods, though he respected his predecessor profoundly.

"There had been great controversy as to Negro education. Negroes themselves and their friends were divided—as to whether the need was for some peculiar kind of education such as was supposed to be offered at Tuskegee, or the classical education traditional in American liberal arts colleges. It is to Dr. Moton's credit that this controversy died of neglect after he came to Tuskegee. He hated controversy as something wasteful and harmful. He knew that Negroes needed whatever education other Americans needed and he quietly went about working for that kind of an educational program at the school. It is significant that his closest educator friend was Dr. John Hope, a classically trained man and able leader of a liberal arts college. These men made common causes and I am sure never spent an hour in controversy as to what was proper education for Negroes. Under new leadership, Negro education began to present a united front that has had its final fruit in the annual United Negro College drive—so significant now. Tuskegee took its place as an important link in the total educational forces of the country.

"Negro colleges had been for the most part founded and supported by the church. The task became too large for the church. Dr. Moton came to Tuskegee just as the philanthropic foundations were coming into full fruition in American life. Many of the founders of these foundations were known to him and the leaders of these great enterprises came to trust him. Sound financial undergirding had not kept pace with the expansion of Tuskegee. The institution was over expanded and had been carried from year to year by the genius and showmanship of Dr. Washington. Dr. Moton quietly began the task of permanent finance for the school. His wide contacts, his skill in dealing with men of influence were important assets in this. He turned to the great philanthropists and through his influence brought to the entire field of Negro education source of support. He raised vast sums for Tuskegee and Hampton and influenced large gifts to other institutions. He was never a partisan of his own institution.

"Because of his broad and unselfish attitude, Dr. Moton had a profound influence on American giving. There is some truth in the statement sometimes made by lesser men that to get real money for Negro enterprises one had to see Dr. Moton. I knew him intimately during this period and I know that he never used his influence for personal ends or compromised his high sense of honor and dignity in his effort to tap sources of great wealth. If he had done so he would have lost his influence. The doors to great wealth were open to him because the men who controlled it trusted and respected him. This was true of Rockefeller and Carnegie interests, Julius Rosenwald, George Eastman and scores of others. They recognized in turn his sound judgment and his high unselfish purpose in dealing with large sums of money. He contributed much to interesting wealth in taking up the larger task of Negro education and welfare.

"Early in the administration of Woodrow Wilson, Dr. Moton attended an international conference at Lake Mohonk. Distinguished leaders from many nations were present. Eleanor Wilson, who afterwards married Hon. William G. MacAdoo, was one of the group of hostesses at the conference. The morning of his arrival, Miss Wilson talked with Dr. Moton as he waited in the hotel lobby for his room assignment. A New York newspaper reporter observed the conversation and later in the day approached Dr. Moton and inquired about his 'talk with the President's daughter'. Sensing a possible sensational use of the incident, Dr. Moton passed off the conversation by saying that Miss Wilson was inquiring about some colored people down south that she had known in the past. The reporter pressed the matter no further.

"That evening when Dr. Moton went in to dinner, he drew a number seating him at the small table where Miss Wilson was hostess. He remembered the reporter and wishing to avoid any chance of a sensational newspaper story, that might be used by enemies of the President, asked for another number and quietly took his place at a less conspicuous table. The incident was reported by Miss Wilson to her father. The President was so impressed by this as to write a letter of appreciation to Dr. Moton, assuring him that although there was no reason for the precaution, his thoughtfulness had deeply moved his daughter and himself. The President asked Dr. Moton to call on him at the White House. The invitation was accepted in due time. This incident was the beginning of a close relationship between the two men which lasted as long as President Wilson lived. Dr. Moton became one of the President's advisors on matters of policy and appointments in the south, culminating in his being sent to Europe late in World War I as a special representative of the President.

"When Warren G. Harding was elected President, Dr. Moton showed the feeling of apprehension common among thoughtful Americans as to the leadership of the new President. He felt that his contacts at the White House had been useful, but he had no contacts with President Harding and no natural approaches to him. In a conversation about it Dr. Moton asked if I could get one or two outstanding white southern leaders to go with him to call on the President-elect. I spoke to Dr. Ashley Jones, the leading minister of the south, and to Mr. John Eagan, a prominent southern business man, and they consented to join him in such a call.

"The arrangements for the visit were handled by Dr. Moton. An appointment was made for the Ponce de Leon Hotel in St. Augustine, Florida about a month before President Harding's inauguration. Dr. Jones, Mr. Eagan and I went down on a night train and met Dr. Moton at the Hotel. The place was full of politicians and for some reason we had difficulty in getting in to the President-elect. After long delays, we found ourselves in a room on the third floor. There were no chairs, so we waited in discomfort. Dr. Moton's embarrassment was apparent. Finally, a man of distinguished appearance passing through the room greeted Dr. Moton cordially. He was introduced as Senator du Pont of Delaware. The senator seemed irritated that we should have been delayed and in a few minutes presented us to the President-elect.

"Harding was a handsome man, immaculately dressed, very cordial. It soon became apparent, however, that he had no background for dealing with such callers. He had no knowledge of Tuskegee or of Dr. Moton and remembered only vaguely about Booker T. Washington. His mind was in a political groove. He assumed that our visit was political but he could not guess what peculiar political significance was attached to our visit. In his embarrassment he undertook to do all of the talking. Dr. Moton's attempts to set him at ease only brought on more talk, much of it couched in the language of "the smoke filled room" with a good bit of profanity. Dr. Moton was a man of good taste and excellent manners. Our associates were men of culture and dignity—one a minister. The longer we talked the more the confusion of the President-elect became apparent. It was embarrassing to prolong the interview and difficult to withdraw courteously, so for more than an hour we were forced to listen to the political talk of a man who was clearly lacking in any background that would enable him to understand the significance of our interest.

"This was the only time I ever saw Dr. Moton's great tact and courtesy inadequate for the situation. The backgrounds of the two men were poles apart and there was no possibility of a meeting of their minds. By the time he finally got us out of the room, Dr. Moton's starched collar was limp and he was speechless. The tenseness of the situation was broken when we paused in the lobby below by a young man from my staff who said, 'If you eliminated "damn" from that man's vocabulary he could do nothing but stutter.'

"I suppose this was the most embarrassing incident in Dr. Moton's long contact as an advisor to four Presidents—Wilson, Harding, Coolidge and Hoover—for, for nearly twenty years he was an American to whom Presidents turned for intelligent and disinterested counsel and guidance. Again, it may be stated for emphasis, Dr. Moton never used these contacts to advance personal fortune or in any narrow sense to advance Tuskegee. He was unselfishly acting for what, in his judgment, was best for the nation. In these high circles he was a long way from his simple rural beginnings in Amelia County, Virginia, but he never lost his head or yielded to the temptation to feel his own importance. He walked with the rulers of the nation without losing that sense of what was fitting and important. That came, I think, from lessons learned from his mother and his hard-headed New England teachers.

"Dr. Moton's courtesy and tact with people was unfailing. He was one of the most polished gentlemen I ever knew. I saw this put to the test dramatically soon after the end of World War I.

"General Smuts of South Africa was one of the half dozen recognized world leaders coming out of World War I. The General visited this country in the early twenties. A reception was arranged in Town Hall in New York, to which many prominent people from all over the country were invited to meet and hear the General. It was a distinguished audience about one-fourth of whom were outstanding Negro leaders. The Old Hampton quartette sang beautifully. It was seated on the platform by Dr. Moton. As the General, obviously moved by the music, began to speak about Africa, he spoke highly of the character of the native African. He was speaking extemporaneously and closed this part of his address with a tribute to the patience of the native by saying that the native was 'as patient as an ass.' The simile was an unfortunate one for an American audience and one could feel the Negroes present freeze against all the General said further. It was clear that General Smuts knew that something had come between him and his audience. When he finished there was little applause and the whole atmosphere was cool. Before anyone else could move, Dr. Moton addressed the Chair. He paid high tribute to General Smuts, a world leader, and with directness in most tactful and courteous language, pointed out what an injustice the General had done himself in his reference to African natives. The audience was relieved. General Smuts understood at once and thanking Dr. Moton, apologized to his audience with such apparent sincerity as to completely regain their respect and attention. The incident left the audience with great respect for each of the men. I have always remembered this as a superb example of Dr. Moton's great skill in dealing with a tense situation. He did it with the touch of a great surgeon performing a delicate operation. Few other men I have met could have handled this situation with such deftness.

"Dr. Moton always strove to be fair in his judgments. He was always generous and fair in his evaluation of the south when he talked in other parts of the country. The most critical things I ever heard him say about the south was in the south to southerners themselves. He honestly believed that the south, in the long run, would deal with the race problem in the best spirit of our democratic traditions. He was perfectly sincere about this, in part because of his own life and experience in the south, and partly because of his profound faith in the ultimate power of Christianity to transform human attitudes. He believed that the Christian spirit was more powerful than hate and force and that men and women wanted to do right.

"Following World War I the two most influential men in racial matters in America were Virginians, Dr. James H. Dillard, a white man, and Dr. Moton. They were close friends and neither moved in major matters of policy without consulting the other.

"But Dr. Dillard was not the only southerner who sought Dr. Moton's advice and counsel. Southern educators, southern editors, southern officers and southern business men and southern liberals of all types depended on him for guidance. Among the many callers at his office there was always a large number of important southerners. His courtesy, his honesty and his sympathy won their confidence and admiration.

"White liberals in the south following World War I realized that racial patterns must inevitably change and expressed a willingness to work with Negro leaders within the south to hasten these changes. Many Negro leaders were suspicious as to the motives of these white men. One prominent Negro leader expressed this feeling by warning Dr. Moton to 'beware of Greeks bringing gifts.' Dr. Moton ignored the skeptics in his own group and threw himself heartily into the organization and development of the Commission on Interracial Cooperation. This organization marked an advance in southern race relations by attempting to get southern leaders, white and colored, to work together as equals on their common problems. Dr. Moton was one of the great inspirations and supports of this organization. His faith and sympathetic understanding opened the minds of many southern leaders and set them to work with new courage at the task of changing the patterns of human relations in the South in conformity to the best democratic traditions. Increasing liberal movement in the South centered in the

Interracial Commission which could never have existed without the leadership of Dr. Moton.

"During the period under discussion the Southern States greatly extended their expenditures for Negro education. The most significant development in this was the dramatic development of state-supported colleges for Negroes. These were at first, for the most part, weak and inadequately supported institutions. They have become strong and effective forces in education in the South. Today more money is expended by the Southern States for higher education for Negroes than is spent from all private sources. This development was accelerated during Dr. Moton's active work at Tuskegee. Tuskegee was in a sense the mother of these state schools. Dr. Moton was constantly advising governors and state educational authorities who were responsible for extending the volume and improving the quality of work in these state colleges.

"Some people honestly impatient at the slowness of progress and a few, I suspect, envious because of his great prestige, sought to discredit Dr. Moton as a compromiser. It was perhaps inevitable that there should have been such criticism, some of it from sincere people who knew him only superficially.

"Dr. Moton was essentially a man of peace. He believed in reason and the power of righteousness. He made no profession of being a Negro. His friendships and associations were across racial lines. His life was circumscribed by neither racial nor national boundaries. The breadth of his outlook and the catholicity of his way of life were no evidence that he was confused as to ultimate ends so far as Negroes in America were concerned. He sought for Negroes in America whatever rights and privileges were enjoyed by other Americans. On this he never compromised. In a moving extemporaneous talk I once heard him say, 'I have to pray often for patience—patience with whites who are satisfied with so little progress, patience with Negroes who are so slow in grasping opportunities, patience even with God who seems sometimes to move so slowly.' He was restless at the slowness by which change came. He was willing to move rapidly but he was not a child to waste time in irrational emotional outbursts. Neither was he a timid devotee of gradualism. He did not believe that time alone ever solved any problem. He accepted the common human experience that even by the hardest and most intelligent work changes usually came slowly, and seemed slower than they really were to those who strained in the thick of battle. He would have accepted all that he strove for immediately, but he knew no magician who could change the world immediately. So he worked patiently but his patience was never mistaken for confusion or timidity by anyone who knew him.

"Dr. Moton's faith in the white South was put to a severe test in connection with the establishment of the Veterans Hospital at Tuskegee.

"The town of Tuskegee had, before the Civil War, been the flourishing county seat of an important cotton growing county. It was a center of wealth and culture. With the depletion of the soil and the passing of slavery the town had lost prestige and had for years been at a standstill. Tuskegee Institute had come to overshadow completely the town of Tuskegee. The leading people of the town had appreciated Dr. Washington and maintained a sort of sympathetic aloofness to the school.

"After World War I it was decided to establish at Tuskegee a large Veterans Hospital. As the work of construction went forward the town began to enjoy a sort of boom. Large numbers of whites came in to have part in the construction, markedly increasing the population of the town. There was a demand for housing. A new hotel was erected, business was better in the stores and on every side there was evidence of the great benefits of these newcomers to the town.

"The decision of the Government to establish this hospital had been based on a desire to have colored veterans cared for by colored personnel. As construction began to come to an end it began to be apparent that the new prosperity would be much less noticeable when the white construction personnel withdrew and colored administrative personnel came in. There was much talk about this in the village. It was finally decided to request the Veterans Administration to use white personnel in the Hospital. A committee sent to Washington was reminded by government officials that the reason for erecting the Hospital was in order to use colored personnel. Their attention was called to a law in Alabama which prevented white nurses from serving colored patients. The committee sought to get around this state law with the fantastic suggestion that each white nurse should have a colored maid who, under her direction, would actually serve the patients.

"The agitation soon spread beyond the town of Tuskegee and as time went on the leaders became more determined. At first Dr. Moton was requested to cooperate with the local group, which he courteously declined to do. As the excitement spread it became a race issue. White supremacy was said to be at stake, and citizens generally in Alabama were asked to line up. Decent people were intimidated. Finally, a committee of whites came to Dr. Moton and demanded that he join them in forcing the Government to change its policy as to the use of colored personnel. By this time it was the voice of the champions of white supremacy in south Alabama speaking. They were no longer consulting Dr. Moton; they were Alabama whites telling a Negro what to do. It was traditional in this section that under such circumstances a Negro was expected to heed the demand, 'or else.' Dr. Moton stood his ground. It was apparent that the lives of Dr. Moton and Dr. Kenny, the school physician, were not safe. Reluctantly, these men left the campus. The Klan took over and from all over Alabama robed Klansmen came to the aid of the town and paraded at night on the highway which ran through the campus. Because of the wonderful discipline on the campus there was no violence.

"The South outside of Alabama reacted instantly against this outbreak of the Klan. Southern church leaders and newspapers condemned the whole performance. Oscar Underwood, Senator from Alabama, was a candidate for the presidential nomination of the coming Democratic convention. His backers realized that the publicity was bad for their candidate. The labor on a large power development nearby were disturbed and power companies in Alabama have great influence. The local people soon felt themselves isolated from the rest of the South and disapproved of by powerful forces in Alabama. The federal government stood its ground, and the excitement soon subsided and the issue was dropped locally.

"This was a challenge to all Dr. Moton had stood for and for a time seemed to be a repudiation of all his faith in the decency of people and the power of the Christian spirit to prevail when challenged. His courage and quiet dignity through it all added to his reputation and power as a leader and to the influence of Tuskegee in the South. I am sure such an incident could not happen now, or ever again. Dr. Moton won, though I have always felt that the shock of this incident shortened his life.

"The vocational work at Tuskegee and Hampton marked a new departure in American education. We know that it definitely influenced developments in southern education. Moreover, it seems clear that the work in these schools influenced the growth of vocational education in secondary schools throughout the nation, particularly federal aid to education in rural high schools. All of this was in line with the demonstrations that had been made first at Tuskegee and Hampton.

"By the time Dr. Moton came to Tuskegee the work had begun to attract the attention of educators throughout the world. Teachers of education among the masses in Asia and Africa were impressed with the story of Tuskegee. Colonial administrators in the Netherlands and Great Britain saw here an experience that was significant for them. In 1928 I came from Alexandria to Venice on an Italian liner. A fellow passenger was a very interesting young African from Kenya Colony. He had acquired the elements of a western education in mission schools at home. This was his first contact with the outside world. In conversation with him I discovered that he was very critical of the education provided in both mission and government schools in Kenya. He was sure that the schools he had known were not dealing with the fundamental needs of his people. Finally, one day he said in halting English, 'I want to go to your country and see Tuskegee, and learn how to develop that sort of a school in Kenya.'

"This was the desire of thousands of people throughout the world. Many of them came to Tuskegee. During much of Dr. Moton's administration there was hardly a month when visitors from some foreign country did not come to Tuskegee. Dorothy Hall became a sort of International House where educators from the ends of the earth met in their search for information and inspiration. Dr. Moton became a sort of host to the educators of the world. No one could have done it better. He was at his best in such a role. Many of these people went away more impressed with the Principal of Tuskegee than with the details of the program. He

[231]

was an example of the best that American Democracy had produced. Here at Tuskegee he became a sort of stay-at-home ambassador to the world that came to his door. This was one of his most useful services. Under his leadership Tuskegee became in a very real sense an international institution, and literally thousands of foreigners were stripped of any delusion of the inferiority of American Negroes. Here were a man and an institution that could not be brushed aside as secondary or inferior.

"So impressive were Tuskegee and its President and staff in those days that many of these visitors undoubtedly got a wrong impression of the South and of America. Tuskegee was, in a sense, an oasis in a desert of poverty, ignorance and discrimination. Nevertheless, it was one of the most impressive educational institutions in America and because of its world outreach one of the most influential. Dr. Moton stood at the confluence of the forces that made it and seemed well cast in his role as a world figure.

"When Dr. and Mrs. Moton made a trip around the world in 1928, they were greeted in many lands by those to whom they had been hosts at Tuskegee, and they had the satisfaction of seeing many evidences of the influence of the institution over education for America and the South.

"I cannot close without a personal word. At the end of World War I I was thirty-five years old. The war had sharpened for me the issues of democracy. I did not feel that I could go back to the conventional life I had lived in the South. I went to see Dr. Moton and one night we walked on the campus for hours, talking about America and the South. That conversation helped to determine what I would do for the next thirty years. So long as he lived we were friends. His friendship was the source of great inspiration and strength to me. Now that he is gone, I am still conscious of the power and beauty of his friendship. I enjoy the twilight of a sunny winter day in the South, as the glory of the day departs and the majesty of the night comes on. Such an hour never loses its power to move me. Sometimes, I afterward try to understand the meaning of such an experience. Its mystic mystery cannot be put into words. It is nature at its best, and the great meaning and mystery back of nature has come close to me. As I recall Dr. Moton I have the same feeling. In him the meaning and mystery of nature at its best spoke to us who knew and loved him."

Contributors

WILLIAM ANTHONY AERY was born, reared and educated in New York City. He received his doctorate in educational research at Columbia University in 1906. In the fall of 1906 he joined the Hampton Institute Academy Staff, became publications secretary in 1908. He held this office until 1922 when he became Director of the School of Education. Dr. Aery retired in 1939 after thirty-three years of service to Hampton Institute. During this long period he wrote 675 publications including one hundred fifty Negro periodicals with constructive race relations stories. While he was publications secretary for Hampton he traveled some fifteen to eighteen thousand miles yearly over the Southern states as Hampton's educational observer. During the past twenty years Dr. Aery has prepared annually "A Review of Negro Education" for the *American Year Book*. He continues his work as local correspondent for the *New York Times* which he began in 1906 at the request of Dr. Hollis B. Frissell. For a full decade Aery and Moton were intimate colleagues on the campus at Hampton, and for two more decades their paths frequently met in the field of Negro education.

JESSIE DANIEL AMES (Mrs. Roger Post) was born in Palestine, Texas. During her busy life she held the following positions:—

General Field Secretary, Commission on Interracial Cooperation; Organization Officer—Organizer and President—League of Women Voters, Texas; League of Women Voters, Georgia; Organizer and President, Texas Branch, AAUW; Organizer and Executive Director, Association of Southern Women for the Prevention of Lynching. Delegate-at-Large for Texas, National Democratic Convention, 1920, 1924 and alternate delegate-at-large for Texas, National Democratic Convention, 1928. Mrs. Ames is the author of *A New Public Opinion on Lynching; Whither Leads the Mob; Are the Courts to Blame; Why We Lynch; Death by Parties Unknown; Changing Character of Lynching;* articles on race, propaganda, education, prison reform and lynching for numerous periodicals.

CLAUDE A. BARNETT, founder and director of the Associated Negro Press, graduted from Tuskegee Institute in 1906 and received the honorary degree, Doctor of Humanities, from that institution in 1949. Dr. Barnett has had an unusual opportunity through the regular and extensive functions of his office not only to be informed concerning the various interracial movements of the nation, but to render significant aid in their steady advancement and accomplishment. He is a trustee of Tuskegee Institute; a member of the Board of Directors of the Phelps-Stokes Fund; a member of the Board of Directors of the Supreme Life Insurance Company of Chicago, one of the three largest life insurance companies owned and operated by Negroes; and a member of the Board of Governors of the American National Red Cross. Since 1942 Dr. Barnett has been Special Assistant to the U. S. Secretary of Agriculture. He was closely associated with Dr. Moton in a number of worthy causes.

CHARLOTTE HAWKINS BROWN, a North Carolinian by birth, was reared and educated in Cambridge, Massachusetts. As a protégé of Alice Freeman Palmer of Wellesley College fame, she had long friendships with such persons as George H. Palmer, George Eliot of Harvard and other New Englanders who pointed the way to success. She has been connected with practically every national group interested in race relations. Dr. Brown is a charter member of the Southern Interracial Commission, on the Executive

Board of the Negro Business League, one time member of the National Board of Y.W.C.A. and an active member in numerous other civic and business organizations.

Dr. Brown is founder and president emeritus of Palmer Memorial Institute at Sedalia, North Carolina, the only finishing school for Negro teen-age youth in America.

WALTER R. BROWN was graduated from the academic-normal course at Hampton Institute in 1913. After two years of teaching in the preparatory division of Morehouse College in Atlanta, Georgia, he returned to Hampton as a member of the staff in the commandant's office. He was appointed Dean of Men in 1930; secretary of Hampton Institute and of its Board of Trustees in 1944. In 1950 he retired to become assistant to the Director of Public Relations.

During World War II Major Brown, with the assistance of his office staff, kept in contact through regular correspondence with eighteen hundred Hampton men and women in military service extending to every continent and to numerous islands in the Pacific. He is one of the founders of the National Association of Personnel Deans of Men in Educational Institutions and was its secretary for the first ten years of operation. Since coming to Hampton as a student Major Brown has served his Alma Mater untiringly in countless ways and has endeared himself to thousands of students, alumni, and friends of this institution.

SPRIGHT DOWELL, president of Mercer University, Macon, Georgia since 1928, was formerly an educator in Alabama. As State Superintendent of Public Instruction and afterwards as President of Alabama Polytechnic Institute at Auburn, a period of twenty years, Dr. Dowell had many cooperative contacts with Tuskegee Institute. This was especially true in the field of agriculture.

Dr. Dowell was the Moton Memorial speaker in Tuskegee Institute Chapel on December 4, 1949.

ALBON L. HOLSEY, sometime secretary to Dr. Moton, began service at Tuskegee Institute in 1914 as assistant to Dr. Emmett J. Scott, secretary to Booker T. Washington. Before coming to

Tuskegee Mr. Holsey was advertising solicitor engaged in the preparation of advertising copy for a number of Negro business enterprises. From 1916 to 1936 he served successively as secretary to Dr. Moton and as director of campaign publicity under President Patterson. In 1921 he became executive secretary to the National Negro Business League, an organization founded by Washington with headquarters at Tuskegee Institute. He served in this capacity until 1945. In 1930 he received the Harmon Gold Medal for "outstanding achievement in the field of business." In 1938 he was loaned to the information section of the Southern Division of Agricultural Adjustment Administration, Washington, D.C. He returned to Tuskegee in 1944 as assistant to the President in charge of Public Relations and as Secretary to the Board of Trustees.

On January 16, 1950, Mr. Holsey's unexpected passing came as a great shock to his many friends everywhere and especially to his more intimate friends on the Tuskegee Institute campus where he had served so faithfully and effectively over a period of thirty-five years.

WILLIAM HARDIN HUGHES was born in Savannah, Missouri, in 1881. He received an M.A. from the University of Chicago and an Ed.D. from the University of California. Dr. Hughes has had a wealth of teaching experience in schools and colleges in California, at Fisk University, Atlanta University, Tuskegee Institute, and Talladega College. Among his published work is *The Negro in Our Economy* and numerous articles in education and sociology journals. Dr. Hughes was associate editor of the *Negro Year Book* in 1947.

G. LAKE IMES was for twenty-five years a member of the Tuskegee Institute staff, serving for five years with Booker T. Washington and for twenty years with Dr. Moton. He began his association with the school as a teacher of English but was transferred the next year to the Phelps Hall Bible Training School of which he later became Dean. While serving as Dean he was chosen as Assistant to the Principal and Secretary of the Institute. In 1922 he accompanied Dr. Moton to the Scottish Churches Missionary Congress in Glasgow, Scotland. From that time on he traveled extensively with the Principal to all parts of our country. In 1933 he accompanied Dr. Moton to Haiti as Secretary of the United States Commission on Education in Haiti of which Dr. Moton was appointed Chairman by President Hoover. Over a period of years Dr. Imes spent the greater part of each summer with Dr. Moton at his summer home in Virginia.

In these and other ways he had close contact with Dr. Moton during the greater part of his administration and came to know him with an intimacy that was possible to very few of his official family. He writes, therefore, from close association in both personal and official relations. He is known to have enjoyed the Principal's complete confidence and to have served him with a loyalty and single-minded devotion which only a great man could inspire.

ALVIN J. NEELY, one of sixteen children, was born in Newberry, South Carolina. He entered Tuskegee Institute in 1901 where he pursued, in addition to the general requirements of the school, the course in brick masonry. He received his diploma in 1909. Appointed by Booker T. Washington as director and manager of the Tuskegee Male Quartet in which he sang second tenor, Mr. Neely traveled throughout the country singing and speaking in the interest of fund raising for the school. He served his Alma Mater as registrar, dean of men, and manager of the Tuskegee Institute Choir at the opening of Radio City and the unveiling of the bust of Booker T. Washington in the Hall of Fame in New York City. Mr. Neely became full-time Executive Secretary of the Tuskegee General Alumni Association in 1941, a position which he still holds. His several relationships and positions on the campus of Tuskegee Institute qualify him to speak from direct experience concerning any one of its first three presidents and their respective contributions to the institution.

FREDERICK DOUGLAS PATTERSON, Director of the Phelps-Stokes Fund and former president of Tuskegee Institute, was born in Washington, D.C. in 1901. His professional career began in 1923 when he became instructor of veterinary science at Virginia State College after his graduation from Iowa State College. Dr. Patterson serves in many and varied educational, humanitarian and civic capacities. He is a member of the Board of Trustees of Tuskegee Institute, Hampton Institute, Bethune-Cookman College and Bennett College, National Foundation for Medical Education and the National Society for Crippled Children and Adults. He is on the Board of Directors of the Southern Educational Foundation, Citizens Committee for the Hoover Report on Reorganization of the Federal Government, National Committee on Civil Defense, and a member of the Board of Governors of the American National Red Cross. Dr. Patterson is also a member of the National Committee of the National Urban League, the Advisory Committee of the Institute for International Education, the National Council of the Boy Scouts of America and past Director of the American Heritage Foundation. He was also a member of the International Bank Mission to Nigeria in 1953.

Founder and President of the United Negro College Fund, the organization which pioneered cooperative fund raising for private institutions, Dr. Patterson has received numerous awards for public service. He holds the National Foundation for Infantile Paralysis Award, New Farmers of America Award, Alumni Award from Iowa State College, Masonic Achievement Award and the Silver Beaver Award from Boy Scouts of America.

Aside from the degree of Doctor of Philosophy which he earned at Cornell in 1932, Dr. Patterson holds honorary degrees from six institutions of higher learning.

JOSEPH L. WHITING, psychometrist for the Atlanta University Center, was advisor in Industrial Arts Education at Tuskegee Institute for twenty years, 1910-1930. In addition to his experiences with Dr. Moton as a member of his staff at Tuskegee, Mr. Whiting was also with one of the units assigned to Dr. Moton for inspection during World War I. He is the author of *Shop and Class* written at Tuskegee in 1941.

www.ingramcontent.com/pod-product-compliance
Lightning Source LLC
Chambersburg PA
CBHW020343270326
41926CB00007B/297